NAVY SEALs
A HISTORY PART II

Also by Kevin Dockery

NAVY SEALS: A HISTORY OF THE EARLY YEARS

NAVY SEALs
A HISTORY PART II

THE VIETNAM YEARS

KEVIN DOCKERY

From interviews by Bud Brutsman

BERKLEY BOOKS, NEW YORK

Most Berkley Books are available at special quantity discounts for bulk purchases for sales promotions, premiums, fund-raising, or educational use. Special books, or book excerpts, can also be created to fit specific needs.

For details, write: Special Markets, The Berkley Publishing Group, 375 Hudson Street, New York, New York 10014.

A Berkley Book
Published by The Berkley Publishing Group
A division of Penguin Putnam Inc.
375 Hudson Street
New York, New York 10014

First edition: August 2002

Visit our website at
www.penguinputnam.com

Library of Congress Cataloging-in-Publication Data

Dockery, Kevin.
Navy SEALs : a history part II : the Vietnam years / Kevin Dockery.
p. cm.
Includes index.
ISBN 0-425-18348-3
1. United States. Navy. SEALs—History—20th century.   I. Title.

VG87 .D63   2002
359.9'84—dc21   2001052926

PRINTED IN THE UNITED STATES OF AMERICA

10 9 8 7 6 5 4 3 2 1

DEDICATED TO THE MEMORY OF
MASTER CHIEF AVIATION ORDNANCEMAN
MIKE BOYNTON, USN (RET.),
WHO WAS TAKEN FAR TOO SOON.

My friend, we are diminished by your loss.

Contents

Foreword

Although the subject of this book is the UDT/SEAL teams of the 1960s, the warriors that evolved into the "teams" started their journey during World War II. Some of the original members of SEAL Team One and Two, who are commonly referred to as the "plankowners," a term that was used in the early days of the Navy to describe the first crew of a ship, were battle-hardened veterans of two wars.

The formation of the first teams was not a romantic knighting of the best cadets from the Naval Academy. From all accounts, the genesis of this group was more akin to something out of the dirty dozen. Most of the Navy's wildest, craziest, and eccentric enlisted men some how all volunteered for the first SEAL teams.

The concept of Special Operations is not new to warfare, but in the context of the modern-day American military, Special Operations would not have been possible if it wasn't for the efforts of one man. Born to an aristocratic family, he quickly became a leader in both high school and college, but perhaps the biggest development of his leadership skills came during his tenure in the Navy, where he emerged as a bona fide World War II hero. He went on to serve as our thirty-fifth president. In my humble opinion, John F. Kennedy had an immense and undeniable influence in shaping today's Special Operation Units. Armed with forward thinking and an inside knowledge regarding the looming conflict in Southeast Asia, Kennedy pushed the military to form an "unconventional warfare" capability. With his roots in the Navy, the message was heard loud and clear. After a few short months of normal Navy red tape and paperwork, the time had come to put an idea into much needed action. Orders were given to select, train, and equip the new top-secret team, custom-made for unconventional warfare.

Transition

But as important as the history of Special Operations is, the spirit of being elite is always about today. In a world that seems to become increasingly unstable, Special Operations are more relevant than ever. The events of September 11 have painfully shown that, without a doubt, terrorist groups are now inclined to commit indiscriminate acts of violence and hostility on a mass scale. As we again do battle in the Middle East, it is important to note that our Special Operations teams need our support at all times, not just in times of war. It's convenient to join the Spec Ops bandwagon when they make our country proud on the battlefield. But not on any news channel do we ever see the battles they must fight at home.

—Bud W. Brutsman

Chapter 1

THE ARENA

Southeast Asia is made up of the Indochinese and Malay Peninsulas as well as a number of large island groups. The area is bordered on the north by China, to the west and south by the Indian Ocean and the Indian subcontinent, and to the east by the Pacific. Countries contained within Southeast Asia include Brunei, Burma, Cambodia, Indonesia, Laos, Malaysia, the Philippines, Singapore, Thailand, and Vietnam.

At the easternmost edge of Southeast Asia is Vietnam. Bordered to the west by Cambodia and Laos, and to the north by China, Vietnam's entire eastern and southern boundaries lie along the South China Sea and into the Gulf of Thailand. Prior to the end of World War II, the entire area of Laos, Cambodia, and Vietnam was part of Indochina, popularly called French Indochina. With the fall of France to the Germans early in the war, the French government's control of Indochina grew loose.

The power held by Japan over French Indochina had grown stronger even before France's fall to the Germans. By March 1941, the Japanese dictated a peace settlement regarding Indochina in order to end an invasion by Siamese (later Thai) forces into what was later to become Laos and Cambodia. The Japanese had encouraged Siam's invasion. With the peace settlement, French Indochina became, in effect, a Japanese protectorate, complete with occupying troops.

The people of Indochina had suffered through a war between the French and the Germans before. During the First World War, 100,000 Vietnamese labored in France to help the French war effort. During that time, Nguyen Tat Thanh, from Hanoi, was living in Paris. Becoming politically active for his people during the First World War, Nguyen changed his name to Nguyen Ai Quoc, which translates to "Nguyen the Patriot."

Fascinated by the Communist revolution in Russia and their overthrow of the czars, Nguyen went to Moscow. After studying there during the early

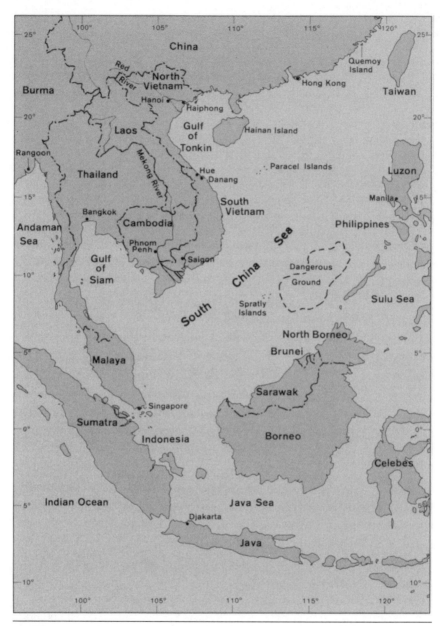

Southeast Asia.

U.S. Navy

1920s, he became a staunch Communist and believer in the Communist doctrine. Struggling for the independence of his people from French rule, Nguyen eventually returned to Indochina after the beginning of the Second World War.

Back in his home country, Nguyen established the Viet Nam Doc Lap Dong Minh, the League for Independence of Vietnam, commonly called the Viet Minh. The Viet Minh was a coalition of both Communists and nationalists who wanted to see their country become independent. Nguyen also changed his name, this time for good. It was by this name that he would be identified for decades to come—Ho Chi Minh.

The Viet Minh fought both the Vichy French and the Japanese forces in Indochina during the war. Ho Chi Minh even met with representatives of the OSS in April 1945. In exchange for training and weapons, the Viet Minh combined forces with the United States in their campaign against the Japanese Empire.

With the Japanese surrender in August 1945, the Viet Minh moved quickly to secure their own country before the return of the French. The Democratic Republic of Vietnam was established on 2 September 1945 with Ho Chi Minh as president.

But Chinese and British forces moved in to occupy the new Vietnam in preparation for the return of French rule. The British secured the area of Vietnam south of the sixteenth parallel while the Chinese moved 200,000 troops into the north area. The Viet Minh agreed to allow French troops into the north area in order to help get rid of the Chinese, but after the Chinese had left, the French remained.

By November 1946, war had broken out between the Viet Minh and the French. Fighting the same kind of guerrilla war they had conducted against the Japanese, the Viet Minh operated under Ho Chi Minh's military commander, Vo Nguyen Giap. The Viet Minh were winning out against the French forces until the United States responded to French requests for aid in late 1949.

During the early 1950s, the United States recognized the Bao Dai government of Vietnam, based in Saigon. Bao Dai had been the puppet ruler of the area during the Japanese occupation. But Bao Dai was not a Communist, and anti-Communist feelings were running strong in the United States, especially with the beginning of the Korean War in 1950.

In spite of their situation, the Viet Minh successfully fought the French

Ho Chi Minh.

in the north of Vietnam until the Battle of Dien Bien Phu in 1954. With the defeat of the French during that epic conflict on 7 May 1954, the Viet Minh won the first Indochina war.

With the Communist government under Ho Chi Minh in control of Hanoi and the Bao Dai government in Saigon, the country was divided into North Vietnam and South Vietnam along the seventeenth parallel according to an agreement reached in Geneva in mid-1954. This was intended to be a temporary situation until nationwide elections could be held the next year.

But Bao Dai left Vietnam before the agreement went into effect, appointing Ngo Dinh Diem as prime minister. The United States, never having signed the cease-fire accords, supported the democratic government of South Vietnam over the Communist one to the north. By early 1961, the U.S. was backing the Diem government with military support. In the countryside and jungles of South Vietnam, the Viet Minh, veterans of years of conflict with the Japanese and the French, moved in to conduct a guerrilla war against the government of South Vietnam. These guerrilla fighters would soon become well known to U.S. troops as the Viet Cong.

■ ■ ■

PHYSICALLY, the whole of North and South Vietnam is over 1,000 miles long with a wide northern and southern area connected by a "waist" fewer than forty miles wide at one point. The country is shaped roughly like the letter *S*, and both parts of it total only about 128,000 square miles, roughly the size of the state of New Mexico.

Geographically, the two countries range from mountains in the north, snowcapped throughout the year, to a huge area of mangrove swamps and flat river-delta terrain to the far south. The land in between these two extremes includes jungle areas and triple-canopy rain forests that contain a wide variety of animal, reptile, and insect life.

All of Vietnam has a tropical monsoon climate. Seasonal temperatures in North Vietnam range from about 62 degrees F. in the winter (January) to 100-plus degrees F. in the summer months (from mid-May to mid-September), the hot and humid wet season.

Temperature changes in South Vietnam are less severe, averaging from 78 to 84 degrees throughout the year. But the humidity level is high, especially during the rainy season, which lasts from May to November. Torrential downpours are constant occurrences during the height of the monsoon season. During June and July, the average monthly rainfall is normally over a foot, peaking again in September.

This heavy rainfall, combined with the rich soil of the Mekong Delta, makes the southern part of South Vietnam some of the most fertile land on earth. The Mekong Delta makes up close to a quarter of South Vietnam's landmass, with an area of some 14,000 square miles. As the Mekong River passes through the delta, it splits into two major tributaries, the Bassac River to the south and the Mekong to the north. About halfway through the delta on its trip to the sea, the waters of the Mekong split again into three smaller tributaries, the My Tho River to the north, the Ham Luong River in the center, and the Co Chien River to the south. The major rivers of the Mekong Delta are interconnected by various smaller tributaries, which are themselves connected by a vast network of streams and canals. In all, there are nine major tributaries in the Mekong Delta, dozens of streams, and hundreds of canals. Almost no area of the delta is more than a mile or so from a waterway that eventually connects to the South China Sea or the Gulf of Thailand.

The alluvial sediment that makes up the Mekong Delta is the reason the area is so fertile. Rice paddies are seen throughout the producing farmland. In between them are areas of twisted mangroves, especially along the banks of the many waterways. But there are also fields of huge elephant grass, which can grow ten feet high and completely block any view of the land.

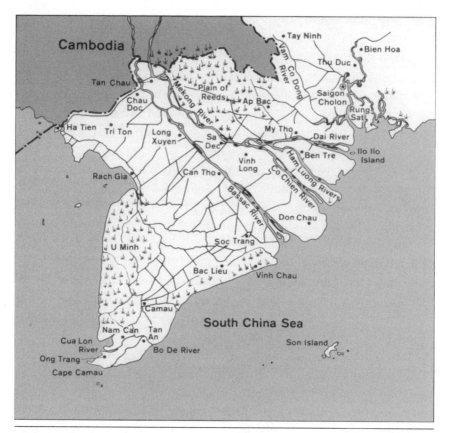

The Mekong Delta.

Banana groves are also scattered throughout the area, along with pineapple fields and areas of bamboo, nipa palm, and even full-sized forests.

Southeast of the South Vietnamese capital of Saigon, bordered on the south by the Soirap River, on the north by the Long Tau River, and on the east by the South China Sea, lies the Rung Sat (Vietnamese for "dense jungle") swamp. Known to the Vietnamese as the Forest of Assassins, the Rung Sat Swamp was called the Rung Sat Special Zone or RSSZ by U.S. forces.

The almost 400 square miles of the Rung Sat contain rich soil that encourages plant growth, a fact illustrated by the heavy jungles found throughout the region. Twisted mangrove roots line the banks of the hundreds of waterways that crisscross the Rung Sat. Among the mangroves

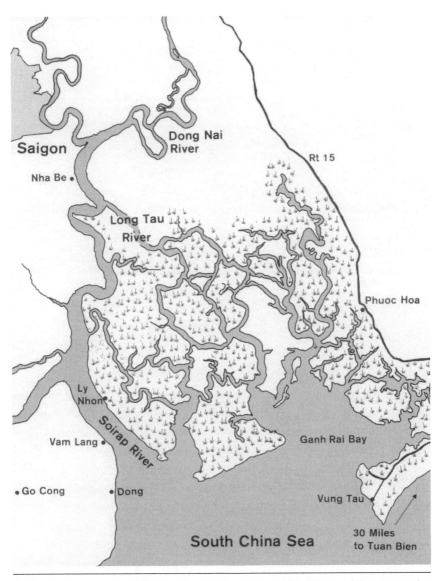

The Rung Sat Swamp, southeast of Saigon. Known to the SEALs as the Rung Sat Special Zone, or more simply, just the Rung Sat.

U.S. Navy

The view of the Rung Sat Special Zone from a helicopter flying overhead. Far off to the upper left is Saigon. It was in this maze of rivers, streams, and canals that the SEALs first took on the Viet Cong on their home ground.

U.S. Navy

grow nipa palm and other hardy plants, making penetration past the banks lining the water very difficult in areas. This same heavy plant growth conceals the areas of land in the Rung Sat between the waterways. For hundreds of years, pirates, smugglers, and other criminals used the Rung Sat for concealment, giving them a base from which they could safely prey on river shipping going into and out of Saigon. The Viet Cong used the Rung Sat as a safe haven just as the pirates before them had done.

This was the area where the SEALs would first see active combat in Vietnam. Within months, their actions would spread farther south from the Rung Sat into the Mekong Delta. In the steaming jungles and thick mud, the abilities of the SEALs would be tested to extremes. And it is there where the legend of the Teams would first be written.

Scott R. Lyon, Lieutenant Commander, USN (Ret.)

In 1952, I enlisted in the U.S. Navy, and that was also the year I first heard about the Underwater Demolition Teams. When I learned about the UDTs during boot camp, I tried to go directly from boot to UDTR training at Little Creek. The trouble was, I wasn't twenty-one years old yet. Because the Korean War was going on, anyone under the age of twenty-one had to have their parents' consent in order to volunteer for the UDTs. I didn't have that consent, so I had to wait.

*There was a movie I saw one time that showed me the Navy Frogmen; in fact, I think that was the title of the film—*The Frogmen. *Since I liked to swim, and I had heard about the adventure you could experience as a Navy Frogman, and I always liked adventure, the UDTs sounded like just the place I wanted to be.*

My route to the Teams was interesting. In those days, the 1950s, there wasn't a lot of paperwork involved in the Navy. I had just completed Explosive Ordnance Disposal school and hardhat diving school. Two classmates of mine, Eve Barrett and Charles Neirgarth, both said that I should go to the Teams. Since I was over twenty-one now, I didn't need anyone's consent, and the Teams still looked very good to me.

My friends and I went down to the Long Branch bar that Friday and had a couple of brews, discussing the situation. My wife and children were both in Washington, D.C., where the hardhat divers' school was located. But without my family even knowing, I went down to Little Creek and was put into UDTR training with Class 25 that night.

I had been looking forward to UDTR training for some time, and now I suddenly found myself right in the middle of it. Having always been kind of a fun person, I just jumped right in and loved every minute of it.

Personally, I didn't have any real trouble with any of the UDTR training. When we graduated, we had the usual party. When someone at the party asked me what I had thought of training, I said I thought it was pretty easy. And I really meant that. But that caused a little conflict among some of the guys who were already in the Teams.

But the simple fact was that I really loved what we did, even in training. Class 25 at Little Creek was a winter class in 1960–61. The second day I was there, it snowed. But in January, we went down to Puerto Rico for further training and that was great. In PR, the water was great, the weather was the same, and it was just fun training.

One night down in Puerto Rico, I had the midwatch in the students' barracks. It was the middle of the night and I was in this building full of sleeping students, making sure the place didn't catch fire and burn down around them.

During that long night, I just decided that everyone else should be up. So I put the lights on in the barracks. With the help of another student on midwatch, Chet Langworthy, I proceeded to wake up everyone there.

Waking the people up, we gave them the instructions to form up in the classroom. Each person was to bring with them one swim fin, one black sock, and their bathing suit. And they were to fall in to class for instruction. These weird instructions were something the instructors had been throwing at us for weeks. So everyone just got up and did what we had told them.

I thought that was a really funny joke. The rest of my class might not have thought so. But they were all so sleepy, they never did figure out who had played that trick on them.

Going through training, I learned something about myself; everyone does. I always thought I had the drive to go forward, to never quit. Whenever I'm given a task to do, I follow through and complete the job to the best of my abilities.

Sam Bailey gave us a lesson in the general attitude toward completing a mission when we first got into the UDTs. When we were being sent out, Sam asked us if we all had some dimes in our pockets. Of course we asked him what for and his answer has stuck with me. Sam said, "Well, we're going to send you out on an operation. And I want you to take that dime and call your mother, because you may not be back."

So I always have a dime in my pocket, because of Sam Bailey.

But in the Teams, we always follow through. It's just part of the job, what we do. The thrill of doing something, of completing something that you haven't even been trained to do. That gives you some real satisfaction and a good feeling of accomplishment.

Class 25 graduated in May 1961 and I was assigned to UDT 21. Working in the UDTs was everything I thought it might be. We deployed all of the time, spending relatively little time back at Little Creek. One very interesting mission was when we were tasked to go and pick up some special boats the Navy was having built and take them down to South America on a mission. Rudy Boesch and I went down to the Bertram Boat Company in Miami, Florida. There, we helped finish up outfitting some special boats and we took them down to Venezuela. There, we conducted what were basically counterguerrilla operations, chasing Che Guevara and his group.

There were weapons aboard the boats and we knew how to operate them. There was a lot of terrorist activity around the oil lines, especially around Lake Maracaibo, near the western border with Colombia, near a little town called Lagunillas on the eastern shore of the lake.

This was a UDT operation, sometime before the SEALs were even created. It was definitely unconventional warfare, and I didn't know why a detachment from UDT was chasing a guy around the swamps and on land in South America. What I did know was that I was very glad to go. What little I knew directly about Che Guevara I had picked up just by reading various articles. He seemed to be quite an adventurer, and I admired him for that. But there was no way I could accept his trying to spread communism through Latin America. We never caught up with him while Rudy and I were down there, but his luck ran out in the end.

We weren't really trained to operate in a riverine environment then. None of us had any prior experience in this kind of counterguerrilla work, but we had the will to get the job done. We had the boats and moving through the waterways was something that came naturally to us. But we did a lot of things we weren't formally trained to do in the UDTs. Whatever we were told to do, we did, to the best of our knowledge. And that usually worked out fine. That may have been a forerunner, a spearhead, of what was to come in Navy Special Warfare.

When the orders came down from higher command, you didn't know who had made them, or even why they had been made. They just said "do this." You didn't always know where you were going, but you knew you were being sent to do something. And when you got there, you just figured out a way to get the job done. Flexibility is always the key, one way or another, we'll figure it out.

Just a few years after joining UDT 21, I was on a Med [Mediterranean] trip with UDT 21 when I first heard about the new SEAL Team that they were forming. That sounded like something even more adventurous than working with the UDT, but when I asked if I could volunteer for the new organization, I was told I had to wait until I returned to the Creek from my Med deployment.

So as soon as we returned to the States, I volunteered to go over to SEAL Team. I was the first person to go from UDT 21 to SEAL Team Two after it was formed. Being in the second group of men going to the SEAL Team meant I wasn't a plankowner, but that difference wasn't much.

Getting into the SEALs was great, I knew it was what I wanted right off the bat. Very quickly, we got into all kinds of training—land operations, weapons, and specialized parachuting. I was already jump-qualified, but in the SEALs we also learned free-falling and other methods of infiltrating from a high-flying aircraft. And we finally got a chance to utilize all of this training when SEAL Team Two deployed direct-action platoons to Vietnam.

In June 1967, I first deployed to Vietnam as the platoon chief of Fifth Platoon. That deployment was a real eye-opener as to just what it meant to fight an unconventional war. My first impression of Vietnam was that it was really hot, and that impression never changed.

Fifth Platoon was in only the second group of direct-action platoons to go to Vietnam from SEAL Team Two. We came in to relieve Third Platoon, which had been in-country since January. Some of the guys from Third Platoon—J. P. Tolison was one of them—took us out on our initial operations, to kind of break us in to operating in their area. At that time I was a chief petty officer and I chose to go out on point for that first operation.

Moving along, I went through some very thick bamboo. After finally penetrating the bamboo, I walked right into a native hooch, just flat put my nose right up against the thatch wall of the building in the dark. Calling back quietly, I told the patrol, "We're here."

So much for quietly sneaking up on a target. Instead, I walked right into it in the dark. So that seemed pretty funny to us, and it helped break the tension we were all feeling from our first operation in a combat zone. But we had a lot of good operations on that deployment.

All the times we went out on operations, I was never really what I would call scared. More like what I would call energetic. And that was probably because of all the adrenaline pumping through my system. Even the first time I was shot at, I wasn't scared—I just reacted quickly. The enemy opened fire and I instantly dropped down, flat to the ground. Then the platoon moved up and we went forward and took out the target. And in all of that, I didn't feel any real fear—more excitement than anything else.

There was one time on a later deployment back in Vietnam when I was scared. Of all of the times I went out on operations, this one time I felt fear. At the time I was one of the first PRU (Provincial Reconnaissance Unit) advisers operating in Vietnam from SEAL Team Two. My unit was 187 men strong and we operated nearly every night. Advisers were told not to go out on operations in the field with their PRUs at that time. But there was no way I could lead these men, earn and maintain their respect, without going into harm's way with them. So I went out into the field on operations with my PRU.

One night, I had my interpreter with me and we were going to meet an NVA snitch who had some information for us. The meeting was to take place in a house, and my interpreter and the NVA informer met easily enough and started their discussions in Vietnamese. After I had gotten the information I wanted from the conversation, I went outside. At that time I was smoking a cigar and I just walked along slowly, enjoying my smoke and thinking about the information and how it could lead to an operation.

I had walked about fifty meters from the house, not going in any particular direction, when the house exploded behind me. Suddenly I was all by myself, just standing on the dike of a rice paddy, and it was obvious that someone hadn't cared for what was going on in that hooch. My PRUs had been spread out in another area and they weren't immediately available to give me any support. Then the bullets started flying.

Diving into the rice paddy, I flattened myself out in the dirty, muddy water as bullets flew by overhead. That was the one moment when I was literally scared in Vietnam. I had no idea how I was going to get out of that situation, but I did get out and I never allowed myself to be cornered like that again.

The SEALs supplied individuals to act as leaders for the PRUs.

Paddling their IBS (Inflatable Boat, Small) toward a surfaced nuclear submarine, these SEALs are coming in from a practice operation launched from this same submarine. Constant practice like this makes the SEALs able to perform real-world operations with minimum notice.

U.S. Navy

We were advisers who would direct operations and see to it that our PRUs were supplied, supported, and paid. We handled the money for them, lived with them, saw to it that their needs were met, and traveled with them.

The basic objective of the PRUs, who were the operational arm of the Phoenix Program, was to capture the high-ranking individuals, the infrastructure, of the Viet Cong. These captures would result in intelligence that could be used by higher command to send in forces against major VC targets. It could be to break up a VC troop movement, uncover caches of weapons and materials, or just to learn the VC's plans for greater operations.

The Phoenix Program was a good program, though I have a hard time saying if it was a major success or not. I operated on a lower level, as a PRU adviser in the field with my unit rather than at a high enough command level to be able to say just how great a success the whole program was. But for its purpose, for as long as it ran, the program, I felt, was a success. But as the war escalated, I felt that the Phoenix Program just couldn't keep up with the speed of the war's operations.

As a SEAL adviser to PRU portion of the Phoenix Program, I can say that our mission was to flat-out kidnap the Viet Cong leadership, not to go out and assassinate them. We could get a lot more information from a living person than we could get from just a body.

The Chieu Hoi Program had been started well before the Phoenix Program, but the two worked so closely together it was almost impossible to separate them sometimes. The Chieu Hoi Program allowed VC and ex-NVA personnel to "rally" or defect from the Communists and receive an amnesty from the South Vietnamese government. Many of the VC and NVA who defected gave intelligence that led directly to PRU operations. Some of the individuals who gained amnesty through the Chieu Hoi Program joined various PRUs and actively operated against their former comrades.

Working with the Chieu Hois, ex-NVAs and VC, didn't really bother me. I thought both the Chieu Hoi and PRU people were very good troops. As far as being fighters went, they were much superior to the regular ARVN [Army of the Republic of Vietnam] troops. In my experience, the ARVNs were very lazy and reluctant to engage the enemy in battle.

My experience with the ARVN troops and their leadership led me to believe that they weren't trustworthy at all. At least not the ones I had direct experience with. Toward the end of my tour, we wouldn't even give the ARVN commanders the locations where we were going to operate. We knew that if we did, the information would be leaked out to the VC.

And this wasn't just paranoia. There had been several incidents in which the information was leaked about where my PRU was going to conduct an operation. When I quit telling the ARVNs where we were going to operate, our targets quit disappearing and the VC weren't waiting for us to arrive on-site.

When I received my commission to warrant officer in early 1968, I was transferred out to SEAL Team One in Coronado out on the West Coast. Before 1968 was over, I would be back in Vietnam, doing a tour with Alfa Platoon of SEAL Team One. There has always been a good-natured rivalry between the Teams stationed on either coast. Most of the joking around is just in good fun. But having served in both SEAL Team Two and SEAL Team One, I noticed some differences between the two Teams.

Since I had primarily been an East Coaster, it seemed to me that the East Coast Teams, both SEAL and UDT, were always together. We did everything together and even our families lived in the same neighborhoods. When I went to the West Coast, I noticed a lot of diversity among the men of the Teams. Everyone had different things that they did—some went bike riding, running, or even horseback riding. On the East Coast, we didn't seem to have all of those opportunities. So we had to stick together and drink beer.

I am very proud to have been a SEAL. Today, I wear a miniature Trident, the insignia of Navy Special Warfare, on the lapel of my suit coat. I don't brag about having been a SEAL, but when people ask me what that is on my lapel, I am glad to tell them. Personally, on the inside, it means a great deal to me to be able to wear that insignia.

Out of my three combat tours in Vietnam, in two of them I led SEAL platoons. During those tours, I went out on probably over 300 operations. On my second tour, when I was a PRU adviser, I had one operation that was a particularly memorable one, even though I couldn't pull it off until my third tour.

Through various sources, I kept getting intel on the existence of a VC-run POW camp somewhere in IV Corps. The sheer volume of intelligence told me that there had to be something to it, and we spent a lot of nights going out and looking for it. It was never there.

On my third tour in Vietnam, this one with SEAL Team One, I was the assistant platoon leader of Alfa Platoon, and directly in charge of Second Squad. In early October 1968, we had just come in from a big cache op when I was called down to get a report of some new information from another SEAL PRU adviser. I was told that two women had just walked into a PRU camp with information about an active VC POW camp. In fact, the women had apparently just come from the camp, where they had visited their husbands, who were detained there. My ears perked right up at that and all I wanted to know was where the camp was and where the women were.

The main armament of the PBR, its twin forward .50-caliber machine guns, are shown in this photograph. The gunner from the River Division has his two weapons aimed outboard to the port side of the boat. The large searchlight is attached to the mounting for the guns. Wherever the light is shining, that's also where the two big machine guns are aimed.

U.S. Navy

Very soon I got hold of the women and was able to interrogate them with the help of an interpreter. I learned exactly where the camp was, or at least exactly where the women thought the camp was. This was very hot intelligence and not something that could be allowed to just sit and wait. Right away I put together an operation to raid the POW camp.

For air support, I called in the Seawolves. There was going to be another large ship, the USS Harnett County *(LST 821), down in the area of the suspected POW camp that would act as a platform for the Seawolf helos. River Division 51 would supply the insertion boats in the form of PBRs. A company of ARVN forces were brought on board for a postoperation sweep of the area of the POW camp the day after the operation. And a platoon from the local PRUs would work directly with us on the op. And topping off the action team was my squad of SEALs from Alfa Platoon.*

Since the intel was hot, the operation was put together very quickly. We took the women with us on board the PBRs well before dawn and they led us in to where they thought the POW camp was located. Inserting at the ladies' direction, we landed on Con Coc Island, part of the Dung Island complex in the Bassac River. But we searched and found nothing. Withdrawing, we moved farther along the shore of Con Coc Island until we came across something the ladies said looked familiar. Then we inserted again.

Inserting from a PBR into enemy territory is quite a problem. Anything could be waiting for you there in the dark. And we had set procedures we followed to maintain security and as much safety as we could. But still, inserting over and over in the same area is pushing your luck.

But this time we had found the right area. We were on the right path on only our second insertion. According to the women, we only had about 200 meters to go inland before we came across a path that supposedly led to the POW camp.

At that point I sent the women back to the PBR. Whether there was anything around or not, I just didn't know for sure. But I didn't want the women around when we tried to sneak up on the camp. And sending them back prevented our having any problem with them if they reacted badly.

As we all went up the path, I stopped the patrol when we came to a rise in the ground. It was sort of a knoll, a rise in the ground, that kept us from being able to see what was ahead of us on the path. Since there could be almost anything waiting for us, I didn't want us walking into any surprises.

With the men crouched down on alert, I slipped up to the edge of the knoll to take a look. It was just daylight now, and there was more than enough light to see. And what I saw was the POW camp right in front of me. Vietnamese prisoners were shackled together, and two of them were secured in bamboo cages. The guards were just getting up, preparing breakfast and getting into their morning routine.

Daylight was brightening rapidly and I wanted to get the raid over with before the guards were all up and moving around the camp. Only one of the guards I could see at that time was armed. As I was looking into the camp, the cages were out on my right-hand side. *There were two small buildings in the camp, hooches really, but I didn't see any activity coming from either of them.*

Withdrawing from the knoll, I went back and briefed my people. The PRUs, I sent over to my left flank. I didn't want them going in ahead of my SEAL squad. It wasn't that I didn't trust them, but once they saw the prisoners in the camp, there was a good chance they would go a little crazy and wipe out any chance of us getting prisoners for interrogation.

So I sent the PRUs over to the left flank and told them not to come in until the firing stopped. Then I took my squad and formed a skirmish line.

When we hit the camp, there was almost no resistance from the guards at all. They were unprepared and we surprised them completely. The interpreter I had with me shouted through a bullhorn he was carrying to all of the prisoners to drop down to the ground, otherwise they might get shot. Several of the guards made attempts to get to their weapons, and a bunch of them just ran off into the boondocks.

In the short firefight, we killed about seven guards and captured another guard and a VC tax collector who just gave up immediately. Facing seven SEALs, three of whom had Stoners and one who had an M60, was looking at a lot of firepower.

Probably the most exhilarating moment of that whole operation was when we unshackled the prisoners and took those two out of the cages. The men just couldn't do enough to show their gratitude. They were kissing our feet and bowing so much it looked like their backs would snap. This went on for more than five minutes. Finally, we had to stop them, since we had searched the camp and the VC could come back and overrun it, just like we had.

We took twenty-six liberated prisoners, and our own two captives, back to the PBRs. The POWs hadn't been fed very well during their captivity, so we gave them the C rations we had available. They thought that food was great and we were glad to get rid of it, so everyone got something out of that.

We took the liberated prisoners back and turned them over to the Vietnamese at Tra Vinh. Some of the prisoners had been at that camp since the Tet offensive, which had been eight months before. The

ARVN sweep of Con Coc the next day indicated that there had been a lot of VC on the island, as many as two battalions' worth. So it was a good thing we pulled out when we did, even though we practically had to drag some of those liberated POWs out, them bowing all of the way.

That was a very successful and satisfying operation. Even though we hadn't liberated any American POWs, it had been a good day for Alfa Platoon.

I was one of the two officers in charge of Alfa Platoon. As the lower-ranking officer, I held the position of assistant platoon leader. But the relationship between officers and enlisted men in the Teams stems from their training together in BUD/S and it's different than I've seen in any other service branch. Everyone, no matter what their rank, would be doing the same things, day and night, during training. Officers and enlisted men did the same exercises, completed the same evolutions, and experienced the cold, the mud, and the water, all together.

This background in working together gave everyone a respect for one another's abilities, experience, and knowledge. Enlisted men in the Teams would often be assigned jobs that required them to lead groups of men, both U.S. and foreign. Sometimes the size of these groups was so big that in any other service, it would require a commissioned officer to do the job "properly." But that wasn't how things happened in the Teams.

When I was a warrant officer in Vietnam with my platoon, after a couple of months of operating, I allowed the petty officers to run ops completely. That meant they did everything—from gathering the intelligence and planning the operation, to giving the patrol orders, and to making sure that all of the equipment and munitions were ready for the op.

When their mission was ready to go, I would go on the op as well. But I went as just another member of the patrol, just a rifleman, M60 carrier, or radioman. The petty officer who had put the operation together would be the man in charge. He would run the op from start to finish. And that would give the platoon, and the Team, a great pool of very experienced petty officers to draw on in the future.

We could work that way. It was just another aspect of the

camaraderie among Teammates, and the mutual respect we had for one another. That was the kind of united men we were in the Teams.

The camaraderie stood out sometimes, even in funny ways. One of the ops we went out on involved us swimming in the Cua Lon River, right at the tip of South Vietnam. We swam the width of that river, and some part of its length, looking for mines. All of this done on Christmas Eve. Since it was the season, while we were swimming, we were all singing "Jingle Bells." We all got along pretty well together.

In the Teams, leadership was much more important than rank. We had some very good leaders among the officers, and we also had some outstanding leaders among the enlisted community. The situations we found ourselves in during missions often called on the most experienced man being in charge. There were several times in the Teams when a detachment was sent off with an officer in charge for the record, but the leading petty officer was the one who was really in charge.

A commanding officer would call both the officer and that leading petty officer into his office and speak to them about the detachment or operation. And that officer could easily be told that he was expected to listen to the leading petty officer. And there was no problems with that situation whatsoever. One time while I was an enlisted man, it happened to me.

There was always close cooperation among the men of the Teams, and this started during our very first days of training. We have the idea of a "swim buddy" in the Teams. This concept is introduced to the students at BUD/S right at the start of their training. A swim buddy is the guy you will eat, sleep, and work with. He is hooked to you, literally sometimes, during training swims. You depend on your swim buddy, and he depends on you. When you get in trouble in the water, you can't call for help easily, and there isn't always time for someone else to show up anyway.

When we used to swim with the early Pirelli and Draeger breathing rigs, we found they were very hard to use and took a lot of experience to operate them safely. A lot of swimmers passed out underwater while training with those rigs. If you had problems or went unconscious, it was up to your swim buddy to make sure that your life was saved. He got you to the surface, and you would do the exact same thing for him.

On actual operations, your swim buddy is the guy who covers your "six" [back, six o'clock position] all of the time. And he expects you to do the same for him. He's the guy who literally turns into your mental twin. He knows how you think and you know how he thinks. When something happens, you already know what your swim buddy is going to do, so you just concentrate on the job at hand.

Probably the best tour of duty I ever had in the Navy was as a BUD/S instructor. I had first phase in Coronado and I did that job for three years. Why I say that was the best tour of duty had to do with the students. Everybody who we put through training had the same problem—they didn't like the instructors, mostly because we were harassing them all of the time.

But later, after the students had graduated and moved on to the Teams, done a tour, and found out what it meant to be an operator, then they would come back. Individuals might call me at my home and ask if they could bring their wives and children over to meet me. And I usually agreed and they would come over with their families.

And to a man, every one of them thanked me for training them the way I had. And that just made me feel very good in my heart, and I've felt that way about it ever since.

While in Vietnam on my last tour I had made a film, just a simple 8mm one, on going into a hooch, exactly how you would do that. I made the film as a training device, and I would show it to every class that went by.

What I emphasized to the students was that they were seeing an actual combat situation, though the person we dragged out of the hooch was really my interpreter. But we showed how we came up to the hooches, how we deployed our people, how we went through the door, pulled the prisoners out, and how we handcuffed and searched them. And I had my own experience that told me how important it was that they all knew how to do this kind of operation.

During that last tour of mine in Vietnam, we had gone into a village and waited for a Chinese guy to show up. We had heard he was coming to this particular village and was giving the people there aid

A Vietnamese "hooch" or bamboo structure. Made of bamboo framing covered with palm frond thatching and woven matting walls, this basic construction was common throughout the Mekong Delta.

Greg McPartlin Collection

and support, and training them in operations against us. So we went in and literally waited all night right outside of his hooch.

When he finally showed up, we jumped in there and grabbed him up. Wrapping him up and bringing him out, we suddenly started taking fire. So it was time to run. I had the prisoner with me, up in front of the patrol. Since I wanted to be sure there wouldn't be any problems with my having the prisoner up in front, I passed him back to one of my men and told him to "take care of him."

Well, the SEAL I passed the prisoner to passed him on again to the man behind him. And with the prisoner went the instructions to take care of him. Finally, we reached the boats and I turned, looking for the prisoner.

"Well," I asked, "where is he?"

"We took care of him," was the answer.

We never got that particular prisoner back for interrogation. And that was why I decided to make that film on how to do a snatch, secure, and transport of a prisoner. And why I showed the film to my students, to tell them how to correctly do it and not take things too literally.

My strategy about training at BUD/S developed because of the quantity of students we had. We used to get about 180 young men in a class, four times a year. Many of these students were "wannabes"—they really didn't belong at BUD/S. They wanted to be SEALs, but they weren't going to be. That isn't to say that they weren't good men, but they just didn't have what it took to get there.

The people who "got there," made the Teams, were the people who knew mentally, deep in their hearts, that being in the Teams was where they wanted to be more than anything else. Physical prowess doesn't really have a big part in getting through training. The larger men had trouble with pull-ups. So you sometimes had to kind of look the other way a bit while they did them. The smaller–framed trainee could do pull-ups all day long; they could scale walls and leap where the larger men couldn't.

But the larger man was stronger, and he could do push-ups or do whatever was a show of pure strength. We had good swimmers, who couldn't do other things well. But the people who got through the course made it through everything, whether it was easy or hard for them. They were the ones who wanted it the most.

As an instructor, it was kind of interesting to watch the students grow as individuals. The first couple of weeks, you didn't really look at anyone in particular much. During those days, the students kind of weeded themselves out for the most part. That was where the wannabes found out what they were really letting themselves in for, and they were gone fast.

Then you started looking at people more closely as individuals. And when you looked at that same person ten or twelve weeks later, you would see a completely different person. They would grow inside, get more aggressive, and feel better about themselves and what they were doing.

Lots of times a student would hurt himself during training. And he would just push it away and keep going. But other trainees might hurt themselves and that would be the end of the program for them.

We tried to make competitions among the trainees. Such as when we had a real fast runner and a slow runner. An instructor would try to pair those two as much as he could, and then just get on that slow runner. And you could just watch that man go. He would get to, and go through, that wall that was keeping him from speeding up as fast as he could. And all of a sudden that slow guy was now one of the fastest runners in the class. I enjoyed doing that immensely, watching these young kids grow to be men.

Nobody likes to be harassed. What it does is bother a person's mind. First off, people feel like you're picking on them, and no one likes that. If they can overcome that, it helps move them forward, teaches them how to ignore what isn't important and focus on the job at hand.

I always wanted to know how the U.S. Marines got their people so motivated during training. We did a very good job, but the Marines do an excellent job in motivating their people. I went over to the Marine training camp several times just to watch them and see how they handled their charges. If I could have instilled that motivation in the trainees at BUD/S, we'd have had even more qualified people for the Teams. But that skill remained a Marine one for me.

One of the things we concentrated on as instructors at BUD/S was building up the camaraderie, the teamwork, of the students. To that end, we had them singing songs and shouting out phrases while they worked. Just like the instructors at boot camp or basic training would teach their students how to march—they would have them mark time and build enthusiasm as a unit by singing cadence songs. That same technique worked for us at BUD/S.

When I was at BUD/S in the early seventies, we didn't really prepare the students for combat. They were taught things that were purely combat-oriented, such as how to do warning orders, patrol orders, and do basic patrolling and maneuvers. It was after they graduated BUD/S that they went on to more specialized training, after they were assigned to a Team. In training areas such as out at Niland, the new operators became efficient in conducting warfare. They would use live ammunition, live demo [demolitions—explosives], and would jump in for an operation. BUD/S gave them the basics, and that was built on later.

Some of what we did with the students at BUD/S was dangerous, though as instructors, we knew it was our job to keep things as

During a capabilities demonstration during one of their reunions, the young men of the Teams re-create a tradition of their UDT forefathers.

Kevin Dockery

safe as possible. Rock portage, where we had the students learn to land a rubber boat and cross jagged rocks while the pounding surf drove down on them—that scared me.

For rock portage, we would put the students, broken down into boat crews of six, into inflatable boats and send them out to sea. Right outside the Hotel Del Coronado, on the shore, are a bunch of large rough rocks. And the students would come in and land at those rocks.

Back during WWII, they had done rock portage as part of the training of the very first UDTs. Later, during the Korean War, the UDTs often had to land on rocky beaches where there was no flat sand or smooth surfaces to ground a boat on. So rock portage remained in BUD/S training because of that history.

But every time we did rock portage with the students, my heart was up in my throat. Someone would come very close to being hurt on almost every landing. Luckily, no one was ever seriously hurt on my watch, but there were a good share of bumps and bruises to go around in spite of that. I have seen broken legs and arms happen during rock portage, but you had to complete that evolution.

Surprisingly, we had people quit rather than face rock portage again. And this was after they had completed Hell Week and some of the more strenuous parts of BUD/S first-phase training. But you never could tell where you might be going in on an op, so rock portage remains a part of training to this day.

The demo (demolition) pits were another important part of training. They were our best chance, as instructors, to expose an individual to the noise and concussion of combat. When you put a man in on a beach someplace during an invasion or operation, he's got a real good chance of being shelled with either mortars or artillery. Some people are deathly afraid of that—the sudden blast of an explosion. And some of them don't even know that they are. The demo pit is a place where we would weed out people like that. If they didn't like being in the demo pit, they really wouldn't like what could happen later on.

The demo pit was this sunken area of black, muddy water and churned-up sand. The students had to crawl around this area while we set off explosions all around them. We even made them eat standing waist-deep in muddy water, trying to shield their food from the dust and debris kicked up by the explosions constantly going off.

The reason for having the students eat while all of that was going around them? Well, that's a harassment. It's hard, miserable, and they have to get through it to graduate. They learn that nothing matters unless you let it matter.

We had a trainee at BUD/S once who I had personally gone out and recruited. That was something we had to do now and then, go out and recruit at the different Navy training centers. When this one young man came to BUD/S, he was the fastest swimmer I had ever seen, and was the best runner I had ever seen as well. When he had to face the obstacle course, he went through it like it wasn't even there. And he was a very good leader, already a third class petty officer when he checked in.

Like all of the Special Warfare operators before and after them, these trainees learn how to take their rubber boat through the rocks. Since the days of the Scouts and Raiders in WWII, rock passage has been an integral part of UDT and SEAL training. Even in calm waters such as these, the trainees could easily injure themselves or their Teammates through a mistake. No man likes this work, and every man in the Teams does it.

U.S. Navy

Just before Hell Week, we would gather all of the students and instructors together. In the meeting, we critiqued each student separately. Each man would get information on whether he was considered good or bad, and why, from every instructor there. And then I would speak to him as well.

For my recruit, all of the instructors said the same thing. To a man, they considered that trainee the best person they had ever seen. And when I asked him if he was ready to go to Hell Week, that student just looked at me and said, "No, I quit."

Just like that. He just didn't want the program. And he didn't have a reason. So I just said, "Fine, put your helmet outside."

Being a BUD/S instructor was hard work, and it was very rewarding. That's what helped make it my best tour in the Teams. And I feel privileged to have been part of the BUD/S training unit.

Today, I've been out of the Navy for quite a few years. And people will look at me and say, "Oh, you were a SEAL." And I sometimes correct them and tell them that I had been in the Teams. That was the key to our success: we were the Teams, we were Teammates. And that is the heart of where we come from.

Most of the people in the Teams don't like a lot of publicity. Especially back in my day, I had a lot of chances to have my picture taken, be the center of newspaper articles. But I chose not to do that. I'm not bashful, but it just didn't strike me as right to advertise that I was in the Teams. I don't publicize it, but when people ask me what the Trident is that I'm wearing, I'll tell them. But they have to ask.

In my opinion, the guy in BUD/S today doesn't have much in common with the operators from World War II or even from my day. In a practical sense, things have changed so much as to be almost unrecognizable in terms of the kind of missions performed and the gear they do their ops with. In my day, we still trained with a lead line and slate, measuring the waters' depth just as they had in WWII. Today, these young men are computer-oriented. They have all the gimmicks that can be found. They're smarter than we were, and have accomplished a lot.

If there is something missing from today's SEAL Teams, it's maybe that they aren't as battle-tested as we were. But I think they have a lot more going for them today. Back when I started in the Teams, we were learning how to do everything. The men of the Teams today have built on what we did, and gone much further with it than we even thought possible.

If there is one thing that everyone who serves in Navy Special Warfare has in common, it is that they are all part of the Teams. And once you have completed that long road to get into the Teams, and have served with your brothers, you will never completely leave. I know I will never leave the Teams behind—never.

Chapter 2

THE HISTORY OF THE TEAMS

Naval units and organizations are required to maintain a log or history of their units. These documents are sent in yearly to higher commands as the unit's official command and control history for the reported year. Even units as secret as the Navy SEAL Teams have had to maintain these historical records.

Initially classified confidential or secret, the command and control histories list the Teams' actions throughout the year, the officers and men, who they were and what they did. They are the best single source of data on just what happened to the Teams, especially during years of active combat in Vietnam. These are excerpts from those records:

SEAL TEAM ONE
Excerpt from SEAL Team One, Command and Control History 1967
Enclosure (1)
SEAL Team ONE, COMMAND HISTORY UPDATED TO DECEMBER 1966
Pages 1–3. [DECLASSIFIED from CONFIDENTIAL]
SEAL Team ONE was commissioned on 1 January 1962 at the U.S. Naval Amphibious Base Coronado, California, under the command of Lieutenant David DEL GUIDICE, U.S. Naval Reserve. Five officers and fifty enlisted personnel from Underwater Demolition Teams ELEVEN and TWELVE comprised the initial personnel complement.

SEAL (Sea-Air-Land) Teams are identified as Navy units trained to conduct unconventional or paramilitary operations and to train personnel of allied nations in operations involving the naval or maritime environment. As with every fleet unit, the ultimate goal of SEAL Team ONE is to serve as a superior weapon in time of war and to attain maximum combat readiness in time of peace. This posture of readiness is particularly crucial since military efforts in a "COLD WAR" situation often preclude any clear-cut distinction between war and peace.

Lieutenant James H. BARNES, U.S. Naval Reserve, relieved Lieutenant DEL GUIDICE on 19 June 1964, as Commanding Officer. At that time, SEAL Team ONE consisted of six operating platoons. Each platoon was assigned administrative responsibilities, but was primarily an operating entity, capable of a diversity of skills and tasks. Personnel were extensively cross-trained to ensure the maximum efficiency of each platoon in the field.

Although young in years, SEAL Team ONE has matured rapidly into a close-knit, highly trained force of dedicated officers and men. Almost from its very beginning, SEAL Team ONE has played an active role in various trouble spots of the world. The first actively employed SEAL units in Southeast Asia were deployed in July 1962. There have been SEAL detachments in Vietnam ever since. In February 1966, SEAL Team ONE sent a pilot group of three officers and fifteen enlisted men to Vietnam, under the operational control of Commander Naval Forces Vietnam. From 26 March through 7 April 1966, these personnel were employed in Operation "JACKSTAY," the first amphibious landing in the Rung Sat Special Zone (RSSZ). Operation "JACKSTAY" was also the first joint UDT/SEAL and Marine operation in Vietnam.

On 15 July 1966, LCDR Franklin W. ANDERSON, USN, ******, took command of SEAL Team ONE. Since that time, SEAL Team ONE has intensified its operations in Vietnam and has increased the size of the RSSZ detachment [Detachment Golf] to five officers and twenty men. Operations conducted in the RSSZ include, but are not limited to, harassment of the enemy, hit-and-run raids, reconnaissance patrols, intelligence collection, and curtailment of guerrilla movements by ambush/counterambush tactics. The intensification of these operations afforded by the increased detachment size has proven the value of SEALs in combat situations.

Ambushes make up a high percentage of the operations conducted by SEAL detachments in the RSSZ. Although the enemy kill rate is not high,

---

the SEALs have placed a great psychological burden on the Viet Cong and have provided an effective deterrent to all VC travel.

On 19 August 1966, SEAL Team ONE had their first combat casualty. Petty Officer Billy W. MACHEN, who was point man on a reconnaissance patrol, triggered a Viet Cong ambush and sacrificed his own life in order to save his comrades. He was posthumously awarded the Silver Star for his gallant action.

On 7 October 1966, SEAL Team suffered one of their most unfortunate casualties. Two SEAL squads were transiting one of the smaller rivers in the RSSZ on an LCM-3 when they were attacked by a large number of Viet Cong. The boat received a direct mortar hit and sixteen of the nineteen men on board were wounded. LTJG William PECHACEK, Petty Officer First Class HENRY, and Petty Officer Third Class PENN were subsequently retired from Naval Service for disability due to their extensive wounds. Despite the adverse conditions, intelligence reports later indicated that during the firefight forty VC were killed by this gallant group of men. In October 1966, the commitment for SEALs in Vietnam increased to a total of seven officers and thirty men.

One of the basic missions of the SEALs is the gathering of intelligence information. This information is utilized by the SEALs and by higher authority to more effectively combat the enemy. Although not wholly indicative of the intelligence gathered, the following figures do show the result of SEAL operations conducted during 1966:

VC KIA	86
VC KIA (PROB)	15
SAMPANS DESTROYED	21
JUNKS DESTROYED	02
HUTS/BUNKERS DESTROYED	33
RICE CAPTURED OR DESTROYED	521,600 pounds

Numerous enemy documents have also been retrieved.

On one of the operations [Operation CHARLESTON, 3–4 December 1966], SEAL intelligence led to the capture of a weapons cache including 57MM Recoilless Rifles, 7.92 German machine guns, two U.S. Carbines, one U.S. M3A1 Submachine gun, and 10,000 rounds of assorted ammunitions. SEAL intelligence has been and is being used by friendly forces conducting operations throughout Vietnam; additionally, SEALs have aided these forces by locating VC base camps, helo landing zones, high ground for friendly base camps, and determining VC commo-liaison routes.

In the wake of the increasing manpower commitments to Southeast Asia, SEAL Team ONE has had their manpower increased to 21 officers and 105 enlisted personnel. This increase was projected for fiscal year 1967, but due to the outstanding performances of SEAL personnel, the increase was accelerated to help meet pressing requirements.

There have been other achievements and activities of SEAL Team ONE, outside the combat zone of Vietnam, that have contributed significantly to the defense posture of the United States Military services. Among them have been the conduct of the operational evaluation phase of the Aerial Recovery System "SKYHOOK." During the evaluation, SEAL personnel made live, two-man pickups during both daylight and darkness utilizing an S2F-type aircraft flying at speeds of approximately 110 knots [127 miles per hour]. Additionally, in August 1966, SEAL Team ONE personnel participated in the first live-man pickup in the evaluation of Air-Sea Rescue system utilizing the DRONE antisubmarine helicopter (DASH).

SEAL Team One's performance since its commissioning has been outstanding. This performance is directly attributable to the devotion to duty and superior capability of the officers and men assigned. Their contributions to the war effort in Southeast Asia and the overall national defense posture have earned distinction for themselves, their unit, and the United States Navy.

Excerpt from SEAL Team One, Command and Control History 1969
Enclosure (3) (b)
Subj: Presidential Unit Citation; recommendation for (U)
Pages 1–3. [DECLASSIFIED from CONFIDENTIAL]
2. SEAL Team ONE was commissioned on 1 January 1962 by direction of the late President John F. KENNEDY, with an allowance of 5 officers and 50 enlisted men. Since that period, due to increased demand and requirements placed on SEAL Teams, they have increased in numbers and

presently have 32 officers and 132 enlisted personnel on board. Since July 1962, SEAL personnel have been deployed in Vietnam under the operational control of Commander Military Assistance Command, Vietnam and/or Commander U.S. Naval Forces Vietnam. It is strongly felt this small elite unit has fully lived up to the expectations and reasons for its formation. Recommendation for this award is based on the achievements of SEAL Team ONE for duty, primarily in the Republic of Vietnam.

3. One of the primary missions of SEAL Team ONE has been to conduct Naval Unconventional Warfare operations against the Viet Cong in the Republic of Vietnam. There are four separate detachments presently located in Vietnam. Detachments ALFA and GOLF consist of seven officers and thirty enlisted each. These detachments are located in the Mekong Delta and Rung Sat Special Zone (RSSZ) respectively. The Rung Sat Special Zone contains the primary sea access to Saigon, and therefore is an area of great strategic importance. It is imperative that the RSSZ remain under direct government control in order to maintain this vital logistic channel. To assist in the insurance of that control, there is a constant requirement for factual and timely intelligence data. This task is one of the main objectives of detachment GOLF. Detachment BRAVO is assigned to MACV and operational in III and IV Corps for special operations, and Detachment ECHO, also under MACV, is assigned to Danang for special operations; these detachments consist of one officer and twelve enlisted men and two officers and twelve enlisted men, respectively. Due to the limited number of trained personnel available, the austere operating conditions, and the casualty rate, personnel have been required to rotate on a port and starboard basis, and in many cases much more rapidly. In some instances these fast turnarounds are voluntary; others are dictated by personnel requirements and increased operational commitments. A large number of SEAL Team members have completed as many as five to six tours in Vietnam and some with as little time as one month in CONUS between tours. Additionally, these men are required to be away from their families a great amount of the time while in CONUS, attending schools and other training functions.

4. The environmental conditions in Vietnam that SEAL Team personnel are subjected to in the conduct of their operations is extremely difficult and

hazardous. Exposure to almost impenetrable mangrove swamps, mud, tidal flats, prolonged immersions in water, and infestations of crocodiles, snakes, and other tropical animals, insects, and diseases, in conjunction with enemy boobytraps, punji stakes, and direct contact, have become a matter of routine on patrols, ambushes, and listening post operations. In areas of the RSSZ, a hardworking, well-conditioned squad can cover no more than a few hundred yards in one day. On occasion, ambush and observation teams have had to wait quietly for over four days in these insect- and reptile-infested jungles and swamps in order to successfully carry out their assigned mission. SEAL Team members usually operate in small units, i.e., two to six men on listening posts, where stealth and concealment are paramount. Intelligence gathering missions take these units/squads within very close proximity of enemy forces, often within earshot and/or a few yards distance. Should a larger enemy force ever detect a SEAL unit of this size, deep within this terrain, outside assistance would be virtually impossible. In spite of the severity of the operating conditions, SEAL Team members have maintained a heavy operating schedule, with many personnel having participated in over forty combat missions in a single deployment. All detachments have been highly successful in carrying out their respective missions, whether they be gathering intelligence data, training indigenous personnel, or interdicting Viet Cong operations . . .

SEAL TEAM TWO
Excerpt from SEAL Team Two, Command and Control History 1972
Enclosure (1)
SECTION V—OVERALL HISTORY OF SEAL TEAM TWO
Pages 1–5. [DECLASSIFIED from CONFIDENTIAL]
REPORT ON THE U.S. NAVY'S SEAL TEAM

1. (C) History

a. SEAL Team was established in J[anuary] 1962 to fill a need for military combat units specializing in unconventional warfare. President John F. Kennedy was one of the principal initiators behind the organization of counterguerrilla forces. These forces were needed not only by the U.S. Army but also by the U.S. Navy to counteract guerrilla activity in the world's rivers, harbors, and inshore areas.

b. The Navy had one unit oriented toward these areas already, the Underwater Demolition Teams. However, their primary mission was hydrographic reconnaissance and demolition of beach obstacles, mainly for the successful operation of an amphibious landing by the Marine Corps. SEAL Team was formed for a more exclusive mission, namely "clandestine operations in maritime areas and riverine environments." The name SEAL was chosen to signify the methods of entry into a hostile environment capable by this unit: by sea, by air, and by land.

c. In 1962, SEAL Team became involved in the growing Vietnam conflict. An advisory group from SEAL Team, called a Mobile Training Team (MTT), was sent rather than a combat unit. MTTs were sent to I Corps region of Vietnam until 1968. In 1967, SEAL Team combat platoons also became involved. They operated mainly in the MEKONG DELTA region until the necessity for combat platoons ended in 1971. SEALs served as Provincial Reconnaissance Unit (PRU) advisers in the IV Corps region from the time of the PRUs inception in 1966 until late in 1970. SEAL advisers to the Vietnamese are still being sent at this time [1971].

2. (C) MISSION.

a. The mission of SEAL Team is stated in reference NWIP 29-1 (A).

b. A SEAL Team is a Navy fleet tactical unit commissioned to conduct naval special warfare in the following areas:

1. Unconventional warfare.

2. Counterguerilla operations.

3. Clandestine operations in maritime areas which include sabotage, demolition, intelligence collection, and training and advising of friendly military or paramilitary forces in the conduct of Naval Special Warfare.

c. Some of the possible tasks of a SEAL Team are:

1. Destroy or sabotage enemy shipping ports and harbor facilities, railway lines, and other installations in riverine environments.

2. Infiltrate and exfiltrate agents, guerrillas, evaders, and escapees.

3. Conduct action undermining the military, economic, psychological morale, or political strength of the enemy forces.

4. Conduct reconnaissance, surveillance, and other intelligence tasks and capturing key personnel.

5. Ambush, counterambush, and interdict enemy waterway lines of communication.

6. Accomplish limited counterinsurgency civic action tasks such as medical aid, elementary civil engineering, boat maintenance, and basic education of the indigenous population.

7. Organize, train, assist, and advise U.S.-allied and other friendly military or paramilitary forces in the conduct of the above tasks.

3. (C) TRAINING

a. Training for prospective members of SEAL Team is located at the Naval Amphibious Base in Coronado, California. A twenty (20) week course called Basic Underwater Demolition/SEAL Team (BUD/S) Training begins several times each year. Applicants must pass an initial screen test and be physically and mentally qualified to undergo one of the most rigorous training programs in the world. A normal training class has an attrition rate of 66 to 75 percent. In addition, officers and enlisted men must train together, creating an atmosphere of camaraderie. Graduates of BUD/S training go to either UDT or SEAL Teams on both East and West Coasts. BUD/S training consists of these phases:

1. Phase I (five weeks): consists entirely of physical training, runs, swims, obstacle courses, night problems, IBS training, and climaxes with "HELL WEEK": a physical endurance test that allows no sleep all week.

2. Phase II (eight weeks): concentrates on SEAL and UDT operations, i.e. hydrographic reconnaissance, demolition training, weapons, patrolling, and land warfare.

3. Phase III (seven weeks): teaches the trainee diving operations, including SCUBA, Mark IV, and Emerson diving apparatus, diving medicine, and diving physics.

b. A graduate of BUD/S Training who goes on to SEAL Team gets even more extensive training including:

1. Parachute Jump School

2. Basic Intelligence

3. Naval Gunfire Support

4. Combat Medicine

5. Survival, Evasion, Resistance, and Escape

6. SEAL CADRE Training

With his oxygen mask firmly in place, this SEAL practices a free-fall as part of a HALO jump.

U.S. Navy

In addition, six (6) months observation and experience are required before a team member is officially qualified.

c. Numerous other schools are available to Team members in their specialties and in special warfare operations. Some of these are:

1. Jumpmaster
2. Parachute Rigger and Packer
3. Ranger School (U.S. Army)
4. Instructor School
5. Leadership School
6. Foreign Weapons
7. Explosive Ordnance Disposal
8. Language School
9. Raider School (U.S. Army)

d. In addition to these schools several joint operations within the U.S. Army and our foreign allies are held each year. Some of these Fleet Training exercises are:

1. FLINTLOCK. An annual NATO exercise in which SEAL Team TWO provides personnel for various joint staffs and operating platoons working in conjunction with the operating forces of our various NATO allies and taking place throughout the European Theater.

2. EXOTIC DANCER. An annual Atlantic Fleet Exercise conducted in the vicinity of Camp Lejeune, North Carolina, in which the scenario involves a combination of both conventional and unconventional warfare forces of the Army, Navy, Air Force, and Marine Corps. SEAL Team TWO provides personnel for various joint staffs, operating bases, and several platoons for the operating forces.

3. STRONG EXPRESS. An additional NATO exercise recently begun in August 1972 that possibly will develop into an annual exercise. SEAL Team TWO provides personnel for various joint staffs and one operating platoon.

4. (C) Organization

a. A SEAL Platoon consists of two (2) officers and twelve (12) enlisted men which can be divided into two (2) squads of one (1) officer and six (6) enlisted. Each platoon is intended to be a self-sufficient unit, and therefore has at least one man from each specialty area. These areas are: ordnance, submersible operations, intelligence, communications, engineering, air operations, and medical.

b. SEAL Team TWO is organized into ten platoons and is supported by the aforementioned departments. Each officer is both a department head and a platoon commander (or assistant). SEAL Team TWO has seventeen (17) officers and one hundred and fifteen (115) enlisted men [NOTE: these are 1972 numbers]. Administrative control is diagrammed in figure (1). It should be noted that SEAL Team ONE is located in California and is larger in size.

5. (C) OPERATIONAL CONTROL

a. Operational control of a typical SEAL platoon is shown in figure (2). Operational control is difficult to diagram because it was constantly changing in the Vietnam situation. At one point in time, two (2) SEAL platoons working in the Mekong Delta were responsible to their respective detachment commands, who, in turn, reported to COMNAVSPECWARGRU "V" in Saigon. Because of the distance between

```
            ┌─────────────────┐
            │  CHIEF OF       │
            │  NAVAL OPERATIONS│
            │  (CNO)          │
            └─────────────────┘
```

COMMANDER-IN-CHIEF, PACIFIC	COMMANDER-IN-CHIEF, ATLANTIC
COMMANDER-IN-CHIEF, PACIFIC FLEET	COMMANDER-IN-CHIEF, ATLANTIC FLEET
COMMANDER, AMPHIBIOUS FORCES, PACIFIC	COMMANDER, AMPHIBIOUS FORCES, ATLANTIC
NAVAL INSHORE WARFARE, PACIFIC	NAVAL INSHORE WARFARE, ATLANTIC
NAVAL SPECIAL WARFARE GROUP, ONE	NAVAL SPECIAL WARFARE GROUP, TWO
SEAL TEAM ONE	SEAL TEAM TWO

Figure 1

U.S. Navy

commands, SEAL platoons for the most part operated independently. Status reports were sent up a dual chain of command as illustrated (figure [2]).

6. (C) CONCEPT OF OPERATIONS

a. SEAL Team began sending combat platoons to Vietnam early in 1967 and were used almost exclusively in the Mekong Delta. Their mission, as stated above, in many cases evolved into a single objective: to identify and neutralize paramilitary units, i.e. sapper teams. Usually this involved obtaining intelligence on one person who after his capture would then lead you to the next senior man. This activity required an extremely accurate and quick intelligence collection system.

b. SEALs utilized a variety of intelligence sources:

   1. Provincial Reconnaissance Unit

   2. Static Central Grievances

   3. Revolutionary Development Teams

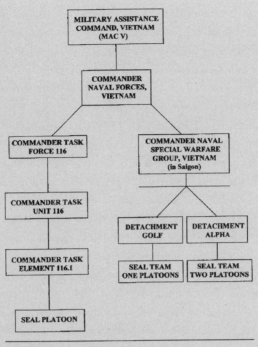

Figure 2

U.S. Navy

4. District Intel and Operating Center

5. Police Special Branch

6. Civil Operations Revolutionary Development Support

7. Province Chiefs

8. District Chiefs

9. U.S. Military Intelligence

10. Vietnamese Military Security Services

*11. Hoi Chan Center

12. U.S. or VN S-2 Dept.

13. SEAL informants

14. Naval Intelligence Liaison Officers

15. Regional Forces

16. Popular Forces

The Hoi Chan Center and SEAL informants provided the most accurate and most recent intelligence, and therefore proved to be the best SEAL platoon usage. Two (2) independent sources of intelligence were needed before it would be considered reliable information.

c. SEAL Teams achieved very good results by organizing missions on the basis of captured intelligence from these sources. The main reason for this success must be attributed to the organization and readiness of the SEAL platoon. In most cases all necessary equipment was ready and quickly available on short notice, and a full SEAL squad remained on base, ready to respond to new information at all times. After several months of operating together, platoon members needed only the most basic information about any imposed operations, which eliminated the need for lengthy briefings and preparations.

d. The platoon leader was responsible for keeping himself current on all intelligence in his area of operations. When critical information was received at any time of the day, he could clear a mission quickly through the Tactical Operations Center, coordinate necessary support (boat, air, artillery), gather his squad together, and be on his mission within an hour.

Excerpt from SEAL Team Two, Command and Control History 1966
Enclosure (1)
COMMAND HISTORY OF SEAL TEAM TWO
CHRONOLOGY
Page 1. [DECLASSIFIED from CONFIDENTIAL]
20 September 1962–30 January 1963 MTT 4-63 Under direction of Ensign DORAN and coordinated with LTJG A. C. ROUTH (SEAL ONE) SEALs instruct Republic of Vietnam Biet HAI (Junk Force Commando Platoons) in UDT/SEAL type operation.

Excerpt from SEAL Team Two, Command and Control History 1966
Enclosure (1)
COMMAND HISTORY OF SEAL TEAM TWO
2. OPERATIONS, ACTIVITIES, AND SPECIAL TOPICS (NARRATIVE) 1962
Pages 6–7. [DECLASSIFIED from CONFIDENTIAL]
DM2 WAUGH and SK2 BURBANK were the first to see action in Vietnam as

Surrounded by crates of supplies and ammunition, these SEALs are conducting a final briefing before going out on an operation. Their tiger-strip camouflage uniforms and heavily made-up faces will help these men disappear into the jungle and the shadows on their operation.

part of Mobile Training Team 10-62, which was under the command of LTJG HOLTZ of SEAL Team ONE. It was the purpose of the MTT to establish an indigenous training staff capable of maintaining training and operational readiness of the Vietnamese Navy Commando Platoons, with a minimum of U.S. assistance. They were further to act as advisers in the development of tactics, equipment, and operating procedures of these Vietnamese Junk Force Commando Platoons, or Biet Hai. MTT 10-62 was relieved by MTT 4-63, which was composed of one officer and seven enlisted men from SEAL Team TWO; personnel were ENS. DORAN, BM1 KUCINSKI, HM1 SCHWARTZ, CS1 TOLISON, BM2 TOLISON, HM2 McCARTY, AO3 BUMP, MN3 CLARK, and AT3 GOINES. The detachment was under control of LTJG A.C. ROUTH of SEAL Team ONE. Training for Biet Hai was coordinated through LTJG NINH, Vietnam Navy, and was similar to that conducted by MTT 10-62 with emphasis on land navigation, guerrilla fare, ambush and counterambush, and raiding techniques . . .

While being observed by their American SEAL advisers, these Biet Hai commandos train with IBS's near Danang in the early 1960s.

U.S. Navy

Both SEAL Teams had now entered Vietnam; they would not leave completely until more than ten years had passed.

Barry Enoch, Chief Gunner's Mate, USN (Ret.)

Back when I was a young man going to a military school, the Columbia Military Academy, there was a magazinelike book in the library that showed the men from the WWII UDTs, what they did, and how they did it. It was probably from the moment of my reading that book that I wanted to be a Navy Frogman.

In 1955, I enlisted in the U.S. Navy specifically to volunteer for the UDTs. But at that time you couldn't go directly to the Teams right after your enlistment. So I spent several years on board a heavy cruiser and then another two years as a crewmember of a destroyer escort. It was when I reenlisted that I was able to put in for UDT training and was accepted.

Class 24 UDTR, West Coast, was exciting, tough, and something I had been waiting a long time for. I was really glad to have been able to get into it and I really enjoyed it overall. There wasn't a question of what I was letting myself in for; I pretty much knew the training would be hard. But I didn't know how bad it would hurt.

Like for so many others, the hardest single part of training for me was Hell Week. During that week, I injured my knee and just had to reach down into myself and grab up that little bit of extra to get through.

We had been doing night rock portages on the beach behind the Hotel Del Coronado. I was the number-one man starboard, which meant I was the guy who was supposed to clamber out on the rocks and pull the line in to start securing the rubber boat. Only our boat bent in the middle and suddenly straightened out, flipping me forward and into the rocks. My knee hit the rock hard and took some damage. At any rate, I had a lot of swelling in it. So I just had to tough out the situation and keep on going. All of the swimming and cold water must have helped it a bit, as it healed up and I was fine.

The thing that got me through that long week was what I think gets so many others through; the desire to want to do that, to be a member of the Teams, more than anything else in the world. What I wanted was to be a Navy Frogman, a diver, and that was something I had wanted for a long, long time.

Like so many other training classes, not many of the students had the desire to get all the way through to the end. Class 24 started with sixty-three officers and enlisted men, and when we finally graduated, it was with six enlisted men and two officers. Our graduation ceremony wasn't very long. But it was a nice day, and we were all wearing our white uniforms under the Southern California sun.

After graduation, we were assigned to UDT 12. Going into First Platoon, I soon found myself one of the volunteers picked to join a small contingent of UDT operators going to the arctic for Project IceSkate. A few men were chosen from three different UDT platoons and we were flown up to Point Barrow, Alaska. From there, we caught an icebreaker, the Staten Island (AGB-5), which took us 800 miles into the arctic ice pack until we hit the solid kind of pack ice they call "gray ice."

On board the ship were some civilians from Washington, D.C. Our mission for Project IceSkate was to test a new kind of explosive and explosive device, what is now called HBX-3. The device had a spe-

cial container with a standoff that would let it float up and breach the ice from the bottom.

What they were trying to do was develop an explosive device that could be released from a submarine to open a hole in the ice. The target was to blast a hole through eighteen feet of ice, a hole large enough to let the submarine's sail slip through to the surface. The thickness of the ice was determined by the height of the sail. The idea was to give the submarine crew a means to escape in case of a nuclear accident while they were under the ice cap.

So we swam these devices back under the ice and fired a number of shots. What we soon found was a twenty-pound charge would make a hole big enough to let the whole submarine come up through the ice. It was cold stuff to work in, but we all had a lot of fun on that trip.

Diving under the ice is absolutely beautiful. The water is a clear blue that you can see through for over 180 feet and still recognize who you're looking at. But as you look down, the blue of the water just turns darker and darker underneath you, until it's almost a purple color.

Under the ice, way down below you, you could see these massive icebergs floating with just a slight negative buoyancy. Those huge bergs just slowly slid by, and you would wonder just what would happen if that sucker started to float up to the surface, where you were under the ice cap.

But the underneath of the ice cap is very rough. The surface of the ice might be flat and scoured down by the blowing snow, but under the water, the ice is rough. There were pressure ridges built up from where ice floes moved together, and those ridges could go down as deep as a house, sixty feet or more. Up where we were firing our shots, it was only eighteen feet thick. But it was like swimming against the surface of a cave, so many ice projections stuck down into the depths.

Close to the edge of the ice pack, the water would be slushy with ice, it seemed to be like swimming in a milkshake. And the water was cold, but we had special wet suits made for it that kept us protected.

It was when we came out of the water that we had a problem. The wind was blowing and it was drifting the snow pretty hard. Those conditions made the air feel super cold. When we surfaced and climbed out, or Teammates would quickly pat our faces dry with towels. Then they would put big parkas over us and hustle us into the boat. They got us aboard the icebreaker and into the warmth as quickly as they could. Because once we were out of the water, the cold would quickly freeze us solid. It was so cold that as they patted your face dry, the seawater that dripped off would freeze well before it hit the ground.

It was that coming out of the water into the arctic blast of cold that was more of a shock than getting in to the water in the first place. But we continued with our operations and then headed back to the much warmer climate around Coronado.

It was a few years later, in 1962, when I was deployed with UDT 12 on a Western Pacific tour. During our stop at Okinawa, a number of us were selected to go to parachute jump school. The U.S. Army First Special Forces Airborne Unit had a jump school at their base on the island. So for a while a number of Navy Frogmen learned how to jump out of a perfectly good airplane well before it landed.

After we completed jump school, we climbed aboard another plane that we were allowed to ride in all the way to its landing. That landing was in Yokuska, Japan, where another surprise showed up for a number of us.

It was around Christmastime, and I'm sure of that because I was coming back to the base from a Danny Kaye USO show. When I passed some of my Teammates on the beach, they told me to get over to the Quonset hut where the UDT 12 headquarters were. That wasn't any big deal, but then they told me that there was a set of transfer orders waiting for me there.

That last was something that had me a little bit upset. I had treaded water in the regular fleet Navy for four years waiting for my chance to become a Navy Frogman. And when I arrived in the office, I found out that sure enough, there were sets of orders for a bunch of us. We were all being transferred to something called "SEAL Team One."

No one there knew what a SEAL Team was, and I was raising more than a little racket about being transferred out of UDT 12. Our executive officer at the time was a man by the name of David Del Guidice. He told me that he didn't know what a SEAL Team was either. But Del Guidice went on to say that he was going to be my commanding officer when we got there. So I shut up right quick.

Men from both UDTs 11 and 12 formed the West Coast SEAL Team, SEAL Team One. The East Coast had men from UDT 21 drawn out to form up SEAL Team Two. Both Teams had sixty men, fifty enlisted and ten officers each.

We were flown back to Coronado, where we formed up into the new SEAL Team. At first, we didn't know what it was or what we were going to do. Confusion was pretty common and we were all a little lost. Six months later and the situation hadn't gotten a whole lot better.

We were fish out of water, literally. We had been told that President Kennedy had wanted people from the Navy to create a unit like the Army Special Forces. We were going to be able to train indigenous forces and operate in a riverine-type environment as well as operate there ourselves. And to meet our new responsibilities, we were going to receive a lot of training.

We went to all kinds of schools. We were commissioned as a SEAL Team in January 1962. And we went to schools almost from day one. Within a week of becoming a plankowner of SEAL Team One, I was at Camp Pendleton, going through basic infantry combat training.

Navy, Marine Corps, Army—all of them had training that we went to. Antiguerrilla and guerrilla warfare training from the Marine Corps; Fort Benning and Army Ranger training. Five days after I graduated from Ranger school, I was down in Panama going through jungle warfare school. Navy schools as well; assault boat coxswain training was one we attended. And after that we went to the Berlitz School of languages. Exotic demolitions training, such as atomic demolition munitions school. Almost anything that was available had some SEALs going to it. We had a Priority 2 and could get a billet for a student just by asking for it.

And we went across the country to Fort Bragg and attended Army Special Forces schools such as foreign weapons or kitchen table demolitions. And Special Forces operational techniques were not ignored as we learned how to operate as unconventional forces.

That last training was closer to what we were going to be doing within just a few years. But Vietnam was still down the road a ways, at least for some of us.

Within about a year of the SEALs Teams being founded, a group of us deployed to Da Nang to train commando-type troops. This was my first exposure to Vietnam. It was all brand-new to me and I was pretty excited. I had a new job and I didn't really know what the job was going to be. But all of us always tried to do the best we could with whatever job we were assigned.

Eventually, I became one of the men teaching the Vietnamese weapons handling, marksmanship, and other skills. This course went on for a while. My job was just to be their instructor. Once they were trained, the Vietnamese commandos were taken away and I never did learn what they were going to be used for.

That was in 1963, and I remember the year well as I had returned home just a short time before my son, our third child, was born. And there wasn't much question in my mind that the SEALs were going to be back in Vietnam.

The SEALs had both a cold-war and a hot-war mission to perform. Those first years after our commissioning, we were operating in a cold-war mode, acting as advisers and instructors. None of us really had any idea that by 1965–1966, the war in Vietnam would escalate to what it did. Once it became a hot war, it stayed that way through 1970 and beyond. But we were ready for it when the time finally came around for us to go into direct combat.

During the first several years of the Teams' existence, we continued to go to all kinds of schools in between the times we deployed as detachments to different assignments. By 1966, SEAL Team One was sending detachments to Vietnam to conduct direct-action combat missions against the Viet Cong. It had become a hot war.

For myself, I didn't go out on my first combat deployment until 1968. In 1965, after I had completed my first enlistment with SEAL Team One, I reenlisted to be an instructor at Underwater Demolition Team Replacement training, what was later to be known as BUD/S for Basic Underwater Demolition/SEAL training.

My tour as a UDTR instructor would be three years long. And after that tour was over, I would go back to SEAL Team One. It was with Class 42 in 1967 that I finished my tour as an instructor, and I ended up taking some of those boys overseas with me.

Things were continually changing during those years I spent as an instructor. When you first went in as a young man to be an instructor, you wanted to do everything to those students that you thought had been done to you when you went through training. Fortunately, there were some old vets who worked alongside you as instructors, and you were assigned to one another.

Those experienced instructors would hold you back and prevent you from tearing a student down completely. Because you were supposed to pick the man back up by the end of the day. And they also kept you from getting too extreme with the students. As my stint as an instructor went along, I learned how to do it right. And there were several things that personally happened to me to adjust my thinking.

Since my Navy rate was as a gunner's mate, my specific assignment was to teach demolitions, weapons, and land warfare. One of the experienced instructors who was there had actually taught me when I went through UDTR. Bud Jurick was someone you could look up to easily. He had parachuted into Normandy during D day when he was in the Army. And he had seen combat in Korea. He was kind of my idol, and he taught me how to be an instructor, and kept me from beating up the students too badly.

Time had gone on in the Teams while I was helping to create new SEALs and Frogs. The SEAL combat commitment in Vietnam had started in 1966 and grown throughout the year. And the cost of that commitment also grew.

A young man that I had gone through training with in Class 24, who had jumped from planes with me over Okinawa, and had even bought the house behind mine in San Diego so that our families could grow up together—he was the first SEAL killed in Vietnam.

On 19 August 1966, Billy W. Machen was killed during an ambush of his platoon in Vietnam. He had been walking point during a patrol and opened fire on a VC ambush before his Teammates moved into the kill zone. He saved his platoon, and it cost him his life.

When that time came, I think it shocked the whole SEAL community. It brought us to the reality that we were fighting a hot war over there, and it could cost. So to try and hold down the cost, we started to do different things to improve our skills and knowledge. We would interview any SEAL who had just come back from Vietnam. We learned what they had been exposed to, how the enemy was fighting, what worked, and what didn't.

Training at UDTR didn't really change; instead it was added onto.

A BUD/S instructor points out a fine point involved in the cleaning of the M16A1 rifle. The student, with his disassembled weapon in his arms, looks intently at what his instructor is showing him.

U.S. Navy

When I had first stepped on board as an instructor, UDTR training was sixteen weeks long. When I left, it had increased to eighteen weeks long. It was continually growing, as nothing was taken away from the original course of instruction but more was being added all the time. It became harder because we were trying to teach those things that would help the Teams to deploy as soon as possible.

Our own success was coming back on us in a way. Vice Admiral Elmo R. Zumwalt Jr. was the commander naval forces, Vietnam, as of 30 September 1968. And Admiral Zumwalt wanted more SEAL in-country as soon as he could get them. We had already been sending augmentation platoons to Vietnam, platoons that arrived in-country not to relieve another platoon but to start up operations in new areas. And SEAL Team Two had been sending platoons to Vietnam since early 1967.

All of this added up to making that last year of my tour as an instructor the longest dress rehearsal I was ever on. I wanted to be a SEAL, I wanted to go back to my Team, and I wanted to go back to Vietnam.

Every time I went to Vietnam, it was a learning experience, especially in the beginning. Any individual who goes into combat experiences the fears of that first night. Just because a SEAL is highly trained for combat doesn't mean he won't be scared. And the same fear that was in my heart, I'm sure was in the hearts of the young men I had with me. But you also have to overcome that fear pretty quick or you won't be any use to yourself or your Teammates.

Arriving in Vietnam, I was the leading petty officer (LPO) for Alfa Platoon, following Platoon Leader Rip Bliss and a fine assistant platoon leader, Warrant Officer Scott Lyon. The platoon had another first class petty officer, Harlen Funkhouser, who had done tours up in the Rung Sat, north of the delta, where we were now. Outside of the three of us, all of the rest of the platoon had just graduated from UDTR only six months before our arrival in-country. We had trained as a platoon ever since their graduation.

You worry about kids like that, and I suppose they might have worried about me a bit. They called me the "Old Man," being all of the ripe old age of thirty-two. While we were getting ready to deploy, I remember my daughter going up to my wife crying "How come they're calling Dad the Old Man?"

Those "kids" of mine in the platoon were all of twenty or twenty-one year old men. But they did a great job during our deployment— fabulous, as far as I'm concerned. And I think that one of the reasons we did so well was that my platoon hadn't been exposed to the Rung Sat Special Zone and the tactics used there.

The Rung Sat is an almost 400-square-mile area of nipa palms, mangrove swamps, rivers, streams, canals, and mud between Saigon and the South China Sea. Called the Forest of Assassins by the Vietnamese after the hundreds of years of pirates and smugglers hanging out in it, the Rung Sat, as it was known to us, was the first area of Vietnam where SEAL Team One had begun combat operations back in 1966. That jungle mud and swamp needed a particular style of operating and movement for us to get around in it. Where we were for this tour, the Mekong Delta, it had a different way of making you move through it.

So now our platoon was developing new tactics. It did seem that every time you deployed to Vietnam, you were fighting a new kind of war. Things just changed constantly.

It may have been a little different, this tour for Alfa platoon. It may have been made up mostly of new graduates from training. But they also had their old instructor leading them. They would have to say themselves whether or not that made a difference. But I did notice that they did whatever I said without much trouble at all.

Early on during that deployment, Scotty Lyon went out on an operation that stands out in my mind from that tour. He took his squad, all green men, down to the north edge of the Ba Xuyen province, to the Cu Lao Dung Island complex near the mouth of the Bassac River. Mr. Lyon developed one of the finest operations that I have ever seen.

He had an LST offshore with helicopter gunships on board. From somewhere, Mr. Lyon brought somewhere in the neighborhood of eight to ten PBRs on the Bassac River at the same time. And they all went in and hit a POW camp, liberating twenty-six Vietnamese POWs who had been captured during the Tet offensive over six months earlier. And Scotty did all of this without one single casualty or accident among his men. That was a tremendous job.

We were all proud of how the Second Squad from our platoon had conducted that operation. There is no question that the success of that operation was due to Warrant Officer Scott Lyon and the way he was able to put the operation together and plan it out. That op was probably the highlight of the whole trip to me.

For our first operation, things were a little different. We inserted from an LCPL (Landing Craft, Personnel, Large), one of the older boats. One of the officers from Mike Platoon, who we were relieving, was taking us out into the area for a "breaking-in" op.

We inserted and patrolled in probably some 3,000 meters until we approached a hooch. A light inside the hooch caught the attention of our point man, so we spread out to surround the building. A couple of the guys went into the building and surprised the single VC inside. He didn't want to be taken prisoner and didn't get away fast

A group of heavily armed SEALs on patrol in Vietnam, with his back to the camera in the center of the picture is Greg McPartlin, armed with a Stoner Mk 23 light machine gun. Attached to his carrying harness is an assortment of ammunition, fragmentation and white phosphorus grenades and medical equipment.

Greg McPartlin Collection

enough. So Alfa Platoon had its first confirmed kill. Our platoon was now blooded.

One of our next operations went much the same. Only, on it we were chasing a mortar tube all night long. It was a heavy mortar and we could see the muzzle flashes from it every time the crew set it up and fired. The flash would reflect on leaves from trees and we knew we had to be close to the firing position. We also knew that a heavy mortar was usually protected by a dozen men or so with AK-47s. But every time we could get close to a suspected firing position, they would have moved and were firing from another location.

Finally, we found a large canal and figured out that they must have had the mortar mounted on a large sampan. Beaching the sampan, they would fire a few rounds on the nearby town of Vung Tau. They would fire three rounds and then move to another position. There, they would fire three rounds again and move on. After the third cycle of firing, the mortar stopped completely.

We never did find them, so we went back to our original mission. Again, we found a hooch with a single VC in it. And yet again, the man didn't want to be taken prisoner and we ended up taking him out.

Continuing our patrol, we came across a small bunker that we intended to blow. I had the demolitions with me and set the charge to destroy the structure. When the shot went off, the explosion was a lot more powerful than we expected. There was some VC ammo or other ordnance that my demolition charge had detonated. Just an average Saturday night in Vietnam.

We had no losses during that first tour, and few in the way of injuries. Our first op went down on 18 August 1968, and our last was on 9 February 1969. Alfa Platoon had 101 combat operations during that tour. And within a day or so of our last op, we were on our way back home to Coronado.

My second tour of duty to Vietnam was really more involved than that first one. I was again the LPO, this time of Charlie Platoon. On 31 December 1969, we arrived in Vietnam and Charlie Platoon started operating out of Ben Luc, a small Navy base on the Van Co Dong River. But that assignment wasn't going to last. Within a few months, Charlie Platoon was sent to the Ba Xuyen province as an augmentation platoon assigned to Coastal Group 36, right across the Bassac River from Dung Island.

Dung Island was a complex of nine different islands that had more or less been left alone during the war to that point. It was, of course, the same place to which Mr. Lyon had led Second Squad of Alfa Platoon to liberate that VC POW camp. But we were in the area to take advantage of the information that had been built up about the area.

Up in Saigon, the intelligence folder on the local area was about two inches thick. There was a tremendous NILO (Naval Intelligence Liaison Officer) officer down there who had an individual working for him who was a big help. The man working for the NILO was a Vietnamese civilian who was very good at getting into the Chieu Hoi circuit and gathering intelligence from them.

The Chieu Hoi (Open Arms) Program offered amnesty to Viet Cong defectors. People who wanted to leave the Communists could "rally" into a local Chieu Hoi center, where they gave themselves up with no risk of reprisals. There, they would be interrogated and debriefed on the operations they had done and what they knew about the area.

So we ended up on the shore at Coastal Group 36 living in tents. The situation wasn't the best in the world; we didn't even have a supply of food, or any regular way of getting any. Every now and then a Coast Guard cutter would come up and drop off some supplies, but for the most part, Charlie Platoon was eating off the land and what the local market offered.

The tents were our home for about three months. Then the Navy Seabees came in and built us a regular base. And I've loved the Navy Seabees ever since. The first thing they did was build a mess hall to feed us. And the second thing they did was build us a barracks, even before they built living quarters for themselves.

The base was an old French outpost, set up in a typical triangular formation. There was a small detachment of riverine forces at the base, a Vietnamese unit using a number of the old gray junks with a few machine guns on them for defense. The Vietnamese just kind of patrolled up and down the river in those junks.

We in Charlie Platoon didn't have anything much better in the way of equipment. We had little in the way of reliable boat support; there was no MST (Mobile Support Team) support with their specialized SEAL craft for us then. Instead, we had one Boston whaler with an outboard motor, IBSs, and sampans. That's what we had and it was what we used. The support may have been light, but Charlie Platoon operated.

In my first platoon back in 1968, we had spent 180 days in-country and ran 101 combat operations. In Charlie, my second platoon, we spent 180 days in-country and ran 71 combat operations. And in both platoons, we had over 80 percent enemy contact on our ops.

The operations for Charlie Platoon weren't as big in numbers, but we had learned a little more over the years. Now we went strictly after the VCI, the infrastructure of the Viet Cong, their leadership and support. Our training had emphasized that "dead men don't talk." And that was the lesson that had been driven home with everyone in the Team over and over again. Now we tried everything we could to capture prisoners and to gather information.

Three heavily armed Navy SEALs share a cigarette with a South Vietnamese. It was from their experiences in the early part of the Vietnam War that the SEALs learned prisoners and the information they supplied was one of the most valuable things they could bring back from the jungle.

Back the year before, during Tet of 1968, we didn't know just how badly we had hurt the VC when we stopped their attacks and drove them back. The North Vietnam Army had put a lot of the leadership of the VC in the forefront of the attacks during Tet. When those VC leaders were killed, their places were taken by NVA officers from up north.

But when an NVA officer came down to take up an important position, he was usually a colonel or something like that, unless he was a tax collector. That officer would bring along his own security team, medical personnel, and other support staff. Capturing one of these guys would almost always turn into a firefight because of all the people they kept around them.

We started running into light force, company-sized combat units that were NVA. These troops were dressed like VC, but there were telltale signs we picked up quickly. Their packs and ponchos were different. And their sandals were very noticeable as high-quality NVA sandals rather than the local market products.

And the weapons these NVA units carried were better and more powerful than the norm had been with the VC. Instead of the bolt-action rifles we had seen before, now we were finding the troops armed with AK-47s and SKS carbines. The ammunition and grenades they carried also indicated that they were a well-equipped army rather than a purely guerrilla force.

Probably the thing that stands out most in my mind from that second tour is the end results from the whole tour. The capture of a number of VCI members and the intelligence that we drew from them helped us operate. Some of this information led us to jungle workshops where they had a junk factory hidden. This was a camouflaged factory where the VC had been making huge junks to transport their equipment and people from the South China Sea up the Bassac River to other parts of South Vietnam. It was a big factory, but we demolished it with explosives. On a bunch of operations, we ran into a lot of personnel who were shooting back at us. So during that tour, we had our hands full from time to time.

The most major action for me personally during that last tour took place with only a few of my Teammates around me. One night, we went in with three Americans, including myself, and a ten-man LDNN platoon. The LDNNs were then known as the Lein Doi Nguoi Nhai, South Vietnamese SEALs, the name translating to "the team of soldiers who fight under the sea."

The LDNNs were very good fighters in my opinions. But we went along with them on operations for a number of reasons, one of the big ones being to give them support. Without us—that is, Americans—on the operation, they couldn't call for air support or whatever else might be available from the U.S. forces.

We went in on some intelligence that told us about the location of a Viet Cong infrastructure meeting. We had both the time and probable location of the meeting and started our infiltration at night.

Going in from our insertion point, we slipped through the nipa palm for about three hours. The water we were moving through was so deep sometimes that some of us had to pick the shorter Vietnamese up from the water and pass them along from one clump of nipa palm to another.

Just before daylight, we arrived at the target site. There was a small dike between us and a clearing. On the edge of the clearing was a hooch. Besides the clearing and the hooch, we also spotted an armed guard, sitting down and leaning against a tree, his weapon in his lap. He may have been asleep, but as soon as we came up over the dike, he jumped up.

Two SEALs put out fire toward a camouflaged VC bunker hidden under the hooch in the distance. The SEALs are working in support of Operation CRIMSON TIDE near Vinh Binh in December 1967.

U.S. Navy

When the guard jumped up, he was immediately knocked down. Of course the noise from that alerted the rest of the enemy. When we reached the hooch, there was a short, fierce firefight that resulted in our VCI targets being killed. Later two of the dead VCI were identified as Tu Day, a district security chief and chapter party secretary, and Nam Meo of the People's Revolutionary Committee. Some additional NVA got away, running from the back of the hooch into the jungle nearby.

With my Stoner carbine, I laid down fire on the VC running from the hooch. Other NVA were running toward a bunker at the same time and some of the LDNNs chased them. On the patrol, I was carrying the radio, and when the fighting broke out, I wanted to get that radio to the patrol leader as fast as I could.

As I was running across the field to where the patrol leader was located, something smashed into my back, knocking me down. I smacked into the ground but wasn't hurt. The adrenaline was pumping right then, so I just got up and kept going.

The patrol leader for the LDNNs was a petty officer named Tich. When I saw that young man next, he had been killed, shot right under the left arm near his heart. Ronnie Rodger, the SEAL LDNN adviser, had Tich over his shoulder. When he laid Tich on the ground, we could see that there wasn't anything we could do for him.

That death hit me pretty hard. There had only been ten months between my combat tours to Vietnam. The year before, Tich had been with me. During that deployment, I had even made it to Tich's wedding. And now I was going to attend his funeral.

There were no exit wounds in Tich's body. So I tied his hands together and slipped them around my neck so that his body could hang down across my back. I would carry my friend back out to his people. While I set off to the hooch with Tich, Rodger started gathering up our platoon and pulling them back to the building as well.

Later I thought Tich's body kept breaking my radio antenna. But as we dropped back to the hooch, we could see that the NVA on both sides were jumping into the nipa palm. So we laid down a base of fire with our machine guns.

Now it was time to get some support in there to help us. After unhooking Tich's body and laying it down, I took the radio off from my back, figuring the antenna might have been broken or bent from the weight against it.

After examining the radio, I now knew what had knocked me down when I ran through the clearing earlier. The battery pack of the radio had two holes in it where bullets had struck. The antenna was broken as well from a third bullet's impact. But when I tried it, the radio worked great.

The first thing I tried to do was to call in 81mm mortar fire from the Swift boats we had in the river after our insertion. But that didn't work since we were out of their range. There were some Army Cobra gunships that picked up my signal. They came in and offered

In flight, a pair of OV-10A Bronco "Black Ponies."

U.S. Navy

what fire support they had available. But they were running short of fuel and ammunition and had to leave while the VC were still around us.

Now our small platoon of LDNNs and SEALs were surrounded by what was later determined to be an NVA light force company. They had us surrounded and we were already down two men, Tich and another LDNN who was wounded in the face. So the situation was starting to get more than a little tense for us.

But there was some additional support that came in over the radio, some of the OV-10B Broncos with U.S. Navy pilots. These were the armed Broncos of the Black Ponies Squadron. We couldn't have received much higher-quality help right then. The two planes had the call signs Pony 102 and Pony 106.

The NVA forces were all around us, cutting off any escape for the platoon. When the Ponies were overhead, I took out a magenta-colored silk "T" ground-marker panel. With the panel indicating to the Black Ponies exactly where we were, I told them that fifty meters in front of the T were the NVA.

The Black Pony pilot called back down to me, questioning the fifty meters' distance between us and the NVA, a dangerously close distance for them to unload their ordnance on a target and not risk hitting us. The pilot understood the situation immediately when I answered him, "Roger that, fifty meters. And if you don't hurry up, it'll be twenty-five."

Those planes came right down to the deck, flying just overhead to minimize hitting us. That was the closest support I ever had. And it was the best support I ever had, too. The heavy five-inch Zuni rockets from those Black Ponies were like hitting the NVA with heavy artillery.

When the first of those big rockets went off, the blast shook us all hard, and I said a few choice words to reflect my feelings. It wasn't that the pilots had made a mistake, but the rocket had hit a palm tree close by over our heads and detonated early. So I called up to the pilot and asked: "What was that?"

"Five-inch rocket," was the answer that came back over the radio.

Well, I had been used to the 2.75-inch rockets from the Seawolves and other helicopter gunships. These were a lot larger, and louder. But their power was something we would be able to put to use.

The planes just pushed back the jungle in front of us. Then we would catch fire from the enemy coming in from the other side. So I would move the marker T and the Ponies would hit the jungle in front of it again.

Those two planes just stayed with us for what seemed like forever. Finally, Pony 102, the flight leader, called down to me over the radio. He said that they were running low on ammunition, so every other run or so would be a dummy run, with the planes not firing their weapons but still keeping the NVAs' heads down.

So those little OV-10s came in on a strafing run, and the NVA would dive behind whatever cover they had available. Only the planes wouldn't shoot. So when the Bronco passed, the NVA would jump up to try and shoot at the plane, and the next guy coming in would open up on them.

The Black Ponies went back and forth like that for a while, then the flight leader got back in touch with me. He said that they had to leave soon but that two Marines (aircraft) were coming down from Vung Tau and he would stay with us until they arrived.

In Vung Tau, an airman carefully watches the underside of an OV-10A Bronco. His left hand is on the muzzle of one of the aircraft's four (two to a side) wing-mounted 7.62mm M60 machine guns. In front of the unconcerned airman is a pod of four 5-inch Zuni rockets and their large high-explosive warheads. Just visible to the left is an empty 7-round pod for 2.75-inch rockets. This is just some of the ordnance and weapons normally carried by a Black Pony for an operation.

U.S. Navy

Soon there were two more OV-10s; these were Vipers from the Marine Corps, flying overhead, and the Black Ponies went back to refuel and rearm. Those Marines might have been different pilots, but you couldn't tell by the way they flew. They were call-signed 106 and 108. And those numbers were the only difference between those Marines and the Black Ponies.

Those Marines flew just as close and as accurately as the others had. The planes flew by so closely that I could tell you whether those pilots had shaved that morning or not. That was how low to the ground those little fixed-wing aircraft flew. Prior to that operation, Black Ponies had always been fighting for us from way up in the sky. That day, they had been right there in the jungle with us. And I wouldn't be here today telling of the action if it wasn't for them.

When the two Marine aircraft showed up from Vung Tau, the Black Ponies had already quieted down the NVA a bit. So I told those pilots to save their five-inch rockets. On the ground, we were getting low on ammunition, with the LDNNs only having about two magazines apiece for their M16s.

Di Croce, one of the SEALs from my platoon, had a Stoner light machine gun with him. So I had him break out part of his ammo load and pass it out to the LDNNs. Since the Stoner fired the same ammunition as the M16, the LDNNs were able to break down the belts and use the loose ammo to load up two more magazines apiece.

Now we had a medevac come in, and we were able to get our wounded and dead out. But the extraction birds wouldn't come in to get the rest of us out. So I told the Marine pilots to use their five-inch rockets and blow me a hole through the nipa palm.

Once that hole opened up for us, any NVA near it would be down for more than a moment from the blasts. So we took off through the hole and just about ran the 400 meters to the nearest water. But the tide had gone out and the water was low. In spite of the low water, as soon as my damaged radio got wet, it quit talking. But I had managed to turn over air-ground control of the aircraft to my lieutenant, who was on a Swift boat nearby.

Before we hit the water, the Swifts wanted to come in and give us fire support. But I had to tell them not to. They would have had to fire at the enemy right behind us. We already had enough stuff coming at us. For the Swifts to have given us support, their fire would have had to come right at us as well.

But that's what happens when you're encircled.

We finally got out far enough that the boats were able to pick us up. Extracting, the patrol pulled out without any more casualties. Besides the VCI we had killed, we had also captured weapons, ammunition, and documents. And that was probably the most exciting mission I was on.

Ron Rodger and I took Tich's body back to Saigon, to the big cathedral they had there. Then we escorted it to the LDNN base and extended our respects to his comrades and family. Finally, we grabbed a helicopter heading back and returned to work.

That was an expensive operation for us; Tich had been a good friend. But it was pretty expensive for the NVA as well. Later reports added to the body count we had of twelve NVA KIA and fifteen WIA.

PCF-11, a Navy Swift boat of Coast Division 11 making a high speed run. At the stern of the craft is a sailor manning the over/under Mk 2 81mm mortar and .50-caliber machine gun. Above the cabin, another sailor mans the twin .50-caliber machine guns in the gun tub. These boats were able to give rapid service and heavy fire support to SEALs during a mission.

U.S. Navy

Reports from NILO a few days after the op told of the NVA forcing the locals to produce forty coffins.

That was a memorable operation for me, and apparently the Navy thought highly of it as well. Sometime later, I was awarded the Navy Cross, our nation's second-highest award for valor, for the actions I took part in that day.

But I have mixed emotions about that medal. Of course you always feel very proud when someone hangs a medal on you for something that you did. And that wasn't the first one that anyone had ever hung on me. But the feeling of humility also comes in very strongly when I think about the medal.

I don't know of any medal that anybody could give anyone, for any action, in which somebody hadn't done more, or even lost their life, and didn't receive one. As I think about that day, I remember those guys up in the sky with their planes, the Black Ponies and Vipers. I wouldn't be alive today if it wasn't for them. And yet I was the one who received the Navy Cross.

My mentor back during my instructor days, Bud Jurick, explained to a student once what heroics were. Bud said that heroics were when the right man saw you at the wrong time, doing the job that you were trained to do. And I think that's what happened to me.

But a Black Pony will never have to buy a drink while I'm around. Just a short time ago I was able to make contact with the fellow who was the lead pilot of that flight of Black Ponies that day. And I am personally looking forward to seeing him.

Physically, a Navy SEAL can be almost any kind of man. There's heavyweights like me, and skinny ones. There's boys from Brooklyn and boys from Oklahoma, from Texas, Kentucky, California, and all of the other states of the Union. And with them come as many different backgrounds as there are places to come from. And each of them is an individual who has made the decision that "I quit" will not be a part of his vocabulary.

Navy SEALs have been portrayed as being kind of superhuman. And some of that might be their own fault. When you don't talk about something, even to end the rumors, the public tends to answer its own questions with whatever story might come along.

What the men of the Teams are, simply, are well-trained, devoted individuals who are, in a combat sense, workaholics. The Team they belong to is more of a huge family than anything else.

In my records are dozens of addresses of men I know and remain in contact with. There are many more who contact me, by phone, mail, or in person, every year. An old Teammate might call me at 2 A.M., and I'll still be glad to hear his voice.

Our reunions are where we get together on a scheduled basis once a year. And it's tremendous to see all of the guys together like that. You might run into a guy at a reunion who you haven't seen for twenty years, but all at once he shows up and it's like the time didn't happen.

I never did have a brother when I was growing up. But I've got hundreds of them now. And that's the reason I say it's a family. Even our higher command refers to the Teams as being a big family. And we react as one.

Sometime back, I went to Las Vegas to visit with an individual who knew that he had terminal cancer. And he knew that he was going to go. But he made a statement that stuck with me. "I don't care how big and how tough a Navy SEAL is," he said. "They'll always be able to say, 'I love you.'"

And that kind of summed it up to me. I may not be able to say that to another man, but inside the family, it's easy.

When a young man stands in front of the Naked Warrior statue, the monument in front of the UDT-SEAL Museum to the UDT men who went before us, I can't tell you exactly what he sees there. But there is something inside those bronze eyes that he does see, and it's not visible to those people who haven't served in the Teams.

What I do hope they would feel is the determination of spirit, the "I'm going to make it. I'm going to do it until I drop, nothing is going to stop me from being a SEAL."

Usually, guys come to that conclusion sometime during training. And by the time they reach that point, where they know inside their soul that they will not stop, usually by then, all of the others who hadn't made that decision have fallen away and are gone.

■ Chapter 3

FIRST COMBAT

Vietnam was not the first place where the SEALs were sent in to combat as direct-action platoons. Though they were involved in a number of actions during the Cuban Missile Crisis in October 1962, the men of the SEAL Teams did not see active combat at that time.

The Dominican Republic is a country in the Caribbean that shares the island of Hispaniola with Haiti, taking up the eastern two-thirds of the island. In early 1965, rebel factions in the military rose up against the Ried Cabral government, causing it to fall on 25 April. Further uprisings of political groups and citizens added to the uproar of the coup in the country.

The United States Navy prepared to evacuate U.S. citizens from the Dominican Republic within a few days of the initial coup. Fears of a Communist takeover of the rebel movement prompted the United States to act. Without consulting allies in the surrounding countries of Latin America, the U.S. sent in Marines and other troops to the Dominican Republic. Among the troops that were sent in during May 1965 were Army Special Forces and Navy SEALs from SEAL Team Two.

The SEALs were highly trained, but most had never seen active combat. Actual fighting was limited, primarily taking place in Santo Domingo, which was the rebel stronghold. The rebels were not dominated or controlled by Communist forces, and the situation was later turned over to peacekeeping forces from elsewhere in Latin America. But in the Dominican Republic, the men of SEAL Team Two saw for the first time the tremendous destructive power of their still-new AR-15 rifles, the first ones of their kind in Navy hands. It would be several years before the SEALs would use those same rifles, along with a wide assortment of other weapons, in combat again, this time in Southeast Asia.

Excerpt from SEAL Team Two, Command and Control History 1966
Enclosure (1)
COMMAND HISTORY OF SEAL TEAM TWO
CHRONOLOGY
Page 3. [DECLASSIFIED from CONFIDENTIAL]
16 May–5 June 1965—Santo Domingo, Dominican Republic. SEAL Detachment works with Seventh Special Forces teams in the Dominican Republic crisis.

Excerpt from SEAL Team Two, Command and Control History 1966
Enclosure (1)

COMMAND HISTORY OF SEAL TEAM TWO
2. OPERATIONS, ACTIVITIES, AND SPECIAL TOPICS (NARRATIVE)
   1962
Page 12. [DECLASSIFIED from CONFIDENTIAL]
On 30 April, a small detachment of one officer (LTJG DORAN) and five enlisted men reported aboard the USS *LA SALLE* (LPD3) to deploy to the Dominican Republic. On 16 May, a second detachment was called to Santo Domingo to work with the 7th Special Forces in reconnaissance of Samona Bay, on the northeastern tip of the island. LT. KOCHEY was in charge of this 3/10 group. There had been suspicious small-boat traffic in the area of Samona Bay and it was suspected that caves in the bay were being used as arms and ammunition caches. Reconnaissance was conducted by [2] Team personnel [LTJG DORAN & RM2 ROWELL] dressed in civilian clothes, posing as tourists on a fishing trip. Caves were thoroughly searched, but none contained suspicious material or were practical as cache sites. Members of the detachment were also involved in several firefights with rebels in the streets of Santo Domingo. No SEAL Team casualties were suffered. They returned to Little Creek on 28 May.

Mike Boynton, Master Chief Aviation Ordnanceman, USN (Ret.)

In early 1965, I wasn't married yet, though I was dating Mary, who would later be my wife. I was living out in Virginia Beach with a Teammate in a trailer. My transportation was a motorcycle and I considered myself really something hot, zooming into the base every day. Tom Cruise lives, a cool life.

One Saturday, I received a phone call from the quarterdeck at SEAL Team Two. The message was that I had to come in to the Team, that the CO wanted to see me. There was no question that I was going in as quickly as I could, but the thoughts that were going through my head were along the lines of: Oh, geez, what have I done?

I was only a third class petty officer, and I couldn't think of any-

thing I had done recently to deserve the attention of the CO. And it had to be serious if he called me in to the Team on a Saturday.

I had only been in SEAL Team Two for about three months, having transferred over from UDT. It had been a job getting to the new SEAL Team; I couldn't just ship over from the UDT. Instead, I actually had to get out of the Navy and reenlist just to get over to SEAL Team Two. It had been a real hassle, but the end result was worth it.

Most of the guys were long familiar to me; I had known them back in UDT 21. And when I arrived, I started going through the mill, heading out for the various training courses to get my qualifications behind be. Now, three months later, I had most of my quals behind me. The only thing I hadn't done was go to HALO school yet.

So I was qualified to operate, and heading it to SEAL Team Two on a Saturday to see the CO about something that I had no idea about.

Okay, fine, I was heading in on my bike, wondering just what in the hell I had managed to do in the last two weeks since I had gotten back from training. It wasn't like they were going to tell me anything over the phone. It never dawned on me that we might be going somewhere. But that changed the moment I pulled in to the Team.

Here it was a weekend, liberty time, and a whole bunch of the guys were in at the SEAL Team. Oh, it's an op, I thought to myself as I pulled in. There wasn't actually anyone walking around the area, but the parking lot was full of cars. Something was up, no question about it.

Heading inside, I was told to head on back to the briefing room. I went on back to the briefing room and there was the CO, Tommy Tarbox, telling us that we were going to take two platoons down to the Dominican Republic. And we were going to leave tomorrow. And then we got a list of the gear we were supposed to take with us and who was supposed to get what. The rest of the talk was an outline of which platoons were going, how they were being transported— generally, a basic operational briefing.

It wasn't really two specific platoons that were going—we were organized into assault groups then anyway, which was really just a name change. A detachment the size of two platoons, twenty-four men, was being sent out on the deployment. There were guys like me, Bob Gallagher, Frank Moncrief, Swede Tornblum, and Jack Rowell among others, basically just a bunch of the guys from Team Two. Among our officers was Black Jack Macione and Georg Doran.

So we started breaking out the gear and packing it for transportation by ship. Our breathing rigs were these pieces of shit called Westinghouse Emersons. Opinions of the rigs were not high. But they were what we had, so they got packed up. Beans, bullets, this and that, whatever was on the lists, all went into our gray cruise boxes.

One of the new items we had was the first-model starlight scope. This was the newest thing on the market, and we had it mounted on an M14 rifle. That big-ass AN/PVS-1 scope added about six pounds to the rifle, but it let us see in the dark, which was pretty cool.

Okay, so we had all of our gear ready to go. We mustered again to get further instructions. Basically, we were going to muster at the Team Sunday and fly out. Then we were told not to tell anyone where we were going.

Tell anyone where we were going? I barely knew where we were going. And I wasn't going to tell anyone anyway. But I wanted to tell Mary something. So I took her out to dinner that night and said that I had to leave the country but couldn't tell her where I was going. There wasn't much more I could say than that. It was kind of stupid, but I was just a third class, what the hell did I know?

So the next day, we all jumped on a plane and flew on south. Landing in the Dominican Republic, we proceeded to stay at the airport all day and that night. Army Special Forces guys were hanging out at the airport along with us. It looked to me like mass confusion, but I guess somebody knew what was going on.

Macione, Doran, and a couple of others went off for briefings, so they had something to do and were gone all that day. For us, all we did was sit on our asses at the airport doing nothing. All we could do was stay in this hangar. You could tell there had been some kind of combat going on already because a lot of the planes were broken and you could smell things. It was the usual disarray of a battlefield, though not as intense as some I would see later.

But our officers finally came back and told us they were going to hold a briefing. So we all piled on this old plane, that we would never want to get on again, to have some kind of privacy. And the

In a staged recruiting picture, Mike Boynton stands dressed in a camouflage beret and jacket, armed with an M16A1 rifle. With his face camouflaged, Mike Boynton is representing a SEAL. His Teammate stands behind him, geared for an open-circuit underwater swim as a UDT operator.

U.S. Navy

officers started to brief us on the situation. Then some yahoo official of the Dominican Republic came up and told us to get the hell off the plane.

So we had to go somewhere else and complete the briefing. Basically, we were told we were going to go into town and do some fighting. And they had some other things lined up for us. And we were all going to get into civilian clothes so that we could blend in. The only thing was, none of us had any civilian clothes with us. We were all running around in greens; nothing unusual about that for us.

So we went to this one place to get outfitted, the local haberdashery. It was a big setup by the Army Special Forces to issue plain clothes to their men, a "sterile issue," and we were now part of the party. What a joke that was; none of the clothes fit us; the only thing that fit me was the shoes because I have small feet.

Drawing our clothes—it was a regular military supply-room kind of setup. We walked along a table and an Army supply type tossed items at us according to our answers about size. When we came to the part where we received civilian shoes, the sergeant barked, "What size?" So I answered, "Five and a half."

Now I'm kind of a big guy, so this sergeant looked up at me, leaned over the table, and looked down at my feet. Then he kind of leaned back up and asked me, "Do you fall over a lot?"

Ha, ha, very funny. Everybody's a comedian. But at least the shoes fit.

So we put on our blue jeans and whatever. And we looked like a real motley mob. Dressed like some kind of refugees, we were going to go into town now, incognito. This was another carefully planned ruse; it really was a great big joke. To transport us into town they were going to use Army six-by-six trucks. So there we were, in Army trucks with all of this military equipment and us, standing up in our civilian clothes, with American weapons in our hands. Subtle. We really had to have looked like a bunch of idiots.

And our weapons were not the most common thing around. We had brand-new AR-15 rifles that Roy Boehm had got for the SEALs right after they were commissioned. The Army only had a handful of those rifles for their airborne and Special Forces. So that helped us really blend in as well.

But the trip into town confirmed what we had seen at the airport. This wasn't a joke; there had been some real fighting going on between the [reportedly] Communist rebels and the government forces. The first clue we had was the bodies we could see beside the road. Going over the bridge into Santo Dominco, we had a real clue that the fighting wasn't done yet when our trucks started taking fire.

It was exciting trying to get underneath those cruise boxes. There isn't a whole lot of cover in the back of a flatbed truck. We couldn't go anywhere and there was nothing else for us to do. What could we do, jump off the back of the truck? And we didn't know where the fire was coming from, so we didn't have any target we could shoot back at.

All we knew was that the fire was coming from town and heading our way. All of us were a lot more disciplined than to just shoot back randomly. And the fire wasn't that close; it wasn't like the bullets were pinging off the truck. But you could hear the zing of rounds going by. It did manage to concern us a bit.

Our little convoy made it over the bridge and into town with no losses. Our final stop was at this big building. The bottom part was this showroom kind of thing, as if for cars. And there was the parts storage area in the back. The whole place was a two- or three-story job. And the rebels had already been there. The building was shot up a bit and looted.

There was a lot of confusion in town. But we linked up with some Army SFs. What we were supposed to do then, I had no idea. The general plan called for us to do some body snatches among the rebels to gain intelligence on their actions, strength, and intentions. And they had some other shit for us to do on kind of an individual basis.

Two of the guys, Georg Doran and Jack Rowell, were taken out and sent up into the mountains somewhere. Their mission was to search some caves along the shore of a bay to try and find some rebel supply caches or signs of where they were smuggling in gear.

But the situation was a little funny for us, besides the lack of specific direction. We had previously trained some of the Dominican Republic's military people, and apparently they were the nucleus of this uprising. That situation kind of made for some general directions to us about not shooting anybody that we recognized.

That struck me as great. What kind of deal was that? If we met these guys, we were supposed to act like we didn't know them? The training had taken place before my time had begun with the Team. It wasn't like I was going to know anybody. So I just said fine, if I knew the guy, I wouldn't shoot at him.

We camped out in this damned building for two or three days. Everything was dark; there wasn't any power. There were artillery pieces, 105 howitzers, somewhere within range. They were on our side, but sometimes it was hard to tell. The Army would crank off a round at the bad guys now and then, even though they might only be a block or two away from where we were. It was almost like what has been going on in Bosnia today, or it seems close to it, I think.

The population in the city had the good sense to stay out of the line of fire. That is, if there was anybody still in that town after the fighting had been going on. When I manned our sniper position up on the roof of our building, I could see the occasional armed rebel running around down the street. You could time one of the runners moving from place to place and then pop him off.

The Dominican Republic was the place where we first saw just what our AR-15s could do to somebody when you hit them with that small, fast bullet. As far as I was concerned, the M14 was better for the kind of shooting we were doing down there. It had more power and could punch through a wall if you wanted to.

I never really had any preference for the AR-15 or M16 over the M14, except for the weight of the gun and the ammunition you could carry. For myself, I didn't see any of the "explosive" power of the AR-15 bullet. It stopped people, but that was just like any

During pre-deployment training, this SEAL carefully aims his heavy-barreled bolt-action sniper rifle. Sitting to the right of the shooter is another SEAL spotting the bullet strikes. Though most enemy engagements in Vietnam were at 30 feet or less, the SEALs practiced long-range shooting and a limited amount of sniping as part of their combat preparations.

U.S. Navy

other weapon. Once, in Vietnam, I hit a Viet Cong with eight rounds of .223, and he just kept on trucking. None of the shots hit a vital spot and he might have bled to death later on, but those bullets didn't stop him from moving.

And there was a chance to do a little firing during our deployment. More than a few shots came our way as we went from room to room during house searches. And we had to stand watch to secure our own area. There was a password system set up and everything. Though in an outfit as small as ours, the idea of passwords seemed pretty ridiculous. More than once the challenge came back in a familiar voice: "Password, what the hell are you talking about? You know it's me."

I took things kind of lightly because, well, basically I thought it was a farce. The Special Forces didn't, though. They were really pissed at us because of what they thought was our blasé attitude.

The Army Special Forces did have some missions they wanted us to perform because of our special skills. The best one was when they wanted us to go through the sewer system of the city wearing our Emersons. And they wanted us to crawl through the sewers dragging all this demolition [explosives] along with us. That way, we could plant it underneath the building and blow up the radio station. The radio station was a problem because the rebels were in control of it and were broadcasting propaganda to the population at large.

That idea was kind of insane. First off, the sewer system wasn't very big. And there was no telling what was inside of there, besides that stuff that's normally in a sewer. I thought they should just take a helicopter and a pallet full of C-4 and drop it on the station. That would have taken care of the rebel broadcasting problem. I think they did do that bomb drop.

There wasn't a chance in hell that I wanted to go into one of those sewers and run into an alligator or whatever might be down there in the tropics. And that wasn't the only weird thing they were trying to get us to do. But what bothered me was that there was somebody, someplace, thinking up this weird shit. Some second lieutenant probably, straight out of West Point and trying to make a name for himself. Who knows?

There was one operation they had us do that involved us going down to a beach on an inlet of the ocean. Our mission was to render the beach safe so that the Army could take out some politicos or whoever. They had arranged for safe passage to get them out of the country or whatever.

For that one, I had an M14 with that starlight scope of ours. My position was across the river from the inlet. One of the guys was acting as a spotter for me and we had set up a little sniper position where we could see a good part of the beach. If anyone got in the way of the beach group, I would be able to pick them off without much problem.

Personally, I thought the starlight was great. Even later in Vietnam, I liked them in spite of their weight. They were heavy, but that ability to see in the dark was great. There was a problem when I actually fired that M14 with the starlight scope on it. When you fired, the muzzle flash would bloom out the scope, causing the whole thing to just go green for a while. Then it would kind of calm down and you could see through it again.

There wasn't much in the way of action, though I did take a shot or two as those days went on. We got put on a couple of missions, but they all fell through before we could act on them.

One platoon went back to the Creek while another one stayed on. I was in the group that stayed on, so my little adventure continued. Larry Bailey was there as one of the SEAL officers, the officer in charge. All in all, I think I was in the Dominican Republic for over a month, about five weeks or so.

We hooked up with an explosive ordnance disposal unit that was down there and we did a few things with them, but nothing particularly exciting. Then we were told to pack our shit, that we were all going home. Being the low man in the ranks, I took a ship back with all of our gear on board. A boat ride back to the States and my Dominican Republic deployment was over.

■ Chapter 4

THE UDT DEPLOYS

Before the SEAL Teams had been commissioned, the UDTs were operating in Vietnam. By the end of 1961, the USS *Cook* (APD-130) had been assigned the task of surveying certain beaches along the South Vietnamese coats. The *Cook* had aboard her a detachment of UDT operators, the men working off the APD as their forebears had done during World War II and Korea. On 4 January 1962, the *Cook* was moving to her assigned objectives along the coasts of South Vietnam.

The UDT operators on board the *Cook* conducted the same hydrographic reconnaissance they had been trained for and that had been a UDT mission for years. Beach configurations, gradients of the shore and underwater seafloor, tides, and underwater obstacles were all located, measured, and recorded. Charts were created from the UDT data that would allow landing craft to conduct amphibious operations with little

In 1963, the conning tower of the USS *Sea Lion* is exposed as the submarine moves across the surface off Saint Thomas Island in the Caribbean. Waving from the bridge is the submarine's skipper, Commander Bob Bills. The *Sea Lion* was one of the diesel-electric submarines that worked a great deal with both the SEALs and the UDTs during the 1960s.

U.S. Navy

difficulty. By the end of January, the *Cook*'s mission had been completed.

But this was hardly the end of the UDTs' operations in the waters off, and in, South Vietnam. Detachment Bravo from UDT 12 was conducting survey operations off the northern coast of South Vietnam, near Danang, in late February 1963. Working with a team from the Third Marine reconnaissance battalion on board the USS *Weiss* (APD-135), the men of the UDT were the only ones allowed to carry weapons ashore. These arms were for self-defense only, and the UDT operators were not to go farther inland than the high-water line.

On 24 February, the Marine detachment from the *Weiss*, working onshore, started taking sniper fire from the jungle. There were no casualties among the Marines or other boat personnel as the group left the beach area. The Marines from the *Weiss* again came under fire some weeks later, now operating off the Mekong Delta. Again there were no casualties, but the mission was drawn to a close before the men's luck ran out.

Further hydrographic surveys and other missions in South Vietnam were conducted by UDT detachments operating out of Subic Bay in the Philippines. Clandestine UDT ops were conducted using the submarines *Perch* (APSS-313) and *Sealion* (APSS-315). Operations conducted from these two craft allowed the concealment of the UDT detachments aboard. Extensive use was made of the two craft by the UDTs.

In 1965, a detachment from UDT 12 continued forward a tradition from the World War II UDTs.

Detachment Delta, UDT 12 at Camp Tien Sha
A detachment of Frogs from UDT 12, working as part of Naval Beach Group 1, were on Red Beach II, just to the north of Danang, on 8 March 1965. They had a sign hanging between two rubber-boat paddles reading:

WELCOME U.S. MARINES

UDT 12

The landing Marines were also met by a number of Vietnamese schoolgirls who put garlands of flowers around the Marines' necks.

Throughout the Vietnam War, the UDTs would be operating in and around South Vietnam. Inshore UDT operations included demolition, reconnaissance, and diving ops. Though they were not expected to conduct direct-action operations against the Viet Cong, the men of the UDTs saw their share of combat. Three men from UDT 13 and one from UDT 12 lost their lives due to enemy action in Vietnam.

Crouching down on watch, this UDT operator keeps a lookout for enemy activity along a small stream in Vietnam. Behind the UDT operator, his Teammates are preparing demolition charges to destroy a VC bunker.

U.S. Navy

Dee Van Winkle, Boatswain's Mate Third Class

Back around 1960, Reader's Digest *ran a story about the UDTs of the Navy. It was such a powerful story to me that I knew what my life was going to consist of from that point on. The story discussed what the Underwater Demolition Teams had done during World War II, and stressed how they were among the toughest men in the world. From that time on, I just wanted to be one of those Frogmen.*

As everyone has to, to get to the UDTs first I had to enlist in the regular Navy. For six to seven months, I served as a lowly compartment cleaner, sweeping barracks out. Then my paperwork had gone though, and in 1963, I was picked up for Class 30, UDTR, at Coronado.

Class 30 started with 143 students; we graduated in January 1964 with 30 still there, the Dirty Thirty. When I first started training, every day was exciting, and so was every night. It was a great bunch of guys to be with, and we sort of stuck together. There's five or six of us who still communicate to this day.

For me, the training was sheer excitement; I loved every second of it. There were aspects of the training that weren't very fun. Fatigue was the big one. It was just very tiring, exhausting really. Lack of sleep was something that everyone suffered from. Had we been able to sleep more, I think we could have performed on a higher level. But of course that's part of the training, to teach your mind as well as your body.

I remember being so tired that I fell asleep in my food a number of times in the chow hall. And I was hardly the only one to do that. It was startling to wake up with my face down in my plate.

Since I was from Arkansas, the Pacific Ocean was something new to me. But at UDTR, it was something you got familiar with very quickly. Arkansas has a serious winter, and I spent more than a few days in the snow growing up. But the cold of the Pacific was something new.

During training, the cold sank into you. Once it got into your bones, into your entire system, it took a long time for it to get out. After training, I remember being cold for weeks. It was like a mild case of hypothermia, and it's hard to explain to someone who hasn't been exposed to it. But it stays with you for a long time.

Hell Week was one of the big hurdles you had to complete early on in training. I remember the lack of sleep and being constantly on the move. The instructors would have us do things that required a lot of intense physical exertion. The memory of being very, very cold, all of the time, is also something that sticks with me about UDTR.

But one of the really great things about the Teams also started during UDTR. And that was the bond that started forming with all of us. It was a very strong bond, and immense respect, for all of us who went through that experience together. Hell Week was great; I actually really liked that whole week.

It was the people I was with who made getting through Hell Week possible. I felt I could have done more than one of those intense weeks of training, as long as I could have my Teammates with me.

It's not so much your own strength you feel, your own power or *ability to handle any situation. When you're really into it, you feel like when you're with these certain people, you can just go on, and on, and on, forever. It's quite an amazing thing that not too many people understand.*

Hell Week is where you learn to get the job done, but you can't do the job by yourself. You obviously have to have help, and you learn to rely on your Teammates. Just as they rely on you. It is absolutely where you learn the importance of being in a Team.

There were things that were just physically tough in training. Probably the runs in soft sand while wearing boots and after having rolled around in the surf for a couple of hours are a good example of what was physically tough to do. And one of the big reasons for this was not just the running, or the being wet. While you were rolling around in the wet, your crotch filled up with sand. The abrasion of that beach sand against the more tender portions of your body as your legs went back and forth during a run was pretty painful.

We ran for different lengths of time, different distances, and constantly built up our legs for the longs swims we would have to do later. In spite of all the physical output, I never reached the point where I felt my body was just giving out. That just didn't happen with your friends around you. You could be in pain, but you were still invincible.

In my estimation, the extraordinary thing about the people who make up the Teams is not the physical aspect. People who look at the UDTs from the outside think about the big, strong guys, just the physical strength. But that isn't the really important part to me.

In our class, we had a guy who was bigger than most of us. He could outrun us, out PT us. He was just stronger and faster than the rest of us. Many of us looked up to him as a hero. But in spite of all of this guy's abilities, he was the last one to quit from our class. He never graduated. It wasn't the strength, or the speed—it was the heart. He wasn't the same on the inside as he was on the outside. And you have to be that, or it just doesn't work.

The respect that you give after you learn just how strong a person is inside is unlike anything you may have felt before. You know absolutely that nothing, nothing at all, is going to stop that man. He could be a big man, a little man, ugly or handsome. But when you've learned what's inside that person, that shows you real strength. And it is only people like this who make up the Teams, who are your Teammates.

For years, I had been thinking of being in the Teams, or being a Navy Frogman. The thought of quitting just never entered my mind. I wanted to be with these men, to serve and work with them. Nothing was going to make me quit, but 110 other trainees in Class 30 did.

Part of our instruction included learning the traditional cast and recovery techniques developed by the UDT operators of WWII. Rolling off the rubber boat secured to the side of a speeding LCPR was neat. That wasn't the time for me when I looked at myself and said, "I'm a Frogman now." But later, we all received pictures of ourselves doing that training evolution. It was when I saw that picture of myself doing cast and recovery, rolling off the boat into the foaming water, that it hit me. It wasn't doing the act, it was seeing the picture that made me realize, hey, this is pretty cool, I'm a Frogman now.

Standing on the grinder that last day and graduating from UDTR was terrific. It made me feel special, and I still do. It was just an honor to be with such great guys, and to be accepted by them was an even greater one.

After graduation, I was assigned to UDT 12, stationed right there in Coronado. After training, I went on to complete Army jump school at Fort Benning, Georgia, and was parachute-qualified. My first deployment came soon after, to Southeast Asia and Vietnam.

This was before the full deployment of U.S. troops to Vietnam. But the situation there was still a serious one. Instead of doing much in the way of beach surveys, our main function was river stuff. We did a number of river patrols and river recons. During the deployment, we did do some beach recons off of Vietnam in the South China Sea, but only a handful of them.

The UDT mission in Vietnam was mainly the river work, the river recons. We served a couple of different purposes, conducting beach recons, especially before the war escalated. Clearing waterway blockages and obstacles with demolitions. And some general diving, sometimes for intelligence and equipment recovery.

Most of my time was spent on the Hue River conducting recons with my Teammates. The river recons we did consisted of doing soundings and recording the depth of the waters, ensuring that

UDT trainees cast off over the side of a rubber boat during their BUD/S training. As did their UDT forefathers, these men are operating with a minimum of equipment to conduct beach surveys. Around the neck of the swimmer still on the boat to the left is a plastic slate and wax crayon for making notes.

U.S. Navy

boats and ships could make it up and down the river. We also charted the locations of fishing nets, the details of possible embankments. All in all, pretty simple stuff, but done in a very scary environment.

We probably weren't the first ones doing that kind of work in the river. But we were the only ones there at that time. And we were operating from an LCPR (Landing Craft, Personnel, Reconnaissance), which was just a wooden boat. On either side of us were fairly high banks where anyone could have been hiding. We were looking over our shoulders a lot.

This was well before the Swift boats were around. There were no helicopter gunships to call on, no gunfire support from offshore ships, or artillery support from local units. There were no other support craft around.

We were armed with some AR-15 rifles, .45-caliber M3A1 "Grease-gun" submachine guns, and some M1 Carbines. In other words— nothing. The LCPRs each had one .30-caliber machine gun, and we *usually operated in pairs. That's not very much armament. By today's standards, it's no armament. It was a scary situation.*

Going down the river, we felt like ducks in a pond, only we didn't know where the hunters were, and the possibility of enemy fire coming in from both sides was pretty bad. Going out of the river to get back to the USS Cook *out offshore was even worse.*

Right at the mouth of the Hue River was an island. So that meant we could take fire from three sides. Which happened to us; that was where we got hit.

Much later I returned to Vietnam with another deployment for UDT 12, but this one was a combat assignment. The mission involved more river work, only this time we ran into a few firefights. It was a hard time for us; we lost a few men. Those days are still etched in my mind. I still think about them a lot and simply wish they had never happened.

During my first combat op, I was afraid. I think that most people, if they are totally honest with you, will say that they were fearful for their life in combat. But at the moment that the action is occurring, you don't really have time to be very afraid. You just do what you were trained to do. It's only later that you experience the fear about what you just encountered.

The men we lost during that tour were not Teammates; that is, they were not members of the UDT. They were teammates in the sense that we were working together, but they were members of the crew of the USS Cook *(APD-130), the ship we were operating from. One of the men was a .30-caliber machine gunner and another was the coxswain of our LCPR, the boat we took from the* Cook *to our operating site.*

While we were on a river operation, our boat was ambushed at the mouth of the Hue River. During the fight, our coxswain and gunner were both killed the same day. That wasn't the only loss we experienced. In another firefight, a U.S. Marine First Force recon guy who was working with us was also killed. I never experienced the loss of an immediate UDT Teammate while in Vietnam. But the men who were killed worked right alongside of us, and it could just as easily have been one of our own who was killed.

There were friends of mine in the Teams who were lost, but not in combat. These men were lost during training exercises after grad-

An APD, or High Speed Transport converted from an early-model Destroyer. These APDs were made the floating bases for the UDTs, one UDT to an APD. Two of the four UDT Platoon LCPRs can be seen hanging from davits toward the stern of the craft. During WWII, some UDTs spent eighteen months and more aboard the same APD.

U.S. Navy

uating from UDTR. Our duties in the Teams are hazardous, and they proved the point. We lost one of our Teammates during helicopter operations off of Camp Pendleton. His name was Aden Marshall.

The situation was that we were doing helicopter insertions with an inexperienced man at the controls. The pilot didn't realize that every time a 200-pound man with his gear went out of the bird and into the water, the helicopter would increase in speed and altitude. Generally, the insertion ops were 20/20, that is they were twenty miles an hour in speed and twenty feet in altitude. We would go about 10/10, going ten miles an hour faster and up ten feet, every time we deployed an operator. By the time the whole stick was out, the bird was probably doing seventy miles an hour at the seventy-foot level.

That pilot just didn't have the proper training or experience to fly the bird on that kind of operation. Aden Marshall was the last guy in the stick, and he hit the water like a ton of bricks. We didn't recover the body until sometime later, and it was just a mess, a huge mass of black-and-blue bruises.

That was one of our bad situations. But it wasn't the only one. Another time, we lost a couple of divers off the Silver Strand during underwater operations. We were conducting a mock attack on a tar-

A SEAL combat swimmer enters the water having jumped from the "Hell Hole" of a CH-46 Sea Knight helicopter.

U.S. Navy

get ship offshore from the Strand. We were using the Emerson rebreather, a real death trap, as our breathing rig.

In reality, the Emerson can be a very good unit to operate with. But at the time we were T&Eing (Testing and Evaluating) this particular piece of equipment. We were not aware that you should not go beyond a certain depth with it. We also weren't aware that if you overworked (breathed too hard) the rig, you had a bad CO_2 buildup.

Carbon-dioxide buildup in a breathing rig was insidious; it would sneak up on you and kill you before you even noticed it. That was what was thought to have happened to two of our Teammates on that attack swim. Cliff Walsh and Samuelson were two of our better Teammates as far as operating goes, and we lost them both. The sea just took them; we never found the bodies.

This was part of the cost of being a Frogman. We worked in a dangerous environment during almost any job we did. That's why the job was so exciting. The danger is like a drug to some people, to do something exciting every day.

Once you've experienced something like this, the constant dan-

A modern SEAL takes aim with his M4 carbine while moving forward from cover. His uniform, gear, weapon, and skills were directly developed from the SEALs' experiences in Vietnam.

Kevin Dockery

ger and risk in your everyday work, that level of excitement is some-thing you miss. When you get out of the Teams, there are just a lot of the guys who don't handle it very well. They miss the life and don't handle the civilian world very well because of that. After I got out of the Teams, I was very fortunate in that I was still playing rugby a lot. That gave me back something of what I had in the Teams and made the transition a little easier.

In the early 1960s, while I was in UDT 12, the SEALs were still pretty much in their infancy. We just didn't know much about them and I personally didn't really have any feeling one way or the other about them. I didn't feel that I wanted to be a SEAL because the UDTs were still doing the main bulk of the operating. Being an operator, that's what I wanted to do. What I didn't want to do was spend my time going to school, learning everything new. I just wanted to do what I had already been taught.

No one in the UDTs seemed to envy the SEALs very much in the beginning, at least not from what I could see. We had all worked very hard to get into the UDT, and the SEAL Teams were very much an unknown.

And the UDTs had some really exciting and interesting jobs going on. The space capsule recovery operation had been assigned to the UDT. Though I never served on one of the recovery teams myself, a number of my friends did. Every manned space shot NASA put up was met by a unit of men from the UDT when it splashed down. I would have loved to have been on one of those teams myself, but just never had the chance.

Being in the Teams was the high point of my life. I have no regrets at all about having served in the UDT. As I look back on it, it was a great adventure, a terrific ride. And I'm just happy to have been a part of it. It was awesome.

The connection I feel with the older UDT operators is probably no different from what I feel toward my own Teammates. That is, we both basically did that same thing. I'm a little bit more in awe of those World War II UDT operators than I am of even my own guys in some respects. They had a real lack of equipment, and much of their training was being developed as they operated. But inside, they were the same guys then as we have today.

After having seen some of the older equipment, especially the diving rigs, I'm amazed the older operators aren't all dead. Even something as simple as the faceplates (masks) they wore were horrible in comparison to what we had. The rubber rotted, and they were small, uncomfortable, and leaked a lot.

Then of course, having seen the modern equipment they use in the Teams today, I'm stunned we did as well as we did back in my day. With the weapons and gear they have now, the comparison is just unbelievable.

There are a lot of misconceptions about the Navy SEALs, and about the Frogmen before them. The public image of a SEAL seems to be that they are these "bad" guys who walk the streets. And the last thing you want to do is screw with a SEAL.

That's not the way it is at all in my eyes. From what I've seen, a Navy SEAL is probably the most polite guy you'll meet in a roomful of people. And he's probably the most humble person in there as well. That Navy SEAL knows himself and his capabilities. And he doesn't have to prove himself to anyone.

Navy SEALs are no different from anyone else when it comes down to being a person. They have the same feelings, the same emotions, the same blood. They're only different in that they're able to control themselves a little more than most.

The public hoopla about the SEALs just confuses me a bit. I don't know what the public expects the men of the Teams to do, other than be themselves. They have no need to do anything to impress people. In fact, they have no need to impress anyone at all.

I think it's important that everyone knows that the men of the Teams are just normal people. We're just people who have been selected and trained to do a certain thing, and hopefully do it very well. And that's it. The special feelings we have for each other are created by the hardships we all had to endure during our training. Personally, I don't want anyone to look at me as anything other than a regular guy.

When the young SEAL of today looks at the older men of the Teams, I hope he does so with some respect for that person's accomplishments. That respect is probably the only thing I would really hope for, and maybe a little curiosity to get to know that person, and what he did in the past.

The thing that binds all of us together in the Teams, then and now, is the feeling of invincibility, the capability we all have to just get the job done, any job. It doesn't matter if it's just a bunch of us repairing a car together, or lending a hand moving someone's household, or just chopping wood. You know you can do anything better than you normally could when you're with your Teammates.

If the Navy SEALs were a football Team, they wouldn't lose a single fucking game. The reason I can say that is that every football team I was ever on when I was in the Teams, we won. I was on the original Navy rugby team back in the early 1960s. And we didn't *really know what we were doing at first. But that didn't matter; we still won almost every game we played. We would just put all of the other players out of the game, knock them right off the field. Nobody wanted to play us after a while.*

■ Chapter 5

THE SEALs DEPLOY FOR WAR

On 1 November 1963, President Diem of South Vietnam was attacked and the government threatened in a coup. The military and the government of South Vietnam staggered and almost fell during the turmoil of the Diem assassination, which took place only a few days later. Diem had been a staunch anti-Communist, and he had received the support of the United States for some time. There were only a few thousand U.S. military advisers in Vietnam at the time of Diem's assassination, among them a handful of SEAL and UDT operators.

Though the situation in South Vietnam was of concern to the U.S. government and the general public, the news of Diem's death was overshadowed by the assassination of President Kennedy only a few weeks later. The government of North Vietnam hoped to take advantage of the situation to their south before the United States could further support South Vietnam. In the year following Diem's death, several more coups and power struggles took place in South Vietnam. And North Vietnam increased its support of the Communist guerrillas in the south. The Viet Cong started receiving a greater flow of materials, weapons, munitions, and even manpower from the north.

The hoped-for general uprising of the population in South Vietnam never took place, much to the disappointment of the commanders in Hanoi. The increase in the flow of supplies to the south caused the United States to begin a bombing campaign along what would soon be called the Ho Chi Minh Trail.

MTT detachments of SEALs continued in South Vietnam, and a new

A Norwegian-built "Nasty"-class fast patrol boat moving at high speed through Pacific waters. Six of these boats were obtained for operations off the coast of North Vietnam. The crews of the boats first received their training at Little Creek, Virginia, from the instructors of SEAL Team Two.

mission increased the SEALs' mission in Vietnam. Admiral Harry D. Felt had put forward a plan of action against North Vietnam in June 1963. Felt's Operational Plan 34A (OP 34A) centered on conducting covert operations against North Vietnam. South Vietnamese commandos, trained and equipped by the United States, would conduct these operations. For the maritime portion of OP 34A, the Navy SEAls would train the South Vietnamese commandos to conduct operations against the north from a variety of watercraft, including Norwegian "Nasty"-class fast patrol boats.

Though the SEALs themselves would not be allowed to go on the northbound OP-34A missions, they trained the men who did conduct the operations. A number of missions were conducted, with some successes. In early August 1964, in the Gulf of Tonkin off the shore of North Vietnam, Swatow motor gunboats of the North Vietnamese Navy attacked the US Navy Destroyers *Maddox* and *Turner Joy*. The Swatows would have been a match for the "Nasty"-class fast patrol boats of OP-34A, but they were not a match in firepower against American destroyers. In spite of this, the Swatows attacked the *Maddox* and the *Turner Joy* on two different occasions during those early August days.

Torpedoes fired by the Swatows did not impact on the destroyers during

Fast patrol boats PTF-3 and PTF-4 move at high speed near Pearl Harbor, Hawaii. The boats will be deployed to Vietnam to conduct operations as part of OP-34A within a few years of this photograph being taken.

U.S. Navy

either engagement, but some heavy-machine-gun fire and small-cannon fire did hit the American craft. The Swatows came under heavy fire from the Navy ships, taking heavy damage in some cases. But the worst damage of the incident would be the political fallout soon to take place in the United Sates.

President Johnson called on the U.S. Congress to respond to the attack against the ships of the U.S. Seventh Fleet. The Congress and Senate passed the Southeast Asia (Tonkin Gulf) Resolution, which gave President Johnson the power to escalate the war in Vietnam as he needed without there actually being a declaration of war. The buildup of U.S. military forces in South Vietnam was now allowed.

Further actions had taken place in Vietnam during 1964 that would greatly affect the SEALs' actions in Southeast Asia. Admiral Felt created a study team to learn about the movement of supplies to the Viet Cong through the Mekong Delta as well as about guerrilla actions in South Vietnam. The nine-man team was led by Captain Phil H. Bucklew, a highly decorated naval officer who had served with distinction with the Scouts and Raiders during World War II.

Officially known as the Vietnam Delta Infiltration Study Group, the team arrived in Vietnam in January 1964 to begin their work. The final study of the team became known as the *Bucklew Report*. The *Bucklew Report* identified the Ho Chi Minh Trail as the primary route used to get supplies from the north down to the guerrillas in the south. But the report also identified the rivers, streams, and canals of the Mekong Delta as primary routes of movement for the Viet Cong.

To stop the flow of men and supplies through the Mekong Delta area, new naval task forces would have to be established, equipped, and trained to operate both in the offshore waters of South Vietnam and in the inland waterways of the Mekong Delta. Task Force 115 was established on 11 March 1965. Its mission would be to conduct Operation MARKET TIME, the coastal blockade of South Vietnam against smuggling from the north.

Blocking the movement of Viet Cong men and supplies in the inland waterways of the Mekong Delta became the mission of Task Force 116 and their leading of Operation GAME WARDEN. The River Patrol Force became the active component of TF 116 when it was created on 18 December 1965.

The ships and small craft of both TF 115 and TF 116 would operate against the Viet Cong throughout the waterways of South Vietnam. But they would be most active in the Mekong Delta area. To attack the Viet Cong on land, and gather intelligence on their movements and operations, a detachment of SEALs from SEAL Team One arrived in Vietnam in February 1966. Operating primarily in the Rung Sat Special Zone, the SEALs from Team One became Detachment Golf. By the next year Detachment Alfa of SEAL Team Two would be established to operate primarily in the Mekong Delta.

SEALs deploying to Vietnam from 1966 forward would now be primarily part of the direct-action platoons operating against the Viet Cong. The SEALs would now show the world just how they could conduct unconventional warfare. The Teams had found their war.

Robert Gormly, Captain, USN (Ret.)

While I was growing up in Virginia Beach, Virginia, I saw some of the movies that had come out about the UDTs of World War II. The one with Richard Widmark, The Frogmen, *is one of the few I remember.*

But because I lived in and grew up in Virginia Beach, only a few miles from Little Creek, the UDTs were something that was always in the background.

I finally decided that I wanted to become a member of the UDTs one time while I was out on a surfboard off Virginia Beach. While out on the water, I ran into the then executive officer of UDT 21, a fellow by the name of Ron Smith. He told me a bit of what he did, and when I found out that he could be out there surfing whenever he wanted to, it sounded like it wouldn't be a bad life for me either. So that was how I joined the program.

Eventually, I was an ensign with East Coast Class 31, a winter class that started in January 1964. The fact that I had a wife and a kid to support did a lot to help me get through training. My college degree and Ron's help got me into the Navy's Officer Candidate School. So when I reported to the Teams, it was as an officer—a very young, very junior officer.

That incentive of my wife and child did help push me through UDTR training, and I didn't particularly want to go aboard a ship for what I intended to be my three-year stint with the Navy. But once you start something like that training program, you get caught up in it. That, and it just wasn't in my nature to quit.

In spite of the difficulties of training, I can honestly say that I never thought of quitting. The fact that Ron Smith had helped get me so well prepared, with an exercise program, running, and swimming, also helped get me through the tough parts. There were just too many incentives not to quit for me to even think about it. But I didn't know what was coming in the program.

Hell Week was cold, and hot, it was rainy, and it snowed. In other words, a typical East Coast winter Hell Week. It was bad, but mostly it was the weather that made it physically miserable for me. People who know say that the East Coast winter training course was one of the hardest, and coldest, you could go through. But I'm not sure that an East Coast summer class—with the heat, mosquitoes, and all the other things unique to that swampy part of Virginia that you just can't get away from—wouldn't have been worse.

Sometime during training, the word came down to us about the existence of the SEAL Teams. In those days, the SEALs were a very classified outfit. Even people in the UDTs didn't know everything about what they did. So I only really learned about the SEALs well after I had gotten into the Teams.

After spending some good years with UDT 21, I went to SEAL Team Two in March of 1966. There was no inclination at that time for SEAL Team Two to deploy to Vietnam. SEAL Team One had sent only a single detachment to Vietnam the month before to conduct direct-action operations against the Viet Cong. SEAL Team Two was pretty much in the doldrums in terms of money and training opportunities. The major shortcoming was money; guys were having to pay their own way to get training done. Our turn to even think about going to Vietnam wasn't going to start happening until late in the summer of 1966.

When deployments to Vietnam finally did start coming up, I did my best to break a few legs and twist some arms in order to be one of the first people going over there from SEAL Team Two. And this isn't just a figure of speech. The CO finally had to cancel our regular Friday-morning soccer games—too many guys were receiving unexplained injuries. And it seemed the injuries were particularly happening to the men selected to be the first to deploy to Vietnam.

But I was lucky; I tried to get into one of the first two platoons deploying to Vietnam and I made it. Third Platoon deployed in January 1967 with Lieutenant (j.g.) Larry Bailey as the platoon leader and Lieutenant (j.g.) Robert Gormly as the assistant platoon commander.

Starting operations in Vietnam was not what we expected. We had a tough time getting going as the first SEALs in the Mekong Delta. SEAL Team One had been conducting operations for about a year up in the Rung Sat Special Zone, very near Saigon. The Rung Sat had a very different kind of terrain than the delta area did. And it required a different method of operating.

The Mekong Delta is a wide-open rice-paddy kind of area, large flat open areas surrounded by bands of jungle and trees. The Rung Sat was a mangrove-swamp, dense kind of jungle area saturated with water and dozens of canals, streams, and waterways.

When SEAL Team Two's Second and Third Platoons arrived in the Mekong Delta area, the people for whom we would be working, the River Patrol Force, weren't really too sure what they wanted to do

A helicopter view of the smaller rivers, canals, rice paddies, and paddy dikes that covered the majority of the land in the Mekong Delta.

Greg McPartlin Collection

with us. Operations started out with our riding river patrol boats as sort of bodyguards. That was a waste of time and talent.

It took about a month really of hashing with the leadership of the River Patrol Force to determine that (a) we would be operating independently, in support of their mission, which was to keep the rivers clear of the Viet Cong; and (b) we would be pretty much calling our own shots on what kinds of operations we did.

It was when we finally got those things ironed out that SEAL Team Two went to work in Vietnam.

During that first tour, the operation where I was dinged (wounded) is the one that stands out the most vividly in the memory. But it was only one of many.

We really didn't know anything about the delta yet. I think that up to the last minute before we deployed, we still thought we would be sent to the Rung Sat. When we went down to the middle of the Mekong Delta instead, we had to learn the territory. So we started off doing ambush patrols in areas that were designated free-fire zones. Which meant that supposedly everyone who moved in that zone was an enemy. Whether this was actually true or not, I just don't know. But those were the designated areas in which we could operate freely.

Some of us got a little tired of taking shots at the local fishermen trying to beat curfew in the morning. So we branched off into running combat patrols in the areas that we knew were completely controlled by the Viet Cong. Anyone we saw in those areas, we could be certain was the enemy.

The first three or four months we were operating, it was really in an intelligence gathering capacity, mainly for the platoons that were to come after us. We learned what areas might be the best possibilities for conducting successful operations, how to operate, and how to coordinate with the available support.

From about the middle to the end of my tour, we started trying to run operations off of the intelligence net we developed. This was information we received either from people we had captured or from the intelligence structures that existed in the delta, on both the U.S. Navy's and South Vietnamese sides.

So we switched from just going out and doing ambushing to actually trying to target specific Viet Cong leaders in their home hamlets, villages, or whatever.

Operating from our own self-generated intelligence was kind of a unique situation for us as the first SEAL to operate in the Mekong Delta. In fact, we were the only U.S. forces actually doing ops on the ground in the delta area for a while. The U.S. Army's Ninth Infantry Division didn't arrive in the delta until several months after we started operations.

Every time we went out on an operation, we gathered further intelligence for ourselves as well as for others. An area could be checked off as a good place to go or not. Or maybe we should go over to this area over here since we've heard a lot of sampan traffic moving over to that spot.

Of course moving about and operating like this only happened after we had gathered some experience. My first combat operation in Vietnam wasn't in the Mekong Delta, it was up in the Rung Sat Special Zone. This was just a few days after we had arrived in-country, and the notion was for some of the guys from SEAL Team One, guys who had already been there for a while, to take us out on a "breaking-in" op.

The operation was okay, with the high point really being the chance I had to work with an old friend of mine, Lieutenant Irve C. "Chuck" LeMoyne, and with his SEAL Team One squad. That first night, we did an ambush, which was pretty much the standard operation for the Rung Sat at that time. All we did was see a crocodile swim by, then a dolphin swam by, and watched the tide come in. No Viet Cong showed and we ended up treading water in a mangrove swamp.

In spite of the discomfort and lack of action, the op was good. I liked to operate, that was just what I wanted to do in those days. The more miserable the better. Of course, when the croc swam by, I was happy to have an M16 rifle in my hands.

What we all learned over there was what the most vulnerable point in any mission was. And that point was at the interface between the river and the land, where we had to get off the river and onto the land. It didn't matter if you were swimming in or coming in off a grounded boat, the first time you went up on the land, you just didn't know what was there.

There were a lot of butterflies flying around stomachs and a lot of adrenaline surging through our systems at that stage in an operation. For myself, after I had gotten on the land and knew what was around me, I felt I was pretty much in control of the situation. After the insertion, it was a matter of continuing on with the op. The adrenaline stayed up, but it peaked and ebbed. Mostly, it hit a high again as you made contact, or were extracting.

The men I was operating with were great. Any SEAL officer will tell you that the men working for him were the best that were in the Team. And I would expect him to say that. But my guys were a great group, mature and skilled. I had no problems with them at all; they were all smart, aggressive, and confident. I relied on them all quite a bit. When we set up a mission, we would plan the thing together. Their input was important and something I listened to closely. And a lot of times I would do what they suggested.

In my squad was Jess Tolison, one of the finest men I've ever known. He was a tremendous leader himself, and having him working for me just made my job a lot easier. If Jess said to go right during an op, then I turned right.

Any group that you go into combat with, you develop a special affinity for. Each of those men will hold a place in your mind from then on. And the men I led were memorable even before we ever went to war.

Toward the end of our tour, we had a series of operations that all resulted in us doing nothing more than spending time walking around and seeing nothing. All of us were itching to do something that had a greater chance of contact. The operations officer from the River Patrol Force, the guys that ran the PBRs up and down the river, came to me with the suggestion for a good op.

He said that there was an island complex down on the Bassac River that the cruising PBRs had been taking a lot of heavy caliber fire from lately, both machine guns and mortars. He suggested that we might want to go in and look around, maybe destroying some of the offensive bunkers that the VC were firing from. That sounded like a good mission to me, so I agreed and an op was quickly put together. I grabbed up my squad and off we went.

We moved into the area, inserted, and set up a security perimeter. After we had a feel for what was going on around us, we started patrolling along a canal. Along with our normal weapons, we had a load of C-4 plastic explosives with us, each man carrying a twenty-pound demolition charge. Out in the canal nearby, I had a boat with a lot more explosives on board.

As we patrolled, we came across a number of bunkers and blew them up—using the SEAL formula for precise demolition work: if a bunker looked like twenty pounds of C-4 would destroy it, we used forty pounds. That way, we were always sure of complete destruction of the target. I think we had about two resupplies from our boat out in the river.

As we continued the operation, we started setting up a pattern in our patrolling for targets. This was my mistake, and I knew we were making it, as did every man with me. But we hadn't seen anyone on the op except for a few old women and some kids. Things seemed so quiet that we even stopped for a moment so that our corpsman, Fred McCarty, could treat a child who had a bad eye

Patrolling along a Vietnamese waterway, these two Mk II PBRs are running slow and low in the water. The gunners in the forward gun tubs man their twin .50-caliber machine guns as they each watch opposite banks for signs of enemy activity.

U.S. Navy

infection. Things were just going easy, and that's what should have warned me to be a lot more alert.

The squad's point man, Charlie Bump, contracted something from one of the nasty ditches we had crossed along the way. He came up to me and both his legs were badly swollen and he was having a hard time breathing. The corpsman gave him a shot of antihistamine and we sent him out to the boat on the next resupply run.

There were only about five of us on the operation now. Jess Tolison had been sent back to the States early for a well-deserved promotion to warrant officer. Now we had Quan, a South Vietnamese SEAL, attached to our squad. That left Bill Garnett as my second in command (leading petty officer), Fred McCarty as the squad's corpsman and radioman, and Pierre Birtz as a grenadier.

Since Bump had been working as our point man, I took his position. After medevacing Charlie, we moved out of the area with me taking the lead. As I moved down the trail in the point position, I caught a glimpse of some grass moving just off to the side of the trail. Stopping, I looked down and could see where someone had just passed by; the grass was still rising up from their footprints.

Concerned for the moment, I directed the squad to hang a left off the main trail and we headed inland. The grass was lower and lower as we moved along, pressed down by someone's feet just a moment before. About fifty meters from where we turned, I stopped and crouched down to look about. There, about five meters in front of me, I saw a head move, and then a rifle. When I leaned up and opened fire, all hell broke loose.

As near as we could determine later, we had walked down the short leg of a L-shaped ambush that the VC had set up for us. If we had continued walking about another ten or fifteen meters past where we turned off the trail, we would have been right in the middle of their killing zone. As it was, only one man was injured, and that was me: I was shot through the wrist within moments of opening fire.

All in all, we were very lucky. We got out and called in a lot of fire. A bunch of people had a good time for the rest of that afternoon, firing up the area we just left. After I received some quick attention from Fred McCarty, and a shot of morphine for the pain that was building fast, we pulled out in our support boat. I was medevaced soon after we returned to base, and I feel very lucky that none of the rest of my men got dinged that day.

A lot of us had discussed combat, and what can happen during it, well before we left for Vietnam. There weren't any illusions about our being bulletproof, outside of the feelings you have along those lines when you're young. We knew about the UDT casualties back in WWII, which was about all we had to draw on in our history. SEAL Team One had taken some casualties up in the Rung Sat, including a whole boatload that had been hit right before we arrived in Vietnam. And after I was hit, I knew I wasn't bulletproof.

The wound was bad enough to take some time healing. And I had some therapy and surgery to correct the damage done to my wrist. But I wanted to get back over to Vietnam as soon as I could. As soon as the hospital okayed it, I snuck back over there, this time in charge of my own platoon.

A squad of SEALs move through the waterways of Vietnam while on a patrol. The man at the rear is armed with a Stoner light machine gun, belts of ammunition for the weapon draped around his shoulders.

U.S. Navy

On my second tour in Vietnam, I relieved Dick Anderson, who was the platoon leader of Ninth Platoon. Dick was the only officer senior enough in Vietnam to be rotated into position as the officer-in-charge (OIC) of Detachment (Det) Alfa, the SEAL Team Two unit in Vietnam that our platoons operated under. So that was my opportunity to go back.

SEAL Team One had Detachment Golf in Vietnam. During all my time in Vietnam, I never saw any difference between the men of

SEAL Teams One and Two. A lot of good friends of mine were officers in SEAL Team One. In fact, a number of SEAL Team One officers had transferred there from SEAL Team Two after they received their commissions. In spite of the good-natured rivalry between the two Teams, we were all operators.

My opinion of the enemy we were fighting, and the allies we had in Vietnam, was close to being the same. The rank and file of the Viet Cong struck me as being good troops working under hard conditions. The South Vietnamese we were working with, once you got past a lot of the higher leadership, were also decent fighters. They just weren't led very well from the higher levels. Though some of the younger South Vietnamese officers fought hard for their country.

We worked a number of times with South Vietnamese SEALs, their LDNN. An LDNN probably saved my life during that operation earlier when I was wounded. Quan had been close behind me on that patrol and he shot the VC who had first shot me. And I have a lot of time for people like that.

It was only a few years later that the Vietnam War wound down for the SEAL Teams and the U.S. military. My second combat tour had been my last. But a number of other SEALs spent four or five tours in Vietnam. Officers just couldn't always go back as often as they wanted. Instead, I went on to be the XO of UDT 22, also at Little Creek.

There was, wrongly in my view, blame put on the military for the war we fought in Vietnam. This showed in the antimilitary sentiment that was prevalent during the 1970s. A lot of our senior officers were taking a real beating in the press, and maybe from some of the politicians in Washington, over the fact that we hadn't "won" the war. There was sort of a "back off and let things happen" attitude from the higher command.

What was more immediately noticed was that the funding, which had been very good during the Vietnam days, dried up very quickly. SEAL Team One, which had the much larger commitment of platoons to Vietnam, had grown very large during the war. SEAL Team Two had grown, but it still wasn't half the size of Team One.

Both Teams were drawn down considerably in size after the war.

And that was very noticeable in SEAL Team One, which had to actively send men out of the Team to reduce their numbers.

In the SEALs, we hadn't done a very good job in explaining to the Navy hierarchy just what we had done for them in conducting unconventional warfare in Vietnam. Everyone understood what the UDTs did; their mission was tied in to the amphibious force and hadn't changed drastically since World War II. They had their place; the SEALs had lost part of theirs.

We didn't need much in the way of funding; the SEALs just didn't cost as much as the other units in the Navy. But that also meant that taking any money away from us had a much greater impact.

From 1972 to 1974, I was the commanding officer of SEAL Team Two, a big step for someone who originally expected to do only a single enlistment in the Navy. And just like when I had come on board SEAL Team Two back in 1966, the men were forced to pay their own way to get training done. Everyone knew that they had to keep their qualifications up, but we just didn't have any money to send them off to schools. For all the military, the 1970s were hard times financially and otherwise. And that was particularly true for the Teams.

When I was the CO of SEAL Team Two, one of the hardest things I had to contend with was having a whole command filled with Vietnam veterans. The guys were super people; all of them were great operators. But we just didn't have a mission then. Of course we had our historic mission of supporting various Navy commands with an unconventional warfare capability, but we just didn't have a war.

Trying to keep a highly trained group of combat veterans happy after there was no war, particularly SEALs, wasn't enjoyable work. Unlike a lot of Vietnam-era veterans I see who didn't want to be there and bemoan the fact that they were in combat, every one of our guys had wanted to be there. So the biggest challenge for me as their CO was to keep them challenged. And the only way I found to do this was to keep involving them in exercises that pushed the envelope a bit. The only way to keep these men occupied was to keep them challenged, keep the adrenaline flowing.

The low silhouette of the Light SEAL Support Craft is shown as this LSSC noses in to the shore for an insertion.

U.S. Navy

And that adrenaline flow also extended to the CO; only it didn't always come from the fieldwork we were doing. One time while I was out on one of these exercises, the Navy almost decommissioned SEAL Team Two right out from under me.

We had an exercise in Denmark with some of our NATO allies in 1973. After the war had ended, the SEAL community underwent a significant organizational change. Now an organization known as the Naval Inshore Warfare Command had been formed. Ostensibly, all SEALs—explosive ordnance disposal, harbor defense units, and inshore undersea warfare groups—were put underneath this large one-star admiral billet.

The SEAL Teams lost a lot of our clout in the political arena under the new system. There wasn't anyone looking out specifically for the Teams' interests. So, in the process of looking for things to cut because of constantly reduced budgets, the SEALs came under the blade.

While I was in Denmark, the phone rang with a call from my XO, who was still back at Little Creek. He told me that I had better get

Navy SEALs

back as quickly as I could. The news was that the then chief of staff at the Inshore Undersea Warfare Command had just offered up SEAL Team Two as compensation in the next budget POM (Program Objective Memorandum) drill. My answer was short and terse, and I had to quickly find my way back to Little Creek.

The trouble was, we still didn't have any money to just get on a plane. So in the time-honored method of the Teams, I used whatever contacts I had to get the job done. The U.S. Army Special Forces 10th Group commander in Germany listened to my situation and told me that he would just get me back there. I was stuck on a plane en route to the 10th's headquarters in Fort Devens, Massachusetts. And that commander himself bought a commercial plane ticket for me to get from Boston down to Norfolk. In a day and a half, I was back at Little Creek.

The cutting of SEAL Team Two was indeed about to happen. And I couldn't stop it from my level in the command structure. I ended up making a phone call to an admiral whom I had done some business with up in the Pentagon. He was the op 06 at the time, the deputy for plans, policy, and operations for the Navy. He was coming down to Norfolk at his next change of command to become the amphibious-force commander.

When I told him what they were trying to do to the SEALs, his response was to the effect of "don't worry about it." About twenty minutes after that conversation ended, my phone rang again. This time it was the admiral I reported to and he asked me to come into his office for a while. It turned out he didn't know anything about the SEALs being cut either. When I explained the situation, he just told me that it wasn't going to happen.

That was maybe my scariest moment as a CO of SEAL Team Two—when I felt that the command was going to be killed.

Richard Marcinko, Commander, USN (Ret.)

A movie in the 1950s called The Frogmen *was where I first learned about the Underwater Demolition Teams. I saw that movie when I was still in high school. In 1958, I had already quit high school and was planning to enlist in the service. The first Lebanon crisis was* taking place and I was looking forward to seeing the action. The Marine Corps recruiter I spoke to told me that I wouldn't see any of that action, so I just said "the hell with you" and went to the Navy.

The UDT looked like it promised real action, which is what I wanted. I couldn't see myself being what my rate was, which was radioman, which is "clickety-clack, clickety-clack, here come the girls to the radio shack." In other words, carrier wave operation, listening to the dits and dashes of Morse code for hours on end.

But it was later, after I had been in UDT and learned about the SEALs, that I saw where the real action was going to be. SEAL Team Two was where I wanted to be.

When I received my orders to go to Vietnam, my first reaction was one of thanks. The reasons were several. One, because it had been a long dry spell between wars. The last real war the United States had been involved in was the Korean War during the first half of the 1950s.

When "Cuba" broke out—which was not a war, but we prepared for it as if it was going to be—the West Coast SEALs came east to help us out. Our numbers were small then and every SEAL counted a lot. So when Vietnam broke out, the East Coast Team went west to help in the fighting there. I had just come back to the Teams as a commissioned officer. So I went to war as the only SEAL ensign going out there, all of the other officers being lieutenants.

But that's what the SEALs were all about, being able to go to war. So my finally being able to go to combat was a situation I looked forward to.

My first day in Vietnam was really a surprise, though it was hot and that was something I had been expecting. We had flown all the way across the United States, from Little Creek, Virginia, to San Diego, California, aboard a C-130 cargo plane, basically riding on cargo straps. We stopped in California because we had to learn how to fight the war according to someone's decision at higher command.

So we went up to the Chocolate Mountains and fired all of the different weapons, and generally showed the West Coast that we knew how to find the on/off switches on our weapons. Then we went down to Tijuana to work on our escape and evasion plan, and liberty. That means we had a good time, and is why SEALs stands for Sleep, Eat, And Live it up, not SEa, Air, Land.

But going in to Vietnam wasn't quite as much fun. When we were flying in to the airfield at Binh Thuy, the C-130 banked hard and started circling. The air crew told us that they had to circle the field at high altitude to check the situation out, since they had been shot at a number of times.

Just about all of us aboard the plane had cheated and put our M16s in our hanging bags rather than securing them in the cruise boxes. As we were coming down to the airport to land, magazines were being locked and loaded so that we would be ready to engage the enemy the moment we hit the ground.

Well, when that big cargo ramp came down, the only thing we engaged was Jess Tolison, one of our chiefs who had been in the advanced parts. He had some trucks and cold beer waiting for us. So it was really quite a civilized way to start off fighting a war.

As far as details went, we had no idea where we were going to live. Most of us were ready to live in tents out in the jungle. But instead, quarters had been arranged for us and all the amenities put on. This was not immediately the all-out shooting war we had expected; that was going to come later.

I was the assistant platoon leader of Second Platoon, SEAL Team Two, in charge of Bravo Squad. This meant that Ensign Marcinko had five highly motivated, thoroughly trained, experienced SEALs to help him beat up the Viet Cong.

SEAL Team Two had sent two platoons over to Vietnam to establish Detachment Alfa, assigned to the Game Warden forces down in the Mekong Delta. Jake Rhinebolt was with us to command the new det. During our first few weeks in-country, the rest of Second Platoon and Third Platoon went up north to operate with the SEAL Team One guys who had been in-country for a while. As the SEAL junior officer in the det, I stayed behind with my squad in Ben Thuy.

Bravo Squad was made up of myself with Eagle Gallagher, Patches Watson, Ronnie Rodger, Ron Fox, and Jim Finley. The rest of the detachment had gone up to work with the SEAL Team One guys

A Mark II STAB speeds along the Bassac River in the Mekong Delta. The small, fast boats proved their worth in Vietnam but the fiberglass hulls couldn't stand up to the rigors of the area.

up in the Rung Sat. And while they were gone, Bravo Squad was supposed to sit quietly at the base. Not much chance of that happening after we had trained for this moment for months, if not years.

To operate in the area, we first had to learn the river, so we went out with the PBRs and went up and down the Bassac. We were shown where the VC normally crossed and all kinds of aspects of the daily river life in the Mekong Delta. We also went out in our own STABs (SEAL Tactical Assault Boats) to test-fire weapons and run the boats out a bit. We actually engaged the enemy in an all-out firefight during one of our test runs. The fact that the other guys were still up in the Rung Sat Special Zone learning how to fight the war while we had met the Viet Cong let us have a little jump start on them on operating in the delta.

The first combat mission that we were assigned involved us going downriver from our base on the Bassac. We did an insertion off of our own boats, the STABs, that we had developed back at Little Creek. Penetrating inland from our insertion point, we didn't find anything, so the mission came up a dry hole. But there's a learning curve to operating, and we were going to start climbing it fast.

There were some funny things that happened that showed little bits and pieces that we had to learn as well. The Viet Cong were known as "Charlie," a short version of their initials in military lingo, "Victor Charlie." Our detachment had two platoons, Second and Third, from SEAL Team Two. In Third Platoon was a guy named Charlie Bump.

Charlie went out on the perimeter one night, and on his way back in, somebody let us know that he was coming. "Here comes Charlie!" That caused some thought about whether or not it was our Charlie or the one we're supposed to shoot, Charlie. So we decided that Charlie wasn't a good name for our Teammate right then.

A SEAL sits at the coxswain's position in a Mk 1 STAB during the Team's early years in Vietnam. SEAL Team Two converted several civilian boats to this configuration for their initial operations in Vietnam.

U.S. Navy

The insert and extract are the two most critical points during any mission. When you start the mission, you're thinking about Murphy, what things can go wrong. And you are mentally preparing yourself for the actions you will take. When you first get to the jungle, and you're sitting there all night long, a palm frond sways, and you look at it and wonder if that's a bad guy moving. If you stare at things long enough, they start taking shape. Things can fool you when you let your imagination run.

When we first went out there in the jungle on patrol, we were told to take stay-awakes, or No-Doz pills. We queered that in a hurry, as people began to see things that just weren't there. I was jumping into the water and killing snakes. The little lights you could see in the hooches—well, they had angels coming out of them. So we didn't take drugs after the first time or two.

In the jungle, you learned very quickly that the human responses were the best. And the hell with the drugs and medications to try to keep you moving.

So you learned on every patrol. People ask the usual question: "Weren't you scared?" But you were so busy doing things, carrying out your mission and surviving, that you really weren't scared. It wasn't until you were back in the base, cleaning up your gear and sitting down to write up the report, that you realized that you almost lost a load out there.

During the action, you don't realize how close you are to losing it, because you're just too busy. When you're inserting, you're worried about all of the things you're going to do. When you're extracting, you're just trying to get everybody home. And the realization of what just happened doesn't hit you until you're relaxing and just writing up the report.

It's very hard to express the relationship all of the men had with one another in the Teams to someone who hasn't been in (1) the military, and (2) any special operations units. The relationship is somewhat like a pro-football-team locker-room experience. That is, we all have a common experience and a common mission. We all want to win, and the important thing you remember is that the probability statistics of where you're going to die are with your Teammates and not with your family.

Your Teammate is your comrade-in-arms. You'll go back-to-back with him in a bar, and you'll go back-to-back in combat. The trust is there about everything. The SEALs came out of the water of the UDT. In the water, we always had swim buddies. And that philosophy just went up onto dry land with the SEALs, we share everything—girlfriends, booze, and whatever—knowing that we might die together as well.

The camaraderie of the Teams was shown when I built SEAL Team Six. I hand-selected everybody in the Team, including the support people. The only way I could really do that was by being able to know a lot about all of the men in the Teams. You can get that in a closed community where everybody knows everybody else.

Across all of the Teams, we know the grandchildren, we know the wives, and we know the girlfriends of our Teammates. We know this because when we were at home and our Teammate deployed, we took care of his family. If the car broke down or the garage door didn't work, we backed that man up while he wasn't there.

Maybe the best way to describe the Teams is to say that we're kind of a "military Mafia." There's a bond between all of us that's very hard to break or slip in on. We take care of our own, and we really don't care if there's somebody else from the outside there to help us.

We trained so much together that we could read one another without using language. When I watched my point man, it got to where he didn't even have to signal me that he'd seen something. The way he carried himself and moved his body told me that he had spotted something or that something was about to go down.

When we lived together so long, developed that comradeship that is so much a part of the Teams, we learned to think alike, do alike. It was like a symphony; we would just flow together and do things in harmony.

If someone was to draw a bead, take aim with their weapon, on the Teammate next to you, naturally, you were going to kill them. We weren't there to make friends. We were there to wipe out the bad guy. In fact, it took a while before we realized that it was good to save a couple of the bad guys for the intelligence that could be learned from them.

But that was part of the evolution of war, of realizing that you are there and what you can do. When you first got there, you had to kind of "vent your spleen" before you knew what you could do. And then you had to finesse the target from there.

You had to learn from the mistakes you made, chew up its ass

With the coxswain of their LSSC insertion craft looking on from the lower left, these SEALs insert for an operation. The Point Man on the right is armed with an Ithaca pump-shotgun.

U.S. Navy

and make sure you didn't do it again, but knew why. Like some people went out on patrol and were sick. Later the patrol was disrupted by their barfing all over the jungle.

SEALs just think that they're invincible in terms of not having to go see a doctor. They're sure that they can take care of themselves, or just gut it out. And I've had a lot of guys go out who shouldn't have been on patrol. But they didn't want to miss going out on an op.

These are just some of the things you learn about. You also learn about the enemy, his boobytraps, and how he operates. And you pass that information on. It's when someone makes the same mistake twice that you either get rid of them, or they're dead.

Nothing supplants being in combat. It's the ultimate challenge. It takes all that you know and all that you have. And when you win—and that's the name of the game—you feel the best about it.

During my first tour to Vietnam, I was an assistant platoon leader for Second Platoon. During my second tour, I was the platoon leader for Eight Platoon. There was actually very little difference between the two jobs for me. The platoon leader I had in Second Platoon, Fred Kochey, was a passive leader. He led by example, but he wasn't a barking dog; he had no ego.

So Fred kind of gave me a free rein. Of course my squad was kind of a wild bunch, in terms of being ultra-aggressive and ultra-confident. We didn't have to worry about being self-starting. Self-containing maybe, but not self-starting.

Actually, in the beginning of the war, that aggressive attitude was one of my biggest problems. After an engagement, I had to stop people from running down the trail and chasing more VC. I was afraid that they would be sucked into an ambush.

The main difference when I was actually the platoon leader was that I picked my own missions. I felt that instead of having to be in the rivers, the maritime environment we were expected to operate in was anywhere I had my canteen, since I had water in it. That's how my platoon operated up on the Cambodian border, down in the Tranh Forest, and up in the Seven Mountains area.

My expanding of the area where we operated not only let me get Charlie where he felt the safest, but I was also getting major kills. Our platoon wasn't getting just couriers and local runners, we were taking down much bigger targets. If you were to compare my operations with today's drug war, Eighth Platoon wasn't taking out the local street dealers with a nickel bag, we were taking out the truckloads.

To accomplish that meant that we had to go deeper inland. And we had to take bigger chances. But that's what we were built for. And no one stopped me. If somebody tried to stop me while I was out on an op deep in bad-guy country, my radio wasn't on.

Operating like that scares the hell out of the bad guy. Particularly in an Asian culture. We had the green faces from our camo makeup. And there were little things you picked up on after you had been over there for a while.

In the villages we passed through, the little kids used to come out and grab our legs. Being an American, you would just think, as I did, Aw, isn't that cute?

It wasn't until after I had been there awhile that I learned the kids were passing their evil spirits on to me. So once I saw that, I would take my green smudge and rub their heads with it. That would cause them to come back in the next life and do the same things again—at least it did according to their superstitions.

Doing that psychological warfare with them could give you an edge. When you were first in-country, you didn't even understand what they were doing to you. But you learned, and then you used what you learned against them. In any combat situation, jungle or urban, when you can go after the enemy where they feel safest, you upset them.

And Asian cultures can be superstitious ones. Odd things, such as running a small deer through a campfire, is taboo for them. So you learned these things, not to believe in them, but to think as your enemy thought. And then you could use those weaknesses against them.

My own weakness centered around the men I was leading. When one of them was hurt or wounded, that weakness was turned back against the enemy. Having a man injured just pissed me off, as it did the rest of his Teammates. We went into retribution mode in a hurry. He would be protected as best we could, and we would kill as many of the enemy as we could on our way out.

The Vietnam War was fought in the kind of place where neither the Army nor the Marine Corps regular units wanted to really fight. They fought the Viet Cong with the same fire and maneuver tactics that had worked during earlier wars, but Vietnam was a place of guerrilla war, fighting in the dark against an almost unseen enemy. And that was where the SEALs could show their best.

If you look at the cloth of those men who joined the Teams, you see that the harder the job they had to do, the better they felt about it. From a managerial, team-leader perspective on the war in Vietnam, the SEALs were given a shitty job in rough terrain. And that meant no staff puke was going to want to come and see you. So all you had to do was fight the bad guy.

There's something to be said about the purity of a small war. For the SEALs, it was instant gratification. You would write up a patrol order, go out there, and shoot the bastard. Either you'd win, or you'd lose. It was black and white, no gray. And that's music, that is the epitome of life for a warrior. It was us against them, and we got an *instant readout; we didn't have to wait for a report to come out every six months.*

Vietnam was a hard job. And the Teams were ready for that job because (1) Everybody was geared up for it; (2) We felt better about it than anyone else; and (3) No staff puke was going to be on our ass, riding around with us looking for his own medal.

■ Chapter 6

SUPPORT FROM THE SEA, AIR, AND LAND

In spite of their wide range of abilities and skills, the SEALs could not have enjoyed the level of success they did in Vietnam without receiving support of an equally high quality. The three environments listed in the name—Sea, Air, and Land—are the same three environments from which the SEALs of Vietnam received support during their operations.

From the sea and the water came the small craft that moved the SEALs in to their target, pulled them out when the mission was over, and would come in with guns roaring if the Teams ran into trouble. This aid included naval gunfire support from large Navy ships such as destroyers and cruisers offshore. And small craft like the thirty-one-foot Mark I and Mark II PBRs (Patrol Boat, River) of the Brown Water Navy would answer when the SEALs called, carrying firepower that seemed almost too much to be coming from such small and lively craft.

From their own commands, the SEALs received specialized watercraft support from the boat support units (BSUs). These units operated and maintained small craft that were unique to the SEALs' operations. Such craft as the HSSC (Heavy SEAL Support Craft), a converted LCM Mk 6, commonly called the Mike boat, worked with the Teams throughout their years in Vietnam. The Mike boat was heavily converted from its original configuration, carrying weapons and ammunition in bulk behind armor plating,

The Medium SEAL Support Craft, another converted landing craft, moves down the river in Vietnam. A number of .50-caliber machine guns, mounted with shields to protect the gunners, can be seen lining the sides of the boat. On top of the overhead cover is a 57mm M18A1 Recoilless rifle.

U.S. Navy

rather than the large numbers of troops it was originally intended to take into the beaches for landings. Big and slow, the Mike boat would just move in like a lumbering giant, spitting out various kinds of fire from its many mounted weapons, to get the SEALs free of an overwhelming enemy force.

From the air came the most agile and destructive force at the SEALs' command. Air support could be in the form of "fast movers"—jet aircraft armed with a mix of bombs, rockets, cannon, and napalm that could rip apart major enemy formations, the fire from the sky being directed to the target by the SEALs on the ground. The helicopter gunship, originally a UH-1 or "Huey" helicopter with gun packages mounted on the sides, was a unique development of the Vietnam War.

Though they could receive helicopter gunship support from the Army and Marine Corps, the SEALs had their favorite unit in one of their own from the Navy, the Seawolves of Helicopter Attack Squadron (Light) 3. Commissioned on 1 April 1967 in order to provide Task Force 116 with its

The early Mark 6 LCM, or "Mike" boat conversion to a Heavy SEAL Support Craft in Vietnam. Two .50-caliber M2HB machine guns can be seen under the overhead cover. On top of the cover is a 106mm M40 Recoilless Rifle. Many modifications were done to the three boats of this type during the war.

U.S. Navy

own organic means of aerial fire support, observation, and medical evacuation, the Seawolves quickly became as legendary as the SEALs.

There seemed to be no situation so dire, no enemy so big, or no terrain so bad that the Seawolves wouldn't come in to support the men on the ground. The men of the Seawolves flew thousands of air sorties. When no one else would come in to give the SEALs what they needed, the Seawolves would fly. At times when the men on the ground had no other way to survive an enemy situation, the Seawolf crews would strip off their weapons, their primary means of protection, in order to have room to come in and pull the troops out.

The SEALs of Vietnam have nothing bad to say about the Seawolves of Vietnam, except perhaps that there should have been more of them. The men of the Teams readily admit a deep debt to the Seawolves. "If it wasn't for them, there would be a lot fewer of us," is the way many SEALs have put it.

The Seawolves were not the only specialized form of Navy air support during the Vietnam War. Activated in April 1969 was Light Attack Squadron

A "fast mover" in this case, an F-4 Phantom II aircraft from the carrier USS *Coral Sea,* drops a load of bombs over a target in North Vietnam.

U.S. Navy

4 (VAL 4), known by their call sign, the Black Ponies. Flying small propeller-driven OV-10 Bronco aircraft, the handful of Black Ponies in the skies above the Mekong Delta could loiter on-site for hours. And when a target was available, the Black Ponies could swoop in with unbelievable firepower for their size. Rockets, both 2.75-inch and 5-inch Zunis, would roar out from under the wings of the Black Ponies and blast huge holes in the jungle, or in the enemy formations underneath. Cannon fire from 20mm guns and bullets from 7.62mm machine guns would rip through the ground that had been torn up by the rockets. The power of the Black Ponies even impressed the SEALs, some of whom had seen a great deal of other firepower already.

Ground support in the form of military formations and troops, both U.S. and South Vietnamese, came in to the SEALs across the land. But the most common ground-based support the SEALs received came in the form of artillery fire from batteries of cannon. Given their training in gunfire support, the biggest gun in a SEAL squad was the man with a radio on his back. At the other end of that radio could be 105mm and 155mm howitzers and other cannon. At the SEALs' command, steel shells would come whistling out of the sky, having been fired from miles away. Directed to their target, the shells would tear apart the jungle with high explosives and buzzing steel fragments.

The insignia of Helicopter Attack Squadron, Light—The Seawolves as shown on a flag displayed at a Seawolf reunion.

Kevin Dockery

**Clyde Christensen,
Commander, USN (Ret.)**

Before I myself was in the Seawolves, I was in another squadron in San Diego, and I remember there was a lot of talk about the Seawolves going about in the various air units. I had been a helicopter pilot with HC-1 (Helicopter Combat Support Squadron One), which had been renamed in July 1965 from HU-1 (Helicopter Utility Squadron One), the first helicopter squadron in the U.S. Navy.

Even in the mid-1960s, pilots from our squadron had been going over to Vietnam to work with the U.S. Army helicopter units on an advisory basis. It seemed to me that the intent of that advisory work was to get us into the Seawolf mission from early on, but I have no evidence of that.

A lot of stories came back to the squadron about working with the Army and operating their helicopter gunships. Interesting things happened with Navy pilots working with the Army and using their armed helicopters.

With his PRUs alert and a SEAL Teammate armed with a Stoner just to the left of the picture, Frank Thornton speaks over the radio. The radioman and his backpack radio remained within close reach of the PRU adviser at all times so that he could call in the big guns (support) when needed.

Frank Thornton Collection

Following on from the HC-1 detachments, Helicopter Attack Squadron (Light) Three, HAL-3, began operations in Vietnam in June 1967, flying borrowed Army UH-1B helicopter gunships with Navy crews. It was under the call sign Seawolves that HAL-3 really began developing a reputation for itself, and it was the stories of these exploits that piqued my interest in joining the unit.

Things had been heating up in Vietnam and the Seawolves were operating on a continuous basis in support of Navy operations while I was working as the naval instructor at the University of Nebraska in their NROTC program. When I completed that tour of duty, I requested to go to Vietnam and be part of the Seawolves. My

HAL-33, Detachment 7, Dong Tam, Vietnam, 1971 (back row, left to right) LTJG Schilling, John Orth, Fred Whitlock, L. St. Jaques, AOC James Osterburg, LTJG T. Ziemer, Terry L. Mize (front row, left to right) LCDR Christensen, LTJG Reid, Lt. Joe Sullivan, LTJG Schull, Lt. Harrison, Rick Bogle, LTJG Todd, John Ross.

U.S. Navy

request was accepted and I would soon find myself back in the air at the controls of a helicopter.

My arrival in Vietnam occurred in the fall of 1970 when I was assigned as the assistant officer-in-charge (OIC) working off the USS Garrett County (LST 786). After about six weeks of training, I was put in command of my own detachment of Seawolves, Det 7 based out of Dong Tam.

HAL-3 was an established squadron with its headquarters in Binh Thuy. It conducted its mission in smaller units—detachments, or dets—that were spread out around the countryside. That way, Seawolf gunships could fly in support of Navy forces quickly and arrive as soon as possible.

The basic Seawolf mission was to support the riverine forces in

A Seawolf helicopter gunship and a Mark II PBR move along a waterway in South Vietnam. These two crafts were the most common air and water support used by the SEALs in Vietnam.

U.S. Navy

Vietnam. In addition, the squadron was to support any ongoing SEAL operations. It soon developed that the Seawolves also were being used to support Vietnamese troops in the field. There was a large Vietnamese Army base in Dong Tam, and so if we got a call from one of their units who was in trouble, we would take off on a support mission for them.

The Seawolves operated in a different manner than the Army helicopter units. For one thing, it was very common to see an Army helicopter operating singly on a mission. At other times, I've observed so many Army helicopters out on the same mission that it looked as if a swarm of bees had been let loose.

For us, we were always in a pattern where we could put in support for the ship (helicopter) that was making the run in on a target. It was a mutual support thing that worked very well for us. Every detachment had two gunships, and if the det didn't have two operational birds, then you just sat there until you had two craft ready to fly. Only if an emergency came up where you had to answer with just *your single ship did you go out alone, and that did happen a couple of times.*

We operated primarily as a light helicopter fire team, two birds working together. In Det 7, we had two UH-1s armed with 2.75-inch rocket pods fired by the pilot. The lead ship had a heavy machine gun, a .50-caliber, mounted as the door gun. In addition, there was a mini-gun mounted outboard, next to the rocket pods, that could be directed and fired by the copilot. The trail ship was armed in much the same way, except the door gunners had 7.62mm M60 light machine guns.

Even before I arrived in Vietnam, I had heard about the SEALs. Their reputation preceded them and it was an impressive one. The SEALs to me were always a highly professional, well-trained group of people. But I personally didn't have any direct experience with them until after I arrived in Vietnam.

In the Dong Tam area, we were fortunate to have a SEAL platoon that we worked with on a regular basis. In spite of their reputation as hard chargers, the SEALs struck me as wholly professional in their approach to a possible mission. It was my experience that we simply never went out on a joint mission with the SEALs unless the intel for the operation had been done extremely well. The SEALs just weren't going to go out on an operation unless they felt they had a maximum chance of success.

Everything that I observed the SEALs do during our joint opera- tions was extremely professional. It was just a pleasure to work with them. Their reputation for working hard, and playing hard, was one I'm sure they earned, especially from what I observed firsthand. But I never saw anything they did off duty get in the way of an operation. When the day of a mission came, they were always ready to go and completely professional about it.

The typical mission that we did in Vietnam in support of the SEALs would usually start with the SEAL commander coming in to talk to me about his plan. "Clyde," he would say, "I've got this type of a mission. Here is where we're going to have to go. Here is how we want to do it. Here is how many men we're going to want to put in on the ground. And here is how long we think we're going to be on the ground."

The mission would be stated first so that we knew what we were

---

Before a mission, Lieutenant Commander Roland Habicht, in charge of HAL-3 (Seawolf) Det 1, gets a final information briefing from a SEAL.

U.S. Navy

going in for and what the objective was. That would then tell me what we had to do first; perhaps we had to put the SEALs in on the target and then leave the area, something we had to do on occasion because of the type of mission they were going to do.

On other missions, we were required to be overhead during the whole operation. In some cases, a SEALs mission lasted so long that we just didn't have the fuel supply to stay on top of them. Then we had to go back and refuel and return.

Once the original mission was over, we could be called on to come in and get the SEALs out, extract them from the target. And if contact was made, we could come in with very heavy firepower in their support.

The best thing about the helicopter gunship support was that we could put our fire in almost any place it was needed. If a team was in trouble, we could come in almost directly on top of them and

Aviation Ordnanceman Michael Draper slips a 2.75-inch rocket into one of the 7-round rocket pods mounted on this Seawolf helicopter gunship. To the right in the picture can just be seen the mechanisms of the two M60C machine guns that are part of the Seawolf's mounted weapons system.

either suppress the enemy forces or land and get someone out or in. Our biggest advantage to the SEALs was in being their dedicated close air support.

Even though our units were called light attack teams, we could pack a big wallop. Our machine guns had thousands of rounds of ammunition available to them. Our rockets were limited to fourteen, seven to a pod, one pod on each side of the aircraft. But we fired them in pairs and each rocket carried either a six- or ten-pound high-explosive warhead. Those rockets had the impact of an artillery strike, and we could put them in exactly where they were needed.

Our firepower was one of our greatest defenses, but there were times when we had to give up a lot of it to complete a mission. A number of times, just because of the place where we were and the

Slipping a long belt of 7.62mm machine gun ammunition into place, Navy Airman Robert Nunes loads one of the four ammunition boxes for a Seawolf's outboard machine guns. Each of the four long boxes will hold 600 rounds of ammunition for the M60C mounted guns. In front of the airman's knee is an ammunition box with a dozen rounds of 40mm high explosive grenades set nose-up. The grenades would be fired by the Seawolf's crew from an M79 grenade launcher, just visible behind the long ammunition boxes on the far right center of the picture. This is just a small part of the ammunition and weapons load carried aboard a Seawolf helicopter gunship.

U.S. Navy

conditions there, such as being very hot and humid, we were limited in what we could carry and still lift off. We would have to strip down the craft, take some of the weapons or ammunition off, and maybe reduce the fuel load to make sure we could go in and do what we had to do.

When we were the only helicopters available, and the SEALs were in a tight spot, we would strip off all of the ship's weapons and ammunition to have enough capacity to lift out the SEALs. That was just something we had to do. And we called that going in "slick," i.e., not having any armament whatsoever.

According to where you were operating from, adjustments had to be made as to just how much fuel and ammunition you had on board for any operation. When I originally arrived in-country, the LST Harnett County was down in the Ca Mau Peninsula, the southernmost point of Vietnam. Flying off that ship, we always had to work with a reduced fuel load. In that case, we were taking off athwartships—sideways, from the middle of the deck.

When you flew like that, the minute you were airborne and went off, all you had was water below you. The hot, humid air limited the lifting capacity of the rotors and engines, so we never were able to lift off with a full fuel, or ammo, load.

Once I arrived at Dong Tam, I found we were operating off a fairly long strip—it was just PSP (Pierced Steel Planking)—but it was still long enough to give you a forward run on takeoff. Moving a helicopter forward for takeoff increases the amount of lift available to it. So we could operate with a lot more fuel and ammunition on board.

On certain occasions, when the weather was not the most agreeable, we actually had to physically bounce the helicopter down the runway until we could finally get it airborne. And there were still times when we couldn't get the bird up in the air with a full load on board. In those situations, we had to go back and take off some of the fuel or ammo and try it again.

Though it never happened to me, there were times when you had to get the helicopter moving forward under a lighter load, and then suddenly increase the load as soon as it was airborne. The way you did this was by having the crew chief and door gunner run alongside the bird as she went down the runway. As soon as the helicopter was airborne, the crew chief and gunner would jump aboard. That usually resulted in the bird bouncing back off the ground, but she would be airborne. As I say, that never happened to me, but there were a few times when I was mighty tempted to have my crew run alongside.

The enemy we were facing in the south of South Vietnam were a kind of hit-and-run force. We really never knew just what to expect on a given day. That was when you were speaking of the Viet Cong. Things were much different farther north, where you could be facing North Vietnamese Army (NVA) forces.

We never knew when we would be called for a sudden operation, or what kind of op it might be. It could be a small skirmish someplace or a fairly large engagement in another place. We had a group of Vietnamese Army people, more militia really than anything else. One of the Vietnamese officers in that group had been trained in the U.S., so he spoke English very well.

That officer described to me that his situation was more of a "Hatfields and McCoys" feud situation than a war. He had a running gunfight with a Viet Cong unit, and it was almost like they would tantalize each other, each unit trying to draw the other one out into a fight.

This situation resulted in a planned meeting of the two units. They were going to face each other down and fight it out. But the officer told me he had, in effect, to promise the VC that he wouldn't bring in the Seawolves. And then he told me that he wanted me there anyway. And we were overhead at the time that Vietnamese unit needed us. So they won that engagement.

So we did operate in support of the Vietnamese Army. But we worked even more in support of the riverine forces. And this was true even though the makeup of the riverine forces had changed. By the time I had arrived on the scene, the manning of the riverine boats had been largely turned over to the South Vietnamese Navy as part of the Vietnamization program. Now, instead of a U.S. Navy crew on board, there would be just a single U.S. Navy adviser. So that took some of the feeling out of the situation for us.

We had much preferred working for the U.S. forces in-country. We knew that when a call came in from Americans—SEALs or who- ever—there really was a need for us. Unfortunately, sometimes, when we got a call requesting support for a Vietnamese Army unit, we learned when we arrived on target that there really hadn't been a need for our services. But we still had to go up, and put everyone in my crews at risk.

But the Navy rewarded the risks we took in their traditional way. The Seawolves received a lot of decorations in spite of being a rather small unit. There was a point system based on the number of mis- sions flown, how they were reported, and a variety of other factors. I really never understood the system completely. But with the accu- mulation of a certain number of points, you received an Airman's Medal. When I received my eighteenth medal award, I wondered just why I had received it. Sometimes, it seemed that the reporting sys- tem almost overshadowed the event itself. But we did do a lot of mis- sions.

Several of the operations we did during my time there stick in my memories of Vietnam. The first of these was soon after I had first arrived in-country and was still down in the Ca Mau area. As the assistant OIC there, I was not in on all of the whys and wherefores of the integral planning for a mission, even one with the SEALs. But planning was done carefully and completely. In spite of that, this one op didn't go too well.

We had stripped down a couple of the available gunships to a slick configuration for the insertion and extraction of the SEALs. It was a joint operation, so we had additional detachments, three in all, working on the op. So we had plenty of firepower while still being able to move the SEALs in and out with our own assets.

But for some reason, the intel on this operation was not as good as it could have been. As soon as the SEALs were inserted, they were hit pretty hard. Though the exact numbers escape me, I know several of them were wounded. And we had one of our gunships badly shot up, with both the pilot and copilot being wounded.

The crew capacity I was working in at that time was as a copilot. I just hadn't been in-country long enough to act as the aircraft commander. But that was one of my first major operations. And to see it not go well, and not know why, has kept it sharp in my memory. There are a lot of reasons things don't go well sometimes. The intel might have been great, but something else happened to change the situation before we arrived. I just don't know.

After I had moved up north to Det 7 at Dong Tam, it was just so refreshing, after that bad experience in Ca Mau, to deal with the SEALs. To see those folks do their homework so carefully and completely made me very comfortable about going out on a mission with them. And after I'd gone out with the SEALs a number of times, and seeing just how professional they were, that feeling just grew more solid.

But the other mission that really sticks in my mind took place out of Dong Tam, and it wasn't a SEAL operation. We had our own radio set up so that we could respond to calls as quickly as possible. One night, a call came in from a couple of American advisers who were north of Dong Tam. They were surrounded, under heavy fire, and needed air support badly.

It didn't matter to us that it was the middle of the night. We were up and off the deck as quickly as we could. To complicate matters, this was the time of year when the Vietnamese burned off their fields to clear them for the new plantings. Now it was nighttime, with *no lights and a smoke haze dimming whatever light there was. Vietnam at night was dark; there were no light grids on the ground and electricity was a nonexistent commodity in the rural countryside. And we were flying through this darkness to an unknown position.*

The Viet Cong had set up a heavy-machine-gun trap, where they could get an incoming helicopter in a murderous crossfire. And as a detachment, we flew in and put down close air support as directed by the Americans on the ground. And the situation reminded me of the old WWII movies with the flak coming up to take out the bombers. Only this time the flak was the glowing green lights of tracers, and they were coming up at us.

Belts of ammunition for machine guns were not normally loaded just with tracers. There would be four, five, or six rounds fired for every tracer launched. So between the rounds we could see, there were maybe six others we couldn't.

With all of that fire coming up at us from all sides, I figured there had to be some of it hitting the helicopter. But it wasn't hit, and we stayed in the air, putting out our own fire all around the Americans' position.

Finally, we ran out of fuel and ammunition and had to go back for a hot reload. Our ground crews did their jobs quickly and we took off again with another load of fuel and ammunition. We returned to the advisers' position and again put the enemy under fire with directions from the ground. And again, those green tracers rose up to meet us.

But we were finally able to drive the enemy back, and got the situation to the point where the Americans on the ground were no longer under attack. And all during that time, my knees shook. Normally, a helicopter doesn't face heavy ground fire in the form of .50 caliber or better. A fire team is just a poor weapons system against such fire. And we normally wouldn't have fought against that kind of a position unless the situation was as grave as it was that might.

But we had people on the ground who needed our help, and they needed it badly. So it really didn't matter that any of us were scared, and I'm certain we all were. But we had a job to do and our people down there desperately needed us to do it.

You could see tracers floating through the air around us; they appeared to move by unnaturally slowly. And you could hear the occasional round strike the aircraft. But we were all very well trained, and we just continued to do what we had to do.

The Navy figured we had done something pretty well in that night's operation. At least, as the officer-in-command, I was given the Distinguished Flying Cross for leading the attack. But I'll always remember those green tracers, and how my legs shook.

Each helicopter burned through fourteen 2.75-inch rockets, 3,000 rounds of ammo for the miniguns, and another thousand rounds of ammunition for the door guns. But the overriding factor for our remaining in the fight was our fuel situation.

A final pre-op briefing for SEALs ready to go in Vietnam. The SEAL at the top right, wearing the cammo bush hat, is armed with the T223 rifle, a version of the HK 33 tested by the SEALs in Vietnam.

U.S. Navy

But in spite of the fear that came over you in a firefight, you could also have a real good feeling come over you as well. You knew in your heart and mind that the people you were working with were really well trained. And they weren't going to be cutting out on you when things got hot. In fact, they were going to be doing everything they possibly could to make that mission a go. Those things added up to a really great feeling, and I'm sure this was as true for the SEALs as it was for the Seawolves.

Anyone who has been in combat will tell you, if they really think about it seriously, that you grow very close to the people you serve with. When you work that closely with people in that stressful a situation, they become your family. Those men become your brothers, and you don't cut out on your brother. You do whatever you have to

---

do to make the situation work. Yeah, you're scared, but you have to do it.

I was surprised a bit when I first learned just in how high a regard the SEALs held the Seawolves. Surely, I had never considered myself anywhere close to their equals when you took into account the amount and kind of training they went through. And the kind of job they did was incredible. In all of my working with them, I think I only understood maybe ten percent of the job they did. So their thinking well of us is a high honor indeed.

During our flight operations, we always had to worry about going down in enemy territory. It could be while on a SEAL operation, supporting the Riverines, or working with the Vietnamese army. But there was some comfort in the thought I had in the back of my mind.

Without being told in so many words. I knew that if we went down, it wouldn't be very long before there would be some SEALs out there looking for me. And that was a great feeling.

After my tour in Vietnam, I returned to the States. The feeling of being there faded somewhat over time. And then I received the honor of being awarded the Distinguished Flying Cross. But you also had to keep in your mind the other people who may have done a lot more than you did, and they never received a medal for it. Yes, it was an honor, but I know I wasn't doing anything other than what almost every other pilot was doing when they were stationed in Vietnam.

Mark Schimpf, Chief Warrant Officer, U.S. Army

In Vietnam, I was a helicopter gunship pilot for the U.S. Army. My bird was a Huey UH-1B, an aircraft that was first introduced into Vietnam as a troop carrier. The birds were later outfitted with weapons systems and flew as helicopter gunships, the same configuration as those first flown by the Navy Seawolves.

The configuration we used was a thirty-eight-rocket setup, two nineteen-round 2.75-inch FFAR (Folding Fin Aircraft Rocket) pods, one on either side of the aircraft. There were also two door gunners, each man armed with a flexible M60 machine gun. Generally, we didn't fly with any externally mounted machine guns, giving up the

A U.S. Marine Corps Bell AH-1G Cobra gunship in Vietnam. Under the stub wings, this lethal aircraft has mounted both a 19-round (inboard) and 7-round (outboard) 2.75-inch rocket pod. In the chin turret under the nose of the aircraft is a 7.72mm minigun and a 40mm machine grenade launcher. The gunner sat in the front of the cockpit with the pilot sitting at the rear in the slip helicopter.

U.S. Navy

weight of the guns and their ammunition in order to carry the larger nineteen-round rocket pods rather than the smaller seven-round versions.

Small arms were available for everyone on board the helicopter. The personal weapons were in case we had to put down someplace and defend ourselves on the ground. On our bird, the copilot also had a 40mm M79 grenade launcher. When he didn't have anything to do on a mission, he would lean out of the bird and conduct miniature bombing missions with 40mm HE grenades.

With those birds, I flew missions all around the Mekong Delta. I was based in III Corps, not too far from Saigon. But every morning, we did about an hour's flight down to the delta region to fly support missions for whoever might need them.

During our missions, we supported a wide variety of people. You never really knew when you started a flight just where you might end up. Vietnamese, Army Special Forces, Navy SEALs, all of them could call us in when we were in the area. It was kind of an open grab bag as to just who we were going to work with.

SEAL missions obviously weren't advertised as to just when and where they would take place. And we never knew when we were going to work with them while I was in Vietnam. Once we had gotten down into an operational area, we could find out that today we would be working with a group of people on the ground who might not be specifically identified. But we would recognize the SEALs because of their unorthodox appearance and selection of weapons.

The first time I met SEALs in the field, my impression of them was that they were a little comical, since I was used to seeing people in uniforms and with standard-issue weapons, and the SEAL units tended to be a little more "ragtag" in their choice of operational uniforms. Simply put, there probably weren't two of them dressed alike; some might be wearing blue jeans, black cotton tops, bandannas, floppy hats, boots, sandals, or even barefoot. And certainly there wouldn't be two of them in a group armed with the same weapon. All in all, a very wild group and more than a little entertaining, from my point of view.

Generally, we didn't get involved with the SEALs on a fire support mission until they had made contact with the enemy and were in maybe over their heads. Our unit didn't normally start out a mission with the expectation of giving air support to the SEALs unless they were going into an area they expected to be hot. If the SEALs suspected they might be facing a larger target than their normal support could handle, then we would be brought on board to stand by. SEALs preferred to go in to a target quietly, and didn't want a bunch of helicopters flying around drawing attention. We only got called in when things had gone "south" for them and they needed some help.

Since so much time has gone by since those days, all of the missions kind of blur together. Separating one SEALs mission from all of *the ops we flew is hard, but there is one that stands out. A SEAL team had been inserted by boat and had run into a lot of trouble on the ground. A Seawolf helicopter fire team had been assisting the beleaguered SEALs, but the Seawolf birds had expended their ordnance almost right off the bat and they had to go back for a reload.*

The call went out for more fire support. Fortunately, we still had full loads of everything at the time. Because of the mission that the SEALs were working, they really needed precise, close air support since the bad guys tended to be right in on top of them when a fight broke out. As an Army gunship pilot, I can say that we were pretty good at precise fire support. We could put rockets exactly right where they needed to be. And that was just what those SEALs wanted right then.

Our load of ammunition and rockets was a large one, actually a bit more than regulations allowed. But rules were made to be broken. And I think I can safely say that in Vietnam, any rule there was got broken in every possible way. On our missions, we always wanted to carry as much armament as possible.

The doors were left off our birds, since they really wouldn't do anything; by getting rid of their weight, we could carry more ordnance. The door gunners had several cases of ammunition for each of their M60 machine guns, one on each side of the helicopter. We also had a selection of hand grenades, including white phosphorus. And the M79 would have a nice selection of ammo on board. Our personal weapons consisted of M16s, CAR-15s, and even AK-47s, whatever was available. You just hauled as much as you could to fight with.

Sometimes, this heavy load made it difficult to get a helicopter off the ground. On a hot day, after around noon, a refueled and rearmed bird would barely be able to hover. The hot air caused the rotors to lose lift and the engine would be straining to get the bird in the air. She would be hard to move even on the skids. But once the helicopter was moving, the forward motion gave added lift and the bird could be on her way.

It was common practice in these hot, hard lift situations for the crew chief and door gunner to get out of the helicopter. We would begin a slow forward motion, sliding along the leading edge of the skids. As the bird gained a little speed, the crew would decide when it was time to leap aboard. The helicopter would usually bounce off the ground, but it would manage to lumber into the air. Once we got flying, it was okay.

All of the helicopters and their crews shared the same kind of dangers throughout Vietnam. It didn't matter if you were Army, Navy, or Marine Corps. We flew the birds that went right in where the action was and slugged it out with an enemy that could shoot at us with anything they had. So there wasn't much in the way of serious rivalry between ourselves and, say, the Seawolves.

There was a certain amount of envy about the meals the Seawolves had, though. They seemed to eat very well indeed. Whenever we had the opportunity to stop at the Navy base at Nha Be, near Saigon, we ate with them. The kidding from our side got pretty serious. We used to tell them to come on up to our base and see what the real war was like, C rations and all.

The Seawolves didn't have the opportunity to get involved in as many different kinds of things perhaps as we did. And they were champing at the bit; those Seawolf pilots and crews wanted even more action than they actually got into. They did work under a somewhat more restricted, controlled environment than we did. The Army guys were pretty loose.

We had our own little jokes, games, and traditions in our aviation company. Probably the most spectacular of these was the tradition of "Bomb of the Day." That was a little game we played when things got boring. And it's a bad thing to have bored young men and explosives in the same place. That's a really dangerous combination.

Generally, the Bomb of the Day was something like a couple of 2.75-inch rocket warheads wired together. We had the M151, what we called the ten-pound warheads, and the bigger M229 seventeen-pounders. But even the bigger seventeen-pounders only had about five pounds of Composition B-4 high explosive inside of them. But that could be fixed by securing one or two two-and-a-half-pound sticks of C-4 plastic explosive to the assembly. And you might add a hand grenade, probably white phosphorus for light and smoke, to the bomb. And whatever else you felt would make for a better effect.

What you wanted was a good flash and bang so the crowd could see it. The bomb would be dumped out over a hooch in an area where we had been doing some shooting. When you were getting

*ready to throw out your bomb, you would call all of the other pilots'
attention to the area of the explosion. That way they could all grade
your bomb.*

*The object was to try and duplicate a miniature nuclear blast.
Sometimes, the Bomb of the Day turned out to be more effective than
you had planned. Usually, your helicopter was fairly low when you
dropped the thing out, and you got a little concussion from the explosion. That's what happens when young boys have a lot of explosives.*

*Bomb of the Day could be a significant event. If your blast was
graded well by the other pilots, you could plan on drinking free that
night. That increased the value of the Bomb of the Day consid-
siderably.*

*The playing around sometimes made the dangerous situations
we found ourselves in every day a little more bearable. You went
over to Vietnam with the thought that perhaps you were going to
win the war for America and her allies, and carry the flag. What you
quickly found out was that the war was a day-to-day survival event
of trying to just keep everybody alive for the year and be done.*

*There was no distinction at all about working with other services.
When you needed help, you didn't really care where it came from.
And that held true for everybody there. We were always pleased to
help out any of the other services. Assisting the SEALs was even
more important sometimes, because they were hanging out there
pretty far. When we could help them out, we were happy to do so.*

*There's a mystique about the SEALs. And being an Army pilot, I
have an opinion of them formed by the things I've seen of their
training. And they went through an entirely different kind of operating than I did. Since the SEALs are a closed group and not a whole
lot is known about them, the mystique and legend of the Teams built
up in Vietnam continues to live on today.*

*You get used to getting shot at. And some people have a very
hard time accepting that if they've never been exposed to it. But
when you get shot at on a regular basis, that's what becomes the
norm for you. As a result, it just doesn't impact on you as much. So
when someone is in trouble and you go in to get them out, you don't
give a great deal of thought to the danger of the situation.*

"Oh, I might get shot" or "There's a lot of lead coming up here. Maybe I shouldn't do this." That kind of talk just doesn't enter your mind. All you do think about is the fact that you have to go and get that person out of trouble. And you do this because you know that if you were that person on the ground, you would want someone to come and help you. And that was done by everyone in the war. It was a normal course of events.

■ Chapter 7

SEAL AND UDT DETACHMENTS

Both the UDTs and the SEAL Teams operated in detachments, commonly called dets, when they deployed from their bases at Coronado or Little Creek. Dets were normally identified by an alphabetical designation according to the Navy phonetic alphabet: *A* was Alfa, *B* was Bravo, and so on. These dets were not of a standard size, but were adjusted to fit the needs of the mission. Det Golf, the largest SEAL detachment of the Vietnam War, grew from an initial allotment of 3 officers and 15 enlisted men (3/15) to a group of six deployed platoons and a command element totaling 13 officers and 75 enlisted men. This was more men than were in SEAL Team One at its commissioning.

At close to the peak of Navy Special Warfare's involvement in Vietnam in January 1970, the numbers of detachments in Vietnam and their assigned personnel were as follows:

PERSONNEL DISPOSITION AND NUMBERS, JANUARY 1970

UNIT	LOCATION	PERSONNEL
NAVSPECWARGRUV	Saigon	10/11
SEAL Det SIERRA	Cam Rahn Bay	1/7

UNIT	LOCATION	PERSONNEL
SEAL Det ALFA (HQ)	Binh Thuy	1/2
Fifth Platoon	Dong Tam	2/12
Sixth Platoon	Ca Mau	2/11
Seventh Platoon	Nha Be	2/13
SEAL Det GOLF	Nam Can	1/3
Delta Platoon (A Squad)	Rach Soi	1/6
Delta Platoon (B Squad)	Kien Son	1/6
Echo Platoon	Nam Can	2/8
Foxtrot Platoon	Nam Can	2/12
Golf Platoon	Nam Can	2/11
Hotel Platoon	Sa Dec	2/11
Juliett Platoon	Long Phu	3/12
SEAL Det ECHO	Danang	0/3
MST One	Danang	3/16
MST Two	Binh Thuy	1/11
MST Two, Det ALFA	Sa Dec	1/8
MST Two, Det BRAVO	Nam Can	1/7
MST Two, Det CHARLIE	Nam Can	1/11
MST Two, Det DELTA	Dong Tam	2/21
MST Two, Det ECHO	Rach Soi	1/8
MST Two, Det FOXTROT	Ca Mau	1/7
MST Two, Det GOLF	Long Phu	1/7
BJU One TM 13	Binh Thuy	3/16
UDT Det DELTA	Nha Be	1/5
UDT Det GOLF	Nam Chan	1/7
UDT Det HOTEL	Danang	1/8

Detachment identifiers could be confusing. Both the UDTs and the SEALs could have a detachment with the same letter designator in-country in Vietnam at the same time. The mobile support teams (MST) who ran the special boats also used the same system. Only the beach jumper units (BJU) avoided this particular area of confusion.

SEAL DETS

- DET ALFA: SEAL Team Two detachment of direct-action platoon in Vietnam.

- DET BRAVO: combined SEAL Team One and Two detachment under the control of COMUSMACV to supply advisers to the PRU program primarily in the IV Corps area. Expanded on 4 October 1968 from 1/12 to 13/21.

- DET CHARLIE

- DET DELTA

- DET ECHO: combined SEAL Team One and Two detachment under the control of COMUSMACV to supply advisers and trainers to the South Vietnamese unconventional warfare units.

- DET FOXTROT

- DET GOLF: SEAL Team One detachment of direct-action platoon in Vietnam. The largest single SEAL detachment of the Vietnam War.

- DET HOTEL

- DET INDIA

- DET SIERRA

UDT DETS

- DET ALFA: UDT 12 detachment.

- DET BRAVO: UDT 12 detachment; conducted hydrographic reconnaissance along South Vietnamese shores including clandestine missions launched from the submarine USS *Perch*. Assisted in amphibious operations and major landings.

- DET CHARLIE

- DET DELTA: UDT detachment stationed at Camp Tien Sha near Danang.

- DET ECHO: UDT detachment assigned to Amphibious Ready Group conducting standard UDT reconnaissance missions.

- DET FOXTROT: UDT detachment assigned to Amphibious Ready Group conducting standard UDT reconnaissance missions.

- DET GOLF: UDT detachment assigned to riverine forces in the Ca Mau Peninsula.

- DET HOTEL: UDT detachment assigned to riverine forces in the Ca Mau Peninsula.

- DET INDIA: UDT detachment assigned to riverine forces in the Ca Mau Peninsula.

- DET SIERRA

Frank Sobisky, Electrician's Mate, Third Class

In August 1966, I joined the Navy specifically to enter the UDT Teams. When a group of us went down to the Navy recruiters' office, I went along really just to watch my two friends enlist for the Seabees. While at the office, I learned about the UDTs for the first time. Originally, I was thinking about enlisting to go to the war in Vietnam, but as a member of the Army Special Forces. I just had that mentality then, I guess.

But once I was at the Navy office, the recruiter hooked right into me and suggested the UDT. When I asked him what it was, he told me about the Frogmen. The Navy Frogmen were something I had known a little about, at least from popular movies and magazines. Then the recruiter played me along a bit, telling me I could enlist and not have to go for ninety days.

Back when I was that young, ninety days sounded like forever. So I told the recruiter to just sign me up, and I found myself in the Navy. When I first arrived in Coronado months later, I was assigned to Class 42, a West Coast winter class. Training was still called

Coming up from the escape hatch, this UDT swimmer is just clearing the deck grids of a sub-merged submarine. He is using open-circuit SCUBA gear during this well-lit training exercise off Key West, Florida, in 1959.

U.S. Navy

Underwater Demolition Team Replacement training then, and it was a little scarier than I expected. And the training was a lot harder than I expected.

It turned out I wasn't in as near as good a shape as I thought I was once those instructors got hold of me. But I held up and went through Hell Week with my classmates. Class 42 was a winter class, and it was very cold. Everyone jokes about the lack of snow in Southern California, but it did indeed snow on our class at least one day. And for San Diego, that was really cold.

A lot of things helped get me through the training, my class-mates and just my own stubbornness. But what probably got me through all of that training more than anything else was that I wanted to impress my father. Any thought of quitting was just some-thing I had to push back and ignore and just keep on going.

There was the fun of the mud flats during Hell Week. Those stinking stretches of thick black mud that the instructors had us roll around in. And this mud had a very pungent smell to it. We were covered from head to toe in thick, stinking mud. We were crawling in it, sitting in it, and even doing somersaults in it. Then it was time for lunch.

So with us standing waist-deep in the muck, the instructors, being the kindhearted souls they were, gave each of us a nice, nutritious sack lunch. Each of the paper bags held an orange, a hard-boiled egg, and a piece of fried chicken.

We had to eat everything with our mud-covered hands. Peeling open some of the package was interesting—you couldn't set the bag down without it sinking out of sight. And all that was visible of our bodies in the mud was white teeth and eyeballs. It was funny to look around and see all these guys daintily trying to peel their oranges with their teeth so at least they didn't have to eat that mud as well. Here were all these big, bad, tough future Frogmen trying their best to keep these bits of dirt out of their food.

We were all pretty much exhausted, and looking around at these guys trying to eat just struck me as funny. So I just lost it and started laughing. That became contagious, and soon enough we were all looking at one another and busting up. The instructors didn't seem to understand what was striking everyone as so funny, but it was a lighthearted moment during a really miserable time.

I made it through Hell Week, but I didn't make it through training, at least not with Class 42. During land warfare training, I injured my left arm and couldn't continue. Since I was already post–Hell Week, the instructors decided to give me a chance to heal and I was rolled back to wait for the next class to go through training.

So when Class 43 began training, I was right in there with them. But the instructors started me right at the beginning with my new class, and I had the honor of going through Hell Week a second time.

Two classes, two Hell Weeks. But at least my second time through, it was a summer Hell Week. And I thought I had an advantage because I knew some of the mind games the instructors would ruin on us during training. That not only helped me get through, it helped my boat crew as well.

But I never had an easy time of it during training. I'm a big guy, and there's a lot of difficulty being a big guy in training. Just by being big, when you step in the sand, you go in deeper than the others. And when you do log PT, you're reaching higher than the others. And if you have a smaller guy next to you, well, he may be trying to pull his own weight, but you usually end up lifting part of his share of the load as well as your own.

The hardest part of training for me was the runs. I just wasn't a good runner. Swimming came much easier for me, as I was already a good swimmer right off the bat at training. And my swimming is probably what saved me during training. At least it helped make up for my slower times during runs.

But all of the work, and both Hell Weeks, were worth it in the end. Standing there on graduation day and getting into the Teams was probably the highlight of my life. And that thought continues to this day. Completing that training was an accomplishment that relatively few others had done. And my father said that it was his proudest moment to see me there that day. For me, it was a very fulfilling moment.

To be a member of the UDT is to have joined a brotherhood. Of the fifteen or sixteen guys who completed training with me that day, any one of them could call me today and I would drop whatever I was doing to assist him if I could. Since I've gotten out of the Navy, I've done a lot of things in my life. But I have never had the camaraderie that I had while in the Teams.

The training then was done on the bay side of Coronado. Once you graduated training, you were sent to the Teams, who were located across the road on the ocean side of the base. So once you had made it through training, you "crossed over" to the Teams.

Once I had been assigned to UDT 11 for several months, I learned about the SEAL Teams for the first time. To me, the SEALs were the elite of the elite. And at that time in my life, I had the mindset that being with the very best was what I wanted to do. But before I could get to the SEALs, I had to prove myself in UDT 11.

We didn't start operating with our respective UDTs right away. Once the graduates of Class 43 had been assigned to their Teams, we all went off to Fort Benning, Georgia, for army jump school. That was another adventure because I don't particularly care for heights. But the training was part of the job. And it was a lot easier than going through UDTR.

Once we arrived at Fort Benning, the instructors broke us up and spread us out among the other students. But we still had our fun. The very first night we got there, we were just kind of wandering around trying to figure out where we were supposed to be. One of the instructors jumped on us as a group and had us start doing push-ups for him. We were being wiseasses about the whole thing, and I think he was trying to make a point about discipline.

The "hooyah" yell we had learned in UDTR came in handy to organize us against the Army in a way. When you screwed up at jump school, the instructors would have you immediately drop and give them twenty push-ups. Every time one of us was dropped down to "start pushing on Georgia," he would yell out "hooo-yahhh!"

When we heard that yell, all of the rest of us would pick up on it, yell out, and drop for push-ups ourselves. No matter what we were doing or where we were, if a Teammate dropped, we all dropped. We had decided this among ourselves after that first-night episode. The instructors all acted frustrated by our shenanigans. But I think that deep down inside, they really got a kick out of it.

I mean, we were in great physical shape. We had all just completed one of the hardest physical training courses in the world, and here we were with these Army instructors trying to punish us with a handful of push-ups. It was nothing for us to do twenty push-ups. And even though I wasn't one of the best runners in the Team, far from it, I could outrun the Army troops in our class. When our jump school class went for a run, the six of us from my UDTR class would literally run rings around them. As the group was running along, we would be circling them on the outside. That pissed them off and was more than a little fun.

There was an incident in the chow line when we disagreed with the Army way of doing things. Volunteers had to serve chow to everyone going through the line. You didn't serve yourself—the volunteers loaded up your tray. And as far as we were concerned, the Army was feeding these guys insufficient portions.

So we volunteered for server duty during chow. I don't think they allowed anyone from the Teams to serve chow at jump school for a while after that. We filled those guys trays so full, they had a hard time carrying them to the dining tables. The civilian cooks said we were going to run out of food, which we did. So we ended up not getting anything to eat, but we still had fun with the situation.

Still, the first time I heard that phrase—"Stand up, hook up, stand in the door"—I was probably in a daze. Even though I didn't like heights, that first jump didn't bother me all that much. But that was only because I was too stunned to react to it. That made my second jump even harder. But I completed jump training and maintained my jump status while in the Teams.

But every time I had to make a qualifying jump in the Teams, I would tell myself that I might not do it this time. You had to jump so many times a year to keep receiving jump pay. But I figured I would finally just not go out the door. But I always did.

The parachute jumping was something I didn't like about the job. But the camaraderie in the Teams was something I really liked. And that aspect of life in the Teams is something that's very hard to explain to someone who hasn't experienced it. It isn't just the danger, or the working close together. I've been a fireman and I've been a policeman since I left the Navy. And both of those jobs hold a certain amount of danger, and there is a feeling of brotherhood among the men who share that danger.

But as much as we got along together in those jobs, it never came close to what was felt every day in the Teams. For example, only in the Teams did you have the concept of a swim buddy. A swim buddy was the guy you were teamed up with for any kind of swim or dive in the water. They would usually try to pick two guys who were pretty close together in terms of skills, but that didn't always work out.

No matter what, you never left your swim buddy, you never parted. You just stuck with each other, and if he got in trouble, you were there to help him out, just as he was there to help you if the situation was reversed.

While in UDT 11 in 1967–68, I did my first deployment to Vietnam. I remember thinking it was god-awful hot there the moment the plane's doors were opened. Stories about what Vietnam was like had made the rounds of the Teams back in Coronado. So when we stepped off the plane, I was ready for someone to start shooting at us at any moment. It took a while before I finally learned to relax a bit and not expect a bullet to snap by at any moment.

Once we had arrived in Vietnam and got set up, we started conducting a lot of beach reconnaissance operations as part of our mission. At one point during the

The first parachute jumps of Jump School are memorable, even for recent graduates of BUD/S. One parachutist is landing just in front of another, blocking view of his body but not the round canopy of his parachute in this shot.

U.S. Navy

deployment, I was assigned to an ARG repair ship for a while. All that ship seemed to be doing was just going around in circles out in the ocean.

But I made it back to my Team soon enough, and we continued carrying out the UDT mission in Vietnam. The SEAL Teams had a lot more training in the land warfare aspect of combat and they really did the Navy's inland operations during the Vietnam War. The UDTs did more along our traditional operation of beach and river recons, measuring the water's depth and making note of any obstacles.

But what kind of operations you would conduct depended on just where your UDT platoon was assigned. There were a lot of river trips and demolition operations conducted. Not only water obstacles were blown out of the way, a lot of shore-based bunkers and hooches were dealt with by the UDT as well. We just didn't get into a lot of the patrolling and close-in combat type of operations is all. That we left up to the SEALs.

In 1969, I volunteered to go over to SEAL Team One and operate as a SEAL. After being assigned to a platoon, I went through tactical

SEALs listen intently during a pre-mission briefing.

U.S. Navy

training with my Team-mates and we deployed to Vietnam later in the year.

The SEALs went out in what were probably smaller groups than we had worked with in the UDTs. And the SEALs had a little more freedom in choosing the operations they would conduct than we did back in the UDT. It seemed to me that our lieutenant would go get an op and come back and give us a briefing on it. We would sit and hash out the details, each man giving his opinion or suggestions as his experience dictated. Then we usually just went out and did the op.

Hopefully, what we had decided to do worked out during the mission. If it didn't, we would try and determine just what had gone wrong. Then we could adjust our game plan to fit.

During my first combat operation, my spoken Vietnamese was very limited. I knew a few things, like bookoo (French beaucoup) meant "many." We were working with some South Vietnamese, trying to teach them a little unconventional warfare, and the language difference was a real problem for me.

I heard the South Vietnamese troops going "bookoo, bookoo," quite a bit while we were out in the middle of this defoliated area. Not knowing exactly what we were running into, I took cover behind this little stump when the patrol leader signaled. Or at least I tried to take cover. That stump was small and I stuck out from all sides of it.

There was just nothing there for me to hide behind really, and I was thinking, Oh, God, I'm going to get killed here. Just then, three guys came walking down the edge of a little canal near us. One of the guys was a North Vietnamese Regular by the look of his uniform. The other two were the classic, black-pajama Viet Cong.

Even though I had those three guys in my sights, I didn't shoot them. That was my first chance to really engage the enemy and I just didn't take it. Had somebody else opened fire, I would have joined right in. But I didn't think I could just open fire.

The three men just walked right by us and climbed into a sampan stuck onto the canal's bank just a short distance from us. As they paddled away, I was thinking they acted just like they owned the country. Reflecting back on it, I guess they did.

Some thought about taking another life kept me from opening fire on those three men. My mind had been occupied heavily for some time with the thoughts of killing my fellow man. But I'd have never let down my Teammates through inaction if things had come down to that.

There were a lot more chances for me to fire before that tour was over. The first time we got into a heavy firefight, the situation was much like you would expect it to be. The air was filled with the sounds of small-arms fire and the bullets were snapping by overhead. It was like hell, and that proved even more so when the SEAL next to me was shot.

I had a kind of a funny reaction to the situation. When the SEAL next to me was shot, he called over to me, saying, "I think I'm hit!"

All I said back was "What do you mean 'you think'? Keep shooting."

I just didn't want to talk to him at the time. The situation was pretty intense; there was a lot of fire going back and forth. The fight seemed to go on for quite a while. But it was actually probably over with in just a short time.

It was situations like this that kind of showed the difference between a veteran and a new guy. It depended on the circumstances, but a veteran had been there awhile and knew his training would carry him through. The new guys still had to learn that.

I did two tours in Vietnam, one with UDT 11 and one with SEAL Team One. I spent enough time over there to build up a different view of the enemy we were fighting: I kind of envied him. It was a strange thought and I never talked about it to anybody, but I always thought they had kind of a better war to fight. They could see who the enemy was, and where he was.

A lot of the time we were shooting at nothing solid—smoke from where someone had fired, or maybe a muzzle flash at night. They had ships to shoot at, the river craft, helicopters, and us. It just seemed like they had a better deal.

But one of the things we had really going for us was the quality and volume of support we could call on. The Brown Water Navy, the guys who ran the river patrol boats and other small craft, they were absolutely top-notch, fantastic. They probably had a job that I wouldn't ever have wanted to do. During my tours in-country, I had worked with the Marine Corps, Army, and different Navy units as well as with the South Vietnamese.

For myself, I felt so lucky, and so secure, knowing the guys I was with. Because of my Teammates and our support people, I knew that if something happened to me, I would be taken care of.

We had really great air support as well. The air unit that sticks out to in my mind is the Black Ponies and their OV-10 aircraft. When I left the service, one of my desires was to buy one of those OV-10 aircraft. It amazed me what they could do when they flew in support of us. It appeared as if the small twin-tailed craft could turn on a dime up in the sky. And the pilots who flew those craft were terrific.

When we called in the Black Ponies, they showed up fast and hung around a long time. All you had to do was tell them over the radio where you wanted them and they were right on target. They would lay down cover fire and just eliminate a target. They really impressed me.

Depending on what they carried under their wings, they could put out a blizzard of fire. They would cover an area and just suppress anything you were worried about. With a Black Pony covering you, you could make some distance if you had to and no one would show themselves to fire at you. If they did, the Black Ponies made them go away, permanently. While we were stationed down at SEAFLOAT, the Black Ponies were our primary air support. And we were very glad to have them.

The funny thing is, during the one operation we did in Vietnam that really stands out in my memory, we didn't fire a shot.

There was supposed to be a few VC or NVA at a little bend in a river. Our Team went on the other side of the river and set up an ambush position. Another regular military unit, it was either the

In Vung Tau, Vietnam, a Black Pony of Light Attack Squadron 4 takes off. Eight pods of rockets and guns are visible below the wings as the small craft lifts into the air.

U.S. Navy

Marines or the Army, was going to approach the suspected position of our targets.

With the regular troops coming in and raising a lot of noise moving through the area, they would flush out our targets and drive them across the river toward our ambush. When they came out of the water, we would dump them. It was a classic hammer-and-anvil ambush, with my SEAL unit acting the part of the anvil and the regular troops moving through the area as the hammer.

We were all set up, spaced out on the bank, and waiting for this handful of VC to enter our kill zone. Then we got our little surprise. Instead of a handful of VC, maybe just a couple of guys, it looked like a whole town was crossing the river right in front of us. There weren't just a few guys—it looked like a thousand people were starting to cross that river. I know that's an exaggeration, but there were a whole lot of them coming in on us.

That was one of the few times I thought I would eat it [be killed] on an operation. In my mind, I was listing how I could possibly slide into the water after we opened up and all of these VC started to return fire. If I could get into the water when all hell broke loose and we bugged out, then I had a chance of swimming away. But that never happened.

All of those enemy troops just landed on the shore and walked by, only ten or fifteen feet from us. None of us fired a shot; we just let them go by. They all went right over the bank and walked away, none of us making a noise all the while. Even the SEALs use their brains on occasion.

On thing about the men of the Teams, they almost always look to the water as the best avenue of escape. For myself, I always considered the water my best way out. I was always a pretty good swimmer, and working in the Teams always made you think about the water. Even when I was riding in a helicopter, I always wanted to sit by the door. As silly as it sounds, I figured if that bird was going down hard, I would jump out and take my chances in the water. In Vietnam, I had a chance of making it to a pond or canal, any body of water.

The water had always been where the Teams worked. Before the SEALs there were the UDTs and the Teams of World War II. Each unit worked in the water, and they were all stepping-stones to where the SEALs evolved to during the Vietnam war. I can remember one of the instructors telling me during training to just keep my mouth shut. That way no one would know how stupid we were and we could just live off the earlier guys' reputations.

That wasn't true, of course, but the men who had built the Teams before us had raised the bar pretty high. And we had to work hard to live up to that reputation, and maybe raise the bar a bit ourselves.

There's an expression in the Teams: "The only easy day was yesterday." I first heard that back when I was going through training. It means that yesterday is over with, so you don't have to worry about it and you don't know what's coming today, but it's probably going to be worse than yesterday. SEALs are a fatalistic bunch sometimes. And this particular expression seems to be true; at least it certainly was during training.

Things were always growing in the Teams. You were always trying

This class gift from Class 89 plainly states one of the most quoted expressions at BUD/S. And the only reason that yesterday was easy is that it has to be over to become yesterday.

Kevin Dockery

to improve yourself, help your Teammates, and make the Teams better. Sometimes, this meant we didn't play by the rules of the regular military so much. And that had its place, too.

Back when the SEALs were first being developed in the early 1960s, there wasn't any rule book to speak of. The Teams just kind of wrote it as they went along. You would try something to get a job done, and if your technique didn't work, you pulled the good points out and tried something new. When we did break the rules, it wasn't to just buck the system, it was to get a job done.

The SEALs of today are an evolved machine, having come from where my generation was back in the 1960s and the Frogmen before us, all the way back to World War II. From looking at these youngsters in training today, I can see that they're in a lot better shape than even we were. And they are certainly much better *equipped. The whole focus of training is different than it was when I went through. Today, training is geared to help get you though, without making the final product any lower in quality. In my day, training seemed to be directed toward getting you out, to get you to quit.*

But if you were to join the Teams back then or today, you would get some of the same things out of it as we did. A confidence will develop that's almost impossible to find anywhere else. And you will find yourself, you will know what you can do. Quitting will not be an option any longer. Anything you're going to face in life after having been in the Teams, you will know that you can conquer.

■ Chapter 8

LOSSES, THE COST OF WAR

In 1968, over sixty SEALs from both Teams were wounded, and fourteen lost their lives. Some platoons deployed to Vietnam and returned without a single man being injured by enemy action. But these platoons were the exception. Most deployed SEAL units suffered at least a few men injured during their actions against the enemy. Some returned from their deployments with almost every SEAL in the platoon having been wounded at least once.

Some SEALs were hit multiple times on different operations during a deployment. Often, a wounded SEAL left the hospital where he was recovering as soon as he could. And SEALs sometimes left before their doctors released them. These men simply wanted to continue operating with their Teammates back in their platoon.

But some injuries were simply too serious. Men from the Teams were paralyzed, lost limbs, eyes, or hearing. These men usually had to leave the Teams and the Navy. But this did not mean they weren't successful later in life. The lessons the SEALs learned about overcoming obstacles during their UDTR or BUD/S training helped them overcome any physical limitations they might have received.

A SEAL or UDT man could be stopped, but that usually meant he was dead. During their years of active combat in Vietnam, forty-nine men of Navy Special Warfare made the ultimate sacrifice. Thirty-nine men from SEAL Team One were killed during the course of the war. Nine were lost from SEAL Team Two, three from UDT 13, and one from UDT 12. An additional two men were lost, one while attached to SOG and another who had been assigned to Detachment Golf.

The cost of operating with the Teams could be high, but many were willing to pay it. Even the three Vietnam SEAL Medal of

Lieutenant (junior grade) Joseph Robert Kerrey, the first SEAL Medal of Honor recipient of the Vietnam War.

U.S. Navy

Honor holders had all been wounded, two while performing the actions that led to their receiving the Congressional Medal of Honor.

The first SEAL Medal of Honor recipient was Lieutenant (j.g.) Joseph R. "Bob" Kerrey of Delta Platoon, SEAL Team One. On 14 March 1969, while leading his squad against a Viet Cong meeting on an island in the bay of Nha Trang, Kerrey came under fire as he and his SEALs were detected by the Viet Cong. In the fierce firefight that followed, Kerrey was severely wounded when a VC grenade exploded at his feet. In spite of his wounds, he continued to direct his men, call in support, and secure an extraction site. Without further loss to his squad, Kerrey got his men out of the area, almost eliminating the enemy force in the process.

As a result of his injuries, Bob Kerrey was to lose his leg and left the Service, but his loss did little to slow him down. He became a successful businessman and then entered politics. Elected governor of Nebraska, Kerrey later moved even further up the political ladder, becoming the Democratic senator from his home state of Nebraska.

Lieutenant Tom R. Norris was not injured during his extraction of a downed U.S. pilot from well behind enemy lines. But during his sampan-mounted patrol behind enemy lines from 10 to 13 April 1972, he was in more than a little jeopardy on a constant basis. In spite of the difficulties of the operation, and the overwhelming enemy forces the men in his unit slipped through, Lieutenant Norris successfully recovered both downed pilots.

Even for a SEAL, this was a harrowing mission. With only a single Vietnamese LDNN to go with him, Norris paddled a sampan to recover the second of the two pilots. Slipping past North Vietnamese patrols so closely that they could hear them speaking, the SEAL and LDNN made it through with their passenger. Lieutenant Tom Norris was later awarded the second SEAL Medal of Honor for his actions. For his bravery and actions during that rescue, the LDNN with Norris, Nguyen van Kiet, became the only South Vietnamese LDNN to receive the U.S. Navy Cross.

The last SEAL Medal of Honor recipient was Petty Officer Michael E. Thornton of SEAL Team One. During the evening of 31 October 1972, Thornton was working with Tom Norris during an LDNN operation well behind enemy lines in the north part of South Vietnam. During their action, Tom Norris was horribly wounded when an AK-47 bullet struck him in the side of the head.

In spite of being told that his Teammate was dead, Mike Thornton did the only thing that seemed possible to him at the time: he went back through heavy enemy fire to recover his Teammate's body. No SEAL, living or dead, had ever been left behind. Everyone in the Teams always came home.

Finding the apparently lifeless body of his Teammate, Thornton lifted up Norris and ran back through enemy fire. In spite of being wounded across his back and legs by an enemy grenade, he ran with Norris as naval gunfire started landing behind them.

When he was blown off his legs by an exploding shell, Thornton was shocked to hear his dead Teammate speak to him. Norris was alive. Now there was no way that Thorton could leave him behind.

In spite of his own wounds, Thornton carried his Teammate to the sea and swam offshore. In addition to pushing Norris ahead of him, Thornton towed one of the badly injured LDNNs. Even for a SEAL, this was an incredible feat of endurance and strength. The Navy and the Congress of the United States agreed and a year later Michael Thornton became the last SEAL to receive the Medal of Honor during the Vietnam War. And standing next to him was his Teammate, Tom Norris. In its entire history, this was the only time the Medal of Honor was awarded to an individual for saving the life of another Medal of Honor recipient.

Norris recovered from his severe wounds, but he left the service because of them. He continued an above-average career by becoming an FBI Special Agent and setting a high standard even for that agency. Mike Thornton continued his Navy and SEAL Career, later becoming a BUD/S instructor. He was selected to be a plankowner of the very secret antiterrorist unit, SEAL Team Six, when it was commissioned in 1980.

SEALs can be injured, and they can be killed. But they never lose the love they hold for their Teammates and their Teams.

Curtis Williams, Quartermaster, Third Class

In Vietnam, I carried the radio and packed an M79 grenade launcher, which had absolutely nothing to do with my Navy rate of quartermaster. Instead of directing a boat, I was putting out high-explosive grenades and maintaining contact with our support over the radio. That aspect of Team life did cause trouble sometimes with promotions, because you just didn't work in your rate. But the job you did and the people you worked with easily made up for that.

I grew up in Chula Vista down in Southern California. Being relatively close to the Navy base in Coronado, I had a number of friends who were in the UDTs. This was in 1966 and most guys my age were getting drafted if they didn't have some kind of deferment. To pick where I wanted to go, I would have to enlist, and the Teams sounded like a great place to be. So to beat the draft, I enlisted in the Navy.

When I first got into the service, I had no idea that anything like the SEAL Teams even existed. They were only around five years old by then and were still listed as secret. What I did know about was the UDTs and that I wanted to be a Navy Frogman.

When I arrived in Coronado, I became part of Class 41, which started in March, close enough to be a winter class. One thing I hate is the cold, and training exposed me to a lot of it. Even after I

Each graduating BUD/S class for years has met the tradition of leaving a class gift. The gift from Class 63 shown here has been one of the more memorable ones.

Kevin Dockery

left the Navy and became a commercial diver, I still hated cold water. But it was just part of the job and you just tolerated it.

It was really willpower that pushed you through training. There was nothing I've ever experienced like the cold we were exposed to. But you just had to gut it out and keep going. It was probably that exposure to cold that made it possible for me to be a successful commercial diver. You didn't have to like it, but you had to keep going.

For myself, I don't think I ever had any real thoughts of quitting. On my first day of training, I looked around at the over 100 guys we had there at the beginning. And it was while I looked at them all that I made the personal commitment to myself that if only one guy was going to be standing at the end of our training, that guy would be me.

It wasn't that I could shrug off everything the instructors put us through and just keep going. There was a point during Hell Week, something like the third or fourth night, that really got to me.

Training and the pace of Hell Week had been rough and we were all pushing hard to keep going in spite of our exhaustion. And the instructors allowed us to put on dry greens, the fatigue uniforms we wore, and lie down a moment.

Lying in bed, I was just starting to get warm. We weren't falling asleep—it was much more like just passing out. It hadn't been more than fifteen minutes or so when the instructors blasted through the barracks, firing blanks and blowing on whistles. They were screaming at us to get up and get back out on the line. So we all had to get up and move out again.

The closeness and comfort of the dry clothes and warm rack made it hard. And our staggering level of exhaustion sure didn't help build any enthusiasm for getting up and moving again. But there was no way I wasn't going back out that door; it was the only way in to the Teams.

In spite of how I felt, I dragged myself out of my rack. Right next to my bunk was my friend's rack, and he wasn't getting up. He just wouldn't do it, no matter how hard I shook him and hollered at him. It seemed that there were fifteen or twenty guys who just wouldn't leave their bunks, to get up and keep going.

When I finally gave up trying to rouse my friend and left the barracks, it seemed like hardly anyone was left in the class. Class 41 had been a fairly big crowd before the instructors had given us that chance to clean up and get warm. But afterward, we were a lot smaller. From something over 100 guys on our first day of training, we ended with only about 25 guys still standing there on the last day.

And I was one of those twenty-five guys, and the feeling was pretty much indescribable. It was a high; I felt I had finally done it, accomplished my goal in the Navy. All I wanted was to be a Frogman, to put that UDT patch on my shoulder. It just felt so good to know that I had made it.

Then, on that same graduation day, I was called into the main office. "Williams get in here," sounded out, and I thought I was in real trouble.

What I found out was that I wasn't in trouble, far from it. Instead, a number of us were receiving a singular honor.

There was a big board in the office up where the instructors had listed everyone in the class and their standing at graduation. And next to my name was the number one. I had graduated at the top of my class.

All during my training, I figured I was just making it through. I had

---

done my best, but never thought that much of it. Everyone, all of my classmates, was doing the same thing. But that wasn't the only thing the instructors told me at graduation.

"By the way," one of them told me, "we want you to go straight to the SEAL Team."

It turned out that the top six graduates of my class were all being asked to go over to SEAL Team One after graduation rather than report to one of the UDTs.

For myself at the time, I was thinking that the UDTs deployed to the Philippines. Based near Olongapo, the Frogs would deploy over to Vietnam every once in a while. But the SEALs were doing some pretty heavy-duty stuff in Vietnam. And the instructors told me that was pretty much the situation.

So I said that I would prefer to go over to a UDT first.

"No, we want you to go to SEAL Team One now," I was told.

There wasn't a whole lot of point in arguing. So off to SEAL Team One I went. And, outside of those first moments of concern, I never regretted going. The caliber of guys I lived with and operated beside in the SEALs was the best. That time is something I wouldn't trade for anything.

But I was still a young man, and had a young man's thoughts and concerns. On my first deployment to Vietnam, I remember sitting on the plane and, frankly, being a little scared. I was really doing it; I was going to war.

The situation was more than a little scary, but it was also very exciting. Nothing I had experienced up to then had prepared me for the adrenaline rush that comes over you in combat. The level of anticipation that comes over you as you move into a combat situation is incredible. But the discipline that had been driven into us from that first day of training helped us get through all of the excitement and do our jobs.

The other part of training, the teamwork, that is the lifeblood of the Teams. And it was the guys I operated with, my Teammates, who made everything we did possible. These were characters that the most vivid imagination in the world would have a hard time inventing.

At that time I was the youngest guy in the SEAL Team. Going straight from high school to the Navy hadn't allowed me much time *for life experiences. But all of my Teammates around me made every day a major experience.*

These guys lived large, and did things that I hadn't really considered possible. Whether we were fighting the war or partying, everything was done at an all-out level. High speed and low drag.

It felt really good to have these men around me. Looking back on it, I wouldn't have wanted to fight in that war if I couldn't have the Teammates that I did. It was their professionalism, their skill, and their courage that helped bring out the best in me. And it was those same characteristics that helped bring a young kid back home.

Though I didn't have a "sea daddy"—an older, more experienced SEAL who shows you the ins and outs of being in the Teams—there are individuals who really stand out in my memory. One of these men is John Fietsch.

"Killer John" Fietsch was so cool under fire. Nothing seemed to faze him. The confidence and air he had about him just spread. And that really meant a lot to me. Just being with men like him made you know that you were going to come home.

Then there was tobacco-chewing Lewis. "Competent" and "warrior" just don't seem to be enough to describe him. He carried the M60 machine gun when most other SEALs wanted the much lighter, and less powerful, Stoner. He was unbelievable, both in combat and off duty. When it came to party time, Lewis made the top of the list. When he blew off steam, everyone around knew it.

Those two men stand out in my memories, but there were a lot of things that happened in Vietnam that I'll remember for the rest of my days. My first combat operation is one of them.

The people who were taking us out on the operation were making sure it was an easy one. They were from the platoon we were relieving and knew the area very well. So they were taking us out on a relatively simple op to kind of "break us in" to the area. The only thing was, when it's your first time in combat, nothing is easy or simple.

All we did was patrol in, set up an ambush at a likely crossing spot, and then patrol out or extract if the ambush went down. We didn't make contact, there were no shots fired, supposedly an easy day.

But it wasn't easy for me. I was scared shitless through the whole thing. There were people in that jungle who would have liked nothing better than to kill me, and I just knew they could see or hear me.

It was during the first op that I was introduced to another new thing, using drugs to help you stay awake and alert during a long night ambush. For myself, I had no idea what any kind of drugs really were. But the corpsman came around and asked me if I wanted something to help me keep awake.

It was going to be a long night, and everyone else seemed to be accepting what the corpsman was offering. So I took what turned out to be Dexamil, and the next thing I knew, I was wired.

Here I was sitting on my first ambush with my adrenaline already racing along, and I take an amphetamine on top of it. I was positively electric—"alert" just isn't a strong enough word for it. I could hear everything—the lapping of the water, the soft sounds of the swamp—and smell the mud and the water—clearly. The drugs and the situation made for a long, tense operation.

But we didn't make any contact. The ambush was broken down on schedule and we patrolled back out to our extraction point. All of my other operations kind of blend into a blur over the years since then. But that very first one will always stand out sharply in my mind. And I don't think I ever took that Dexamil again.

Though I can't remember the specific operation where we first made contact with the enemy, I'm sure it was an ambush. Almost all of our ambushes were river ambushes, though sometimes we would set up along a trail in the jungle. And we followed the same general procedures for each one.

The patrol would insert along the riverbank a distance away from the planned ambush site. Then we would patrol in and set up along the river or trail. With our weapons facing out into the kill zone, we would then wait for the target to come along. On a river, it would be a sampan that eventually came down and entered the ambush.

The sampan would have two or three guys in it. Even though we operated almost entirely at night, we could still see well enough to make out the weapons in the sampan that identified the men as VC.

In 1968, this SEAL waits cautiously along a stream in Vietnam. He is armed with a Stoner 63A light machine gun fitted with a 150-round ammunition drum. Across his chest are additional belts of 5.56mm ammunition for his Stoner. Slung from his shoulder, across his back, is a 66mm M72 LAW antitank rocket. Lastly, clipped to his belt is an M26A1 fragmentation grenade. His hair is held in place by a 40-inch olive drab triangular bandage which cannot easily slip down across his eyes. The bandage also prevents sweat from running down into the SEAL's eyes.

U.S. Navy

And when the target was centered in the kill zone, the ambush would be triggered.

When we all opened fire at once, it looked like the whole world had turned to flame. It wasn't until we did that first active ambush that I really saw just how much firepower we had. When the muzzle flashes died away, our night vision would be pretty much gone along with them. But there really wouldn't be much to see anymore. The high-velocity slugs from our machine guns and rifles tore that sampan apart—there just wasn't anything left.

I think we had three Stoners, an M60, and a bunch of M16s all open fire at once. They all just blew that wooden boat apart—I had no idea up until then just how powerful all of our weapons together really were. It was pretty amazing.

When we went through all of our training, preparing for that first moment of combat, there was a certain amount of anticipation that built up. Then the sitting on the ambush site just built up the tension even more. The waiting and waiting would just go on, and then, when the action finally happened, the tension release felt like some kind of high.

That was the reward that came from all of our training. We were able to leave as victors, could feel the victory. That was what I had trained for, why we all sat for hours on end waiting for our target to come along; the sudden burst of action was like finally getting the cookie from inside the jar. You had heard about it for weeks and months, and now it had finally happened.

It was just an unbelievable feeling, and there wasn't any thought given to the fact that someone else was dying. Besides that, they had been the enemy and would have just as easily shot and killed all of us.

The VC did manage to get a piece of me toward the end of the first tour in Vietnam. I was blown up and wounded pretty well during an operation. But I lived and recovered from my injuries. Not all of my Teammates were as lucky.

We had patrolled in on one operation and set up an ambush overlooking an empty riverbed. When the tide was up, I'm sure that riverbed was filled with water. But when we were setting up, there wasn't much more between its banks than mud. There wasn't much question that we were well into the VCs' backyard. Where we set up, there were about four or five hooches in back of us, each complete with a VC flag. If the locals were bold enough to put up a VC flag, you knew you weren't in friendly territory.

That situation alone made for an eerie feeling. But we had moved in very quietly under the cover of darkness and set up our ambush. There was no sign at all that we had been detected. But in spite of that, we left nothing to chance. According to our standard operating procedures, one of the members of our patrol set up as rear security. This man, Saunders, was facing the other way, away from our ambush site, just in case someone tried to sneak up on us while we were waiting.

During the middle of the night, we almost nailed a target with our ambush, and it would have been the wrong one, though it might have tasted good.

While we were all sitting there, primed and ready to fire, a pig came rooting along in the kill zone. It was a near thing, for the pig. We almost opened fire, and if we had, that pig would have been shredded pork. But our fire discipline held and we continued waiting for a real target.

The night passed and dawn was coming up as we all held our positions. The plan was that by dawn, if we hadn't made any contact with the enemy, the Seawolf helicopter gunship support we had for the mission would come into the target area. The Seawolves would put out rockets, into the jungle, about fifty yards upriver away from us. That fire should flush any VC returning to their hooches directly our way.

Whether we were in the wrong place or the Seawolves put out their fire on the wrong target, I never did find out. But the helicopters dumped their rockets right into the hooches behind us.

The explosions from the high-explosive warheads on the rockets blew Saunders in between me and the SEAL setup next to me. Now there were people running out of the hooches toward us. It seemed we couldn't get our weapons off safety fast enough to take on all of the targets. The situation was a turkey shoot as all of these VC ran around in confusion.

Those VC must have thought we really had our stuff together to be able to blow up their hooches from the air and nail them when they came running out of the door. They never noticed that we had been facing the wrong way to start with.

We had our own wounded, but nothing on the level of what the VC had. Saunders had been hurt in the face, but it wasn't too bad and he was being bandaged up by his Teammates. I had the radio with me and quickly remade contact with the Seawolves.

Those helicopters were turning around and preparing for another pass. "How'd we do?" the pilots asked. "We're coming around for another run."

"No, you're not," I called back. "Do not fire another thing."

When we walked out of there, you could hear the sounds of

Frozen in flight by the camera, a Seawolf launches a high explosive 2.75-inch rocket. The symbol of the Seawolves can be seen painted on the nose of this helicopter.

U.S. Navy

wounded VC throughout the area. The groans and moaning of the wounded blended in with the almost supernatural appearance of the landscape. The exploding rockets had put kind of a fog all around the area, just a white mist about two feet thick over the ground. The sun was breaking over the horizon and the pink light of dawn gleamed across the fog. The whole effect looked like something from The Twilight Zone.

We walked through the fog, stirring it up with our legs as we stepped over bodies. The sounds of the wounded carried over everything as I led Saunders out. He couldn't see what was all around us, only hear it and be concerned about his own situation. But I could see everything, and it left a picture that won't soon leave my mind.

On that op, Saunders was hurt. But for the most part, we got away pretty clean. On a later op, I was blown up myself, and one of our officers was killed.

We had prepared for that operation carefully. During the day, we had done a helo recon, where we checked out the area in daylight and made certain where everything was. What we saw told us that we were going to have to go in with a larger force than we usually did.

On a normal mission, we operated in units of five or six guys. For that last op, we were going to take ten SEALs in. The target was a sleeping area that the VC would use to lay up. There was a pagoda, a small Buddhist temple, and a hooch at the target. We were going to go in and ambush both targets at the same time. One group of four of us was going to set up around the hooch. The larger, six-man group, which I was a part of, would set up our ambush around the pagoda.

Gene Tinnin was the officer I was with on the op. Since I carried the radio, I moved along right behind him in the patrol. As we moved in, we came up to a small building just visible in the dark. Tinnin turned to me and whispered, "I think that's probably the hooch; I think it's too small to be the pagoda. The point man and I are going to go out and look for it [the pagoda]."

So I gave the signal for everyone to set down on alert, just in case we were sitting around the wrong thing. We hadn't separated into our two ambush teams yet. But after about twenty minutes had gone by without any sight of Tinnin, the other officer with us decided to move out with the smaller element. They went ahead and set up their ambush around the structure right in front of us. There wasn't anything I could do and just watched them leave.

About another twenty minutes went by when I received a call over the radio. The other element had set up around the hooch and was waiting for us to initiate the ambush. According to the plan, the pagoda element would initiate the ambush and the hooch element would open fire on our signal. The only trouble was that we still hadn't found the pagoda.

"Hey, look," I said into the radio, "the patrol leader is still out looking for the objective. You guys aren't even supposed to be set up yet. You may be sitting around the pagoda."

And I left the conversation at that since I didn't want to be talking long. The other patrol wasn't supposed to have moved out yet, but what happened next I'm only guessing at.

What I think happened is that the other radioman didn't relay my message to the other patrol leader. But that was only the second mess-up. The first mistake was that they shouldn't have gone over and set up an ambush in the first place.

But the time went on and the mission continued. After another twenty minutes or so had gone by, Tinnin finally came back. But he was moving in from the opposite direction from where he had left. He had left, moving off to my right. But because there was a tree line just behind us, it was much easier for him to move around the long way and he ended up coming in from my left.

As Tinnin walked up, he whispered to me, "There's nothing over there. That has to be the pagoda," and he pointed out in the direction of the hooch. "The hooch must be somewhere over there." He pointed off in another direction.

Now our point man, Nap, was a big guy, even for a SEAL. He was something like six feet four inches tall. But that night there was no moon, no anything, just darkness. Our conversation was taking place in whispers, the talker putting his lips right up to the other's ear and keeping his voice as soft as possible. As he walked up, Tinnin had noticed that the other guys were missing, "Where's the other guys?" he whispered to me.

I was just getting ready to tell him that they had already set up when we heard the thud of an object hitting the ground near us. Whatever had hit, it seemed to me to be some five or six feet away. Tinnin and I just looked at each other as if to say, "What was that?" We had no idea that it was a hand grenade.

The other four guys had just seen two figures come up from the darkness. And it was too dark for them to make out that our big point man was one of them. So they had thrown a grenade at what they thought to be two VC coming up on them.

Then the grenade exploded.

The blast threw me backward, and as the explosion echoed around, the other guys opened up with their weapons.

Stunned by the blast, I started pulling at the grass, trying to get away. Then a round hit me in the chest and I immediately began gushing blood from out of my mouth.

The other guys must have heard our screams because they stopped firing and came over to help us. In spite of our support, it took maybe an hour to get us all out of there.

A Mark II PBR speeding along during tests. Only the twin .50-caliber machine guns in the bow gun tub and single .50 at the stern are mounted on this PBR. Only half of the keel of the boat is in the water as this small craft planes across the surface.

U.S. Navy

At one point I heard one of the guys say that there was no use in working on Tinnin, that he was dead. So that was when I knew he was gone. But I didn't know how many of my group had been injured. One of my fears was that the VC had come in and everyone had been hurt. But that didn't turn out to be the case.

Our patrol had inserted from PBRs, and the guys in the boat were lying up in the water not too far away. The PBR sailors could hear our conversations over the radio. And when they learned that a bunch of us had been hurt, they came in at a dead run to pick us up and get us out.

At one point the guy on the other radio was talking to a helo when I came around enough to make out what he was saying. And what he was saying was "If you don't bring that helo in here, I'm going to shoot you down."

So apparently, the extraction birds couldn't find a place to set down close enough to pick up the wounded and get us out. Finally, they did find a place and our Teammates got us out. What I remember is two guys each holding me under one arm and just dragging me along with my feet trailing behind.

When I was hit, I thought it had been a concussion grenade going off. The blast had made it feel like every bone in my body had been broken. Immediately following the blast, I tried to drag myself out of the fire zone. But soon after that, every time I tried to move, everything just felt like limp noodles.

Then we reached the helicopter and my Teammates threw me on board first. Tinnin was put in next, his body, or what was left of it, landing on top of me. Then our big point man, Nap, was tossed in on top of Tinnin.

Among the wounded in the bird then, I was the only one still conscious. So I grabbed up Nap's hand and kept talking to him, telling him that it would be all right. Of course I already knew that Tinnin was dead.

Later the corpsmen told me that if I had passed out instead of trying to reassure Nap, I might have died myself. Apparently, I had lost so much blood that it was a wonder that I made it back at all.

Afterward, the incident was investigated and the blame for the accident was placed on Eugene Tinnin. For myself, I think that was just the easy way out and it certainly wasn't Tinnin's fault. As far as I am concerned, the patrol should never have split up without the senior patrol leader, Tinnin, telling them to.

And I had told the other radioman that we were still right where we had been when they moved out. But the message may never have been passed out among the other patrol. I am certain that otherwise they would never have opened up on us.

So two major mistakes caused a SEAL warrant officer to lose his life and the rest of our element to be wounded. And Tinnin had been a real good guy. The three of us—Tinnin, Nap, and myself—were wounded the worst because we had been the only guys standing up when the grenade went off. But all the other guys, even though they had been lying prone in the grass, were still hit, mostly in the upper body and head.

For myself, I had been hit in sixteen different places. All in all, I was very messed up. My right kneecap was blown pretty much *off, and the doctors told me that I'd probably never walk right again.*

My injuries were so severe, they kept me in-country for more than a month just trying to stabilize me for transport. Things were pretty bad; the heaviest dose of Demerol they could give me only cut the pain for about two hours. But they could only give that to me every four hours. So for two hours out of four, I was in immense pain.

Time blurred a bit, and I couldn't tell how long I was on that two-hours-of-relief-and-two-hours-of-pain cycle. But it seemed to be almost the entire time I was in-country. Finally, they shipped me out to a hospital in Japan, and finally back to the States.

For the next four months I was in the hospital trying to heal. And the Navy wanted to give me a medical discharge. I was considered so bad off that they had the papers ready to give me a medical discharge with a 50 percent disability.

But I was getting real tired of being in the hospital, and I was missing being with my Teammates back at my SEAL Team. So I finally walked into the office and told them that nothing hurt anymore and I wanted to go back to the SEAL Team.

Then they told me that they weren't certain that they could do that.

"Well," I said. "That's where I'm reporting for work tomorrow, okay?"

So they canceled the paperwork for my medical discharge and I went back to SEAL Team One. But I didn't have a whole lot of time left in my enlistment. The Team didn't want to send me back out with a deploying platoon, and they had another assignment I could do.

Across the street, on the amphibious base proper, there was kind of a research and development platoon working with the four-man swimmer delivery vehicles (SDVs). The guys that they sent over to the R&D platoon had mostly come back from a real hard tour in Vietnam. Gary Gallagher, a SEAL who later received the Navy Cross, was one of the guys in the platoon along with me. Most of us had been hurt and were out of the hospital at one stage of recovery or another.

And I stayed with the R&D platoon until my enlistment was up and I left the Navy and the active SEAL Team. But in spite of the injuries I received during my one combat tour in Vietnam, I never regretted my time in the Teams.

Of course there had been times—sitting in the mud next to some slow flow of brown water in Vietnam, waiting on an ambush and being eaten alive by mosquitoes, or having fire ants crawling up my pants—when other thoughts would cross my mind. Usually, they were along the lines of what my old friends back home might be doing.

My old civilian friends would have been in college, dating the girls and having fun. Then the question of just how I had gotten where I was would cross my thoughts. But that never lasted long. Being with my Teammates meant a great deal. It was the sort of experience you can't buy for any amount of money. And I have no regrets at all that I did it.

In spite of my being badly hurt, nothing would have been worth my not being with my Teammates. The experience was unbelievable. Even if I had to be wounded all over again, I would not avoid going. All of that was part of what we did, who we were.

Now, if I could go through my experiences with the SEALs, do it all again, and not be wounded, well, that would be nice. But that's not how it is. In fact, I feel pretty lucky about just being here. It was Teammates like Tinnin, and the other losses in the Teams, men who were killed, who I do hold regrets for. I hated to see anyone get killed over there, but there's a special pain in the loss of a Teammate.

In spite of it all, I came back alive. I might have been blown up, but I later worked through my injuries and recovered. A lot of things still hurt, but I'm walking and not in a wheelchair. And my mind still works, in spite of what my Teammates might say.

What each man carried for an operation, in terms of weapons and ammunition, varied a bit from squad to squad. In our squad, our point man carried a CAR-15, a shortened M16 only about thirty inches long. The point man led the squad through the bush, watching for boobytraps and any enemy forces. He was usually the first person to come into contact with an enemy while we were patrolling. The short, handy length of the CAR allowed him to swing that weapon into action even faster than he could a rifle.

The patrol leader usually came next in the order of march. Gene Tinnin, my patrol leader, usually carried a regular M16 rifle. Then I

Wearing a set of mottled camouflage, this SEAL is directing his 40mm M79 grenade launcher toward something that has caught his attention off in the brush.

U.S. Navy

walked behind him. The radioman always tries to stay close to the patrol leader. For a weapon, I carried the M79 40mm grenade launcher along with all different types of rounds.

For my M79, I carried a number of high-explosive, fragmentation grenades, buckshot rounds that turned it into a close-range shotgun, fléchette rounds, which were the same as the buckshot rounds but launched a swarm of finned, steel darts rather than shot. And different-colored flare rounds.

We all carried pistols as well as our primary weapons. Most of us carried a Smith & Wesson 9mm Model 39. In case your main weapon jammed or whatever, it was nice to be able to grab up a handgun and keep fighting. This was particularly true in my case, as the M79 is a single-shot weapon. If something happened and I missed a close-in shot, I didn't have time to put another round in my grenade launcher. I just grabbed up my 9mm.

Sometimes, Tinnin carried a Stoner instead of an M16. A Stoner is a belt-fed light machine gun that fires the same round as the M16 and is much lighter than an M60. It puts out an amazing number of rounds in a minute, or even a second, and you can carry large amounts of ammunition for it.

Behind me usually was Lewis, and he carried an M60 machine gun. The M60 was a very heavy weapon that most guys didn't want to drag around. But Lewis was an animal who could just keep going. He carried not only the M60, but all his own ammunition, hundreds of pretty big rounds. That was a lot of weight for one man, but he liked the M60. In the Army, an M60 gunner would have other guys carrying rounds as well, but Lewis packed all his own.

To augment the firepower of Lewis's M60, the next man behind him in the patrol usually had a Stoner. Rear security, the last man in line, kept a close watch behind us, making sure no one crept up along our trail and surprised us. He carried either another Stoner or an M16.

Our ammunition loads were heavy. I carried rounds strapped all over me, across my front and on my back. A man armed with an M16 had at least seven or eight magazines minimum, each one holding twenty or thirty rounds depending on their size. For the M60, Lewis had crossed bandoliers as well as big pouches on his belt, same thing for the Stoners. We were all pretty well loaded for bear. Any spare place a man had to strap on some ammunition, he usually had it.

If we went in a straight firefight, we had about fifteen or twenty minutes' worth of ammunition. But that would be fired under discipline. Weapons were used in short, aimed bursts rather than just spraying an area with unaimed fire. That fire discipline made our ammunition last longer.

The men I was with in the Team were some of the most unbelievable people I have ever met in my life. And it started with the men who put me through training. Barry Enoch, a SEAL who later won the Navy Cross for his actions in Vietnam, was one of my instructors. Another was Olivera, a big, hook-nosed American Indian.

During our runs, Olivera would pick out a trainee as his target in the group. Then he would run alongside that trainee, sometimes even running backward, while smoking a big cigar. And all along

On line along the shore, these SEALs test-fire their weapons. The SEAL in the center is armed with a Stoner 63A light machine gun, the rectangular pouches on his back holding extra ammunition belt boxes. The SEAL just half visible on the right is armed with an AK-47.

U.S. Navy

that run he would blow cigar smoke in that trainee's face. All you could do was hope it wasn't you he picked that day.

It may have been Olivera who held a record at that time for running the longest time without stopping. But he was just one of my instructors, all of them an amazing bunch. Another instructor was Chief Allen, a five-time heavyweight boxing champion.

And when I passed training and got to the Teams, the guys there were no less impressive. They all worked hard, and they played harder than anybody else I have ever run into in my life. Plus, the loyalty was intense; we would all have given our lives for one another.

When I went to Vietnam, I knew I was going with some very high-caliber guys. These were men I trusted a lot, had confidence in. And that really helped me a lot as a first-timer.

If there was one word for my time in the Teams, it would probably be "unbelievable."

Chapter 9

TET 1968

As early as July 1967, the Communist leadership and military strategists in North Vietnam were preparing their biggest blow against the forces in the south. Ho Chi Minh and General Vo Nguyen Giap had decided to stage a series of attacks all across South Vietnam. Their intention was to overwhelm the South Vietnamese military and their U.S. allies, hopefully causing the collapse of the South Vietnamese government of President Nguyen Van Thieu.

The enemy used a number of feints and deceptions to decoy the U.S. forces as well as the U.S. government. With offers to go to the peace table diverting the attention of President Johnson, attacks such as the siege of Khe Sanh forced the military to concentrate their forces in the countryside and away from the cities. At the same time NVA forces and supplies were moved down the logistics track known as the Ho Chi Minh Trail.

Stockpiles were built up in the safe areas of Laos and Cambodia. Caches in South Vietnam were filled and more were established. As many as 84,000 Viet Cong and NVA troops were in position to conduct the campaign, scheduled to coincide with the lunar new year in 1968.

The Communist Tet offensive was masterfully planned and executed with the primitive communications and supply means available to the VC forces. The NVA and Viet Cong forces' various feints and deceptions caused the American military command to concentrate their forces along the borders of South Vietnam. The staged NVA border battles at Song Be, Loc Ninh, and Dac To worked. However, intelligence reports and suspicions led U.S. commander General William Westmoreland to investigate the buildup of Viet Cong forces that had been noted for over six months.

A Mark II PBR slowly cruising along a waterway in South Vietnam. The firepower of the 31-foot boat is visible in the three .50-caliber machine guns and single 7.62 mm M60 machine gun that can be seen mounted on the boat. Additional small arms would also be on board for the use of the boat's crew.

U.S. Navy

A number of Game Warden assets, including PBRs, Seawolves, and SEALs, were dispatched to the Cambodian border in Chau Doc province as part of Operation BOLD DRAGON I. The mission of these units was to locate and interdict men and supplies that were suspected to be crossing into Vietnam from Cambodia. These Game Warden forces located a great deal more than they expected.

The Tet lunar new year is a very significant holiday to the Vietnamese. It is a period of revelry, fireworks, and time spent with family. It is also a time of reverence for the ancestors of a family. The Viet Cong and the North Vietnamese decreed a truce to cover the period of Tet, 27 January to 3 February, 1968. The actual beginning of the Tet holiday was before daylight on 31 January. North Vietnam decreed that their people would begin their celebration on 28 January and hold their normal three-day celebration before the south held theirs.

In 1789, the Tay Son Montagnards had attacked Chinese troops who were securing Hanoi. Their attack worked only because it was such a surprise to the enemy, coming as it did at the beginning of the sacred Tet holiday. The leadership of the north knew their history, and planned to have it repeat itself.

On 31 January, prior to sunrise, North Vietnamese Army units and the majority of all available Viet Cong units launched attacks throughout South Vietnam. Out of the forty-four provincial capitals of South Vietnam, thirty-six were attacked. Of the six major cities in the country, five became targets that first day. Military airfields and bases also came under fire, with twenty-three of them trying to hold off heavy enemy attacks. Even Saigon, the capital city of South Vietnam, was attacked by eight battalions of Viet Cong.

The attack was sudden and fierce. South Vietnamese forces, many of whom had been recalled from their holiday, wavered and lost ground. U.S. forces were under heavy fire throughout the country. And smaller units in the field who had not been in constant contact with higher command quickly found themselves facing huge numbers of the enemy.

Excerpt from SEAL Team Two, Command and Control History 1968 Page 2. [DECLASSIFIED from CONFIDENTIAL]
During the entire TET offensive, the three SEAL [Team Two] Platoons handled themselves capably and professionally. Much of the fighting consisted of heavy street fighting. The SEAL Platoons in Vinh Long [6th Plt.] and My Tho [7th Plt.], which were almost completely destroyed, were instrumental in thwarting the Viet Cong attempts to overtake the cities. The Eight Platoon, in Chau Doc at the time, together with a small PRU force, succeeded in liberating that capital of that province. A commendation to the Eighth said in part, "The SEALs in vicious house-to-house fighting succeeded in breaking the hold that the Viet Cong had established on the city . . . The members of the CORDS staff in Chau Doc have the deepest admiration for and extend profound gratitude to each member of this platoon of Navy SEALs."

Harry Humphries, Draftsman, First Class

It was in the early 1960s, when I was a sailor in the fleet serving on board a destroyer that I first learned about the Navy's Underwater Demolition Teams. I was doing experimental underwater work with an underwater sound lab out of New London, Connecticut. There was a group of scientists on board our ship who kept talking about these great guys they worked with in their experiments with underwater equipment. The guys they were talking about were the operators from the UDTs.

This was something that I personally found very exciting. I had been a civilian diver before coming into the Navy, possibly the first one in my town. The thought that I could do the same kind of underwater swimming in the Navy that I had done in the civilian world had a lot of appeal to me.

As a result of my desperate desire to get off of that destroyer, I volunteered for the BUPERS (Bureau of Personnel) request for UDT candidates. Nine chits later, I got off the vessel and was sent to Little Creek, Virginia. There, I became a trainee with Class 29, East Coast, a winter UDTR class.

Looking back on things now, I can see that when both the East and West Coast Teams were running their own replacement training, each was a very difficult program. Each coast had its own disadvantages for the trainee, and neither made things easy for the prospective Frogman.

Training was without question the most difficult mental and physical thing I've gone through in my entire life. There is just a black period in my memory, where every moment was a year and every second a week. But at the end of every day, when we did finally roll into our racks, the thought was there that another one was down. And the next day was another down, and another. And we finally all became Frogs.

Hell Week is one of those things that I just don't remember a lot about. Maybe I have a mental block about remembering something that's tremendously horrible. And Hell Week was all of that. It was really demanding, and probably the closest I came to quitting anything in my life.

But maybe it was the pigheadedness and tenacity in my genealogy that wouldn't let me quit. So I stuck it out and graduated with my class.

I don't think that I have ever experienced a greater thrill in my life than I did when Class 29 graduated. It was, first of all, a tremendous monkey off your back—you're there, you'd finally made it.

Looking around, you could see that compared to your first views of the surrounding class, there weren't many folks left.

Without question, to be with those people, and to have suffered what you suffered with them, bound everyone together. Even today, we are all the closet of friends. One of my classmates, John Roat, has written a book called Class 29. And he tried hard to portray the humor, personalities, the difficulty, and all of the things that go along with the UDTR or BUD/S training experience. Everyone in the Teams can relate to the descriptions in that book.

Parts of training still stand out. Cast and recovery, the rolling off a rubber boat on the side of a speeding craft, and later being snatched up with a rubber snare, I think was probably the most dynamic thing that I did during the water phase of UDTR training. By the time we did cast and recovery, and the more technical underwater work, we had moved from Little Creek to Roosevelt Roads, Puerto Rico.

That training was when you really started to feel that you were getting into the advanced stuff. That was real Frogman stuff. But the bottom line was that cast and recovery was really used operationally only during the Second World War, and maybe a little bit during Korea. But you just can't make the boats go quickly enough during high speed combat.

The SEAL Teams were something I really heard about for the first time when I reported aboard UDT 22. During training, there had been rumors about this new Team that had being formed up, but no one really knew what it was. Class 29, which had started up in January 1963, was just getting under way when the SEALs turned one year old.

The scuttlebutt was that it was some top-secret operation and that these guys were doing something very special. No one knew what it was really about, so rumors flew. We had just finished going through the Cuban Missile Crisis less than a year before, just a few months before Class 29 had started training. So there was still fallout from that situation. All sorts of potential warlike clouds were floating around. And we looked at the whole thing as being pretty exciting stuff. The limited rumors about the SEALs just blended in with everything else.

During a swimmer recovery, a combat swimmer has just had the rubber snare slipped over his arm by the snare man as the pickup boat moves along. In this particular system, the snare will pull the swimmer around to the back of the rubber boat where he will clamber aboard, like his swim buddy is just beginning to do at the lower left of the picture.

Once I got aboard UDT 22, I did a couple of platoon deployments. The future CO of SEAL Team Two, Tom Tarbox, had become a friend of mine. He and I had both played football on the amphibious fleet championship team. We kind of hit it off and I asked him about coming over to SEAL Team Two if a billet became available.

My CO at the time was Dave Schaible, who was also my sea daddy and showed me what it was to operate in the Teams. Dave was probably also the sea daddy of 10,000 other SEALs during his career. But in a quiet meeting, I told the skipper that I really would like to go over to this new command. And Dave looked at me in that closed session and said, "I don't blame you, Harry. I'd like to go myself."

Eventually, Dave Schaible did go over to the SEAL Teams, as the skipper of SEAL Team One. But for me, he sent me over to SEAL Team Two when a billet opened. And I became a SEAL.

My arrival at the SEAL Team was the climax of my career in the Navy. When I was at UDT 22, my platoon officer had been a super leader, Irve C. "Chuck" LeMoyne. He was a lieutenant j.g. at that time, and later rose in rank to become one of the first SEAL admirals to serve in the special warfare community. God rest his soul, he passed on a few years back and left a legacy in the Teams that will be a hard one to follow.

Chuck's platoon chief was a man by the name of Dave Casey. The combination of Dave Casey and Chuck LeMoyne made my tour as a new platoon member one of the finest experiences that I can imagine. They were both excellent leaders and true Navy Frogmen. You would die for both of these men, and I was hardly the only one to hold that opinion. They made my break-in period as a new Frog one of the better things that ever happened to me.

After I was broken in to the UDT platoon, I was looking for more. I wanted to advance in my career. And I also wanted to get inland more, because I really did like the inland stuff. The new SEALs were all about inland operations, working from the water and going up on land to conduct operations.

When I came aboard SEAL Team Two, I thought that this was it for me. These men did everything that I ever wanted to do in my military career. Now that I was there, I was going to die at this command. This is where the action was going to happen, and I wasn't going to go anywhere else.

When I first arrived at SEAL Team Two in 1964, I was greeted by the master-at-arms, Chief Rudy Boesch. Rudy was a well-known, top-gun senior NCO in the community. He was probably the most respected bullfrog, and he still is, taking many a new SEAL under his care and making sure they start out right.

As I was one of these very new SEALs, Rudy read the rules to me very clearly and concisely and in a manner that let me know that I was a grown-up now and that I wasn't expected to do anything other than be a grown-up. I would be expected to stand watch every thirty-five days, whether I wanted to or not. Here I was, a guy who had been in the fleet not a long time earlier, and just doing three-section liberty was a lot of fun for me.

But this was when I realized that these men were true professionals. The men were treated as equal to the officers. There really was no difference between commissioned and noncommissioned ranks. The mutual respect between the enlisted and the officers was such that there needed to be no difference. The leader was clearly known, and things moved along from there quite efficiently.

Working in SEAL Team Two the years before Vietnam was extremely different than it was during and after Vietnam. Those years, from 1962 to 1967, were quite a unique period, the formative years of the SEALs. As an E-5 twenty-three-to-twenty-six-year-old in the Team, you were a young kid. Most of the other guys were in their thirties and forties. They had all been career UDT operators, selected as long-term career types because of the intensive training they were going to get. Training was going to be of long duration and cost lots of bucks. And the command wasn't about to waste money on this kind of training on a man who was only going to be in for five or six years.

So the Navy needed to have a career-designated individual, and preferably one with a good deal of prior experience. The Team was still starting up when I arrived, and it needed the collective experience of a lot of veteran individuals to get off and running.

In those days, we were organized into the "assault group" system. Assault groups were similar to platoons. My first assignment was to Assault Group 2. Again, I was extremely fortunate in working under two of the finest leaders that I can think of, though in a different way than back in UDT. These men were a more hardened, combat type. Lieutenant Henry J. "Jake" Rhinebolt was my assault group leader. Jake, who is a dear friend even today, is without question a fine man and great leader.

The guy who I respect and love still today, and would follow to the death, was the assault group chief. That was Bob Gallagher. Without question, Bob Gallagher was the warrior of the SEAL Teams on the East Coast. All of us did our share during an operation, but Bob did his, yours, and everyone else's share of the work on an op. And I am sure that many, many people will remember some of their experiences under Bob's leadership in combat.

Bob set the trail clearly for me as to how a SEAL should operate, and how he should conduct himself, especially in a combat environment. I was fortunate to have that kind of leadership and instruction. It probably helped get me home alive from Vietnam.

Bob Gallagher was called the Eagle by just about everyone in the Team. Maybe because he was just about as tenacious and nasty as an eagle. But he was also a bald-headed son of a gun. In recent years when I've seen him, he's just getting balder. Sorry about that, Bob.

The assault group was organized pretty much like a platoon is today. We thought in terms of boat crews, so that there's at least a coxswain and four or five strokers or paddlers in a rubber boat. So we were organized into twelve-man units in those days. Definitely, there would be one officer in a group, not always two. We often deployed with one officer and one chief, or one officer and one first class petty officer, in a group. That was due in part to the very small number of men in the SEAL Team at that time. There were only around fifty enlisted men in all of SEAL Team Two then. So a lot of assault groups just weren't fully staffed.

As an assault group, you were split up into two IBS crews, manning two IBSs on an insertion. Each boat crew was capable of operating as a fully independent unit. It was as part of an assault group that I went on a mission to France, where we crossed-trained with the French combat swimmers and were tested on our intelligence-gathering capabilities.

After we returned from that mission, I had an opportunity on the outside, out of the Navy, that was very important. So I took that offer up and left the Teams, without knowing that our assault group would soon be deploying to Southeast Asia as a platoon. That information hadn't gone out to much of anyone yet.

So I got out, and after I left, the word came out that SEAL Team Two was going to be deploying to Southeast Asia. That bothered me a lot; I couldn't sleep at night. And there was no way I was going to let this happen and not get a piece of the action. Combat would be the ultimate test at my training and abilities. And seeing action with my Teammates held more appeal than can easily be explained to an outsider.

So I got on the phone and started calling everybody I knew. I was trying to get all of my old buddies to pull strings or whatever it took

SEALs slip in during an insertion from a Zodiac rubber boat fitted with an outboard motor. Wearing a ghilly suit as camouflage, the SEAL at the bow of the craft maintains watch while armed with his M60 machine gun. The SEAL radioman, just stepping of the side of the boat in the center of the picture, is armed with an M16A1/M203 combination rifle and 40mm grenade launcher.

to get me back into SEAL Team Two so that I could deploy as if I had never left the Team in the first place.

So along came Dick Marcinko, who had gotten out of Officer Candidate School as a brand-new ensign just a year or so before. Dick had recently returned from deploying with the first SEAL Team Two platoon that had deployed for combat in Vietnam.

Because of his performance on that deployment, now lieutenant (j.g.) Dick Marcinko was assigned a platoon. He was now the platoon leader of Eight Platoon. Dick went out of his way to do the Marcinko thing and pull strings left and right with the Navy detailers in Washington. He made everybody believe that I was the most brilliant thing that ever walked the face of the earth, and that the Navy absolutely couldn't continue without me. Of course we all know that that's a lie, but it worked.

And I came back into the Navy and the Teams. What the point is, is that Dick had the willingness to bend a little bit, and push, and shove, and coerce, if you will, to do what he thought was best for his men and his Team. The next thing I knew, I was climbing off of a helicopter and charging through a rice paddy somewhere in the Mekong Delta. This was only a matter of weeks after I was having my martini lunch with my executive cohorts in the local pub back in the civilian world.

We were starting to take rounds from the tree line. The cracks of the supersonic bullets were snapping by overhead. And as all of this took place, I had the feeling that it was about time for lunch.

But that was how Marcinko operated, how he got things done, and it was also how I got back into the Teams. Now I was on my first deployment to Vietnam, arriving with the Eight Platoon in December 1967. The officer-in-charge was Lieutenant (j.g.) Dick Marcinko, his assistant was Lieutenant (j.g) Gordy Boyce, and the platoon chief was Chief Boatswain's Mate Louis A. "Hoss" Kucinski. That was quite a team.

The surprising thing to me was that we had a large proportion of kids, young men really, in the platoon, something we had never had before. And that was simply a result of the necessity of SEAL Team Two having to beef up the platoons. We did not have as many of the older, more experienced guys around to staff up and keep a three-platoon rotational system going.

There were three SEAL Team Two platoons doing combat tours in Vietnam at any one time from about the middle of 1967 on. When a platoon deployed, it replaced a platoon that was already operating in-country. That platoon in turn rotated back to Little Creek. Three platoons were in the training cycle to deploy to Vietnam while three platoons were already there. And several platoons were in the process of remanning and reorganizing as well as taking care of other SEAL Team Two commitments in the world at the same time. That took a lot more than the fifty enlisted men who were in the Team with me earlier.

So SEAL Team Two was immediately taking people right out of training to build up the numbers. I didn't like this at first. I didn't think these kids needed to be there yet; they didn't have enough experience. But after I did one combat tour, I realized that those were the guys I wanted with me, not the older guys. And that is what the SEALs became, more of a younger group, and less of a Navy fleet–experienced group. And for our mission in Vietnam, that's exactly what should have happened.

Because of our technique of operating, the ferocity of how we did our job, and the tactics we used, we were very much like the VC themselves, only better. We were much more aggressive. Since we had learned just how the VC were successful, and saw that it worked, we copied it. That action resulted in extremely high kill ratios of VC to SEALs lost during the war—in our favor. SEAL Team Two had zero losses, until Eight Platoon went into Chau Doc during the Tet offensive of 1968.

Eight Platoon had been up on the Cambodian border in January 1968. Our orders had come from a communiqué from General Westmoreland regarding a possible large enemy crossing of the Cambodian border during a given time period. Certain units in the area were to go up and observe whether the crossing was indeed happening.

So Dick had Eighth Platoon up in Chau Doc, which was a border city, on the Cambodian border on the west side of Chau Phu province. Eighth was operating along with about eight PRU individuals, mercenaries really, mostly Cambodians and some Chinese. With these men, we patrolled the border, looking for activity and any signs of crossings.

What we didn't realize was that the activity had already occurred. Our patrol was picked up by an advancing company of NVA—North Vietnamese Army regulars—or Viet Cong. We weren't sure of who we'd run into, but it was a group of company strength.

Prior to our patrol going out, we had set up fire support from two 105-howitzer fans. These were angled cones of fire that the howitzers could put out to cover known zones in our patrol area. So when we made contact with that heavy concentration of enemy forces, we called in artillery fire support. The tubes [guns] came back to us that we could not be supported because all tubes were turned to defending the city of Chau Doc. So we had no artillery support.

Eight Platoon performed a strategic withdrawal. Calling for extraction, we got the hell out of there. Luckily, we didn't lose anyone in that encounter. For a time, it was extremely intense. When the entire tree line opened up with enemy fire, it was nothing but Kalashnikov-colored tracers coming at us. These were green traces, not the red tracers used by the U.S. and its allies.

The PBRs we had called up came in to extract us and we returned to Chau Doc. On the way back, the local PRU adviser, who had been

As two PBRs pour in fire toward the shoreline, a Seawolf helicopter gunship close by overhead launches a 2.75-inch rocket from its rocket pod. The PBRs are part of River Section 523 while the gunship is part of HAL-3, Det 3.

U.S. Navy

with us on the op along with several of his men, got on the radio to report what had happened and get an update on the local situation.

The PRU adviser in Chau Doc was an army sergeant named Drew Dix. He was the only Army PRU adviser in the whole of the IV Corps area, the rest mostly being SEALs. Drew had called his safe house to see about the situation. The PRUs were run by "the Company," and the local Company guys maintained their own safe-house facilities in Chau Doc. What Drew was trying to get was a sitrep—a situation report—on just what was going on.

The reports that came back over the PRC-25 radio, on the Company's own secure circuit, were not good. All of the American strongholds in the area had been overrun. The local Army Special Forces C Team, their battalion headquarters detachment, was in a barricade situation trying to hold off the enemy forces. Basically, the Viet Cong had overrun the entire city of Chau Doc.

One of the concerns was that all of the U.S. AIDs (Agency for International Development) nurses were being held captive by Viet Cong. Drew was clearly distressed about this, in part because one of the nurses was an old friend of his. So we just kind of looked at one another as we all agreed that we had to go in and get them.

Going over to Dick, I said that we had to put a group together to try and get these civilians out. Dick wanted to do the very same thing, but he was restricted to doing his job, directing all of the platoons operations from the TOC (Tactical Operations Center) and maintaining the flow of information to keep all of us alive. He wanted to do the very same thing, but instead he gave me permission to split off from the platoon and go in with Dix to support him.

Our PBRs pulled in to the beach and we all piled off, while taking only sporadic sniper fire. We quickly patrolled up to the TOC, where the poor officer who had the duty that day was located. That was a sight I'm never going to forget. As we entered the TOC, I could see that officer lying on a couch, staring up at the ceiling, with the focus of his eyes some 2,000 feet beyond it. He was a very cool and collected, experienced old Army soldier.

In the background, I could hear the voices coming in over the radio, voices from soldiers at the Army Special Forces bases scattered throughout the area. And those voices were screaming about thousands—5,000 from one voice, 6,000 from another—of enemy troops crossing the Cambodian border. Those SF troopers were out there counting the heads of the enemy as major units were passing their locations. And they couldn't get artillery support to attack the incoming VC.

So this Army officer was just as cool as he could be. Because he knew that in about four hours, all those thousands of enemy troops were going to be here, in Chau Doc, and we were all going to be dead. There were all of like twenty of us there in the city to run the defense. And I was impressed with his aplomb in what appeared to be a hopeless situation.

Drew went out to the back area behind the TOC, where he had parked his jeep before we had all gone out on the op just the night before. It so happened that Drew's jeep had a .50-caliber machine gun mounted on a pedestal standing up from the center of the floorboard. I had already committed myself to accompanying him when he came up to me and waved to me that we were going.

So I jumped up into the back of the jeep and checked out that big gun, firing off a few practice rounds to make sure it was operating correctly, that the headspace was set right and the timing was on. The Browning .50-caliber machine gun is a massive weapon. It puts out a half-inch thick projectile the size of a little finger at around 2,700 feet per second. The rounds can chop down a concrete wall as they fly out of the car-axle-size barrel. The blast of a big .50 has authority; it is loud and distinctive. And I was very glad we had that gun with us.

As we were leaving, I could see the look on Dick's face as he came out of the TOC to watch us go. This was the first time I had ever seen that serious an expression on him. And as he saw I was looking, he said, "Watch yourself, asshole."

Then he smiled with that big grin of his. "Who knows, maybe you'll get laid," he finished.

There's nothing much that can be said to that. But it wasn't the last thing that happened. As Drew and I were leaving, into the jeep popped another SEAL. It was Frank Thornton, who jumped in carrying his M16. And we hadn't gone more than a few feet when another volunteer jumped aboard. This time it was Wally Schwalenberger, Eighth Platoon's dog handler. Only Wally didn't have his dog with him; he had a Stoner instead.

I was absolutely tickled pink with having these two volunteers, these Teammates, aboard. There wasn't much question that two guys in the jeep by themselves just weren't going to make it. But what they did was what the Teams are all about. Volunteering to do the things that you wouldn't expect, and during the most traumatic periods you can imagine. The best in men comes out in these situations.

But these guys just jumped in. Nobody told them to, but there was no way they were going to let me go by myself. And out we went from the TOC compound, into the raging firefight that was Chau Doc city.

How we made it through those streets I don't know. God was with us. It was just one firefight after another. As we were cruising on down the highway, I was looking around and trying to see the sources of the fire that was coming at us. All I could see was the lit-

Frank Thornton (right) and Drew Dix (back to camera) discuss the situation at Chau Doc during Tet 1968. To the left is Drew's jeep with its pedestal-mounted .50-caliber machine gun.

Frank Thornton Collection

tle smoke and muzzle flash of the guns from those pockets of VC troops all throughout the city.

As I spotted the enemy, I would return fire with the big .50. While I was putting out fire, I noticed the jeep was doing this fantastic job of countersniper maneuvering. The jeep was going through these sinuous curves and bouncing off the gutters and so on.

While I was firing here and there, watching my tracers going through windows and blowing walls out, I was thinking, This guy can really drive this thing! He was really impressive, I thought as I tripped off another series of shuddering kabooms from my .50. The knocking thunder of that huge Browning completely blanketed the firing sound of the 5.56mm weapons of my Teammates.

All of a sudden I noticed that we were coming up to a bridge and that the jeep was heading straight at one of the parapets. Oh my God, I thought, Drew's been hit!

Looking down at the driver's seat, I could see Drew with both his hands up to his head. He wasn't hit; he had clapped his hands over his ears. He hadn't touched the steering wheel since I had started firing that .50, the muzzle of which was only about three feet over his head. It turned out that the muzzle blast from that gun blew his eardrums out. To this day, he can't hear worth a shit.

Seeing how much fun Drew was having, I stopped firing the .50 over his head; the VC had pretty much stopped showing themselves anyway. And we continued on our drive, pulling up to the Company safe house a short time later. The safe house had a number of Company types there—spooks, really—as well as some PRU bodyguards. They had held out in their compound well enough and were able to give us some intel on the local situation. The nurses weren't at the safe house, so we decided to continue on to their quarters in another part of the city.

We regrouped and picked up two other civilian types, spooks, as well as another jeep. Drew kept on as the peerless driver of the first jeep, and Frank and Wally jumped over to the other jeep with the two CIA guys. I maintained my position as the .50 gunner. From the safe house, we headed off into the inner city.

The inner part of Chau Doc was saturated with pockets of VC. Every time we turned a corner, there would be five or six of the enemy in front of us. When they got over their surprise at seeing us, the VC would open up on us, and we would of course return fire. Sometimes, we fired first. But before the firefights could turn into much, we would be around a corner and going down another street. And there we would come across another pocket of VC.

But Chau Doc was giving us the cover of a congested city. We had the narrow streets and short blocks of Chau Doc to thank for being able to duck around and past the firefights the way we were doing. Of course, the surprise of the VC at suddenly seeing our two jeeps appear, fire spitting out from a half-dozen weapons in our rapid passage, gave us an edge.

Eventually, we got to the nurses' house. There, our big advantage had disappeared because now we were stopped. Around this house were several pockets of VC, all of them in upper building areas looking down on the nurses' house. The house was an old French colonial building, with a small courtyard in front of the house proper. Stopping the jeeps, the bunch of us dove into the courtyard and scrambled up to the front door of the house. Then we ran into another problem.

The front door of the house itself was open, but across the opening was an accordion type of steel gate, as you see in the front of some jewelry stores. And of course the gate was securely locked.

Hitting the deck in the courtyard, we were immediately taken under fire by the VC all around us. We were pinned down. But we had fairly decent cover in the courtyard with the concrete walls that surrounded it.

Drew yelled into the house, "Maggie, are you there?"

In kind of a whispering tone, Maggie called back, "I'm here. I'm under the bed, and they're inside!"

The fear in her voice was obvious to us all; she was panicked but called out to us in kind of a distressed whisper. Since the door was open, but with the gate across it, we had visual access to the building; we just couldn't get inside of it.

So as soon as the VC heard the voices of Maggie and Drew, they reacted. We could see three or four VC come running down the stairs and out of the kitchen. As soon as that happened, we yelled to Maggie, "Get down and stay down!"

Then we opened fire and just swept the area. We continued sweeping the area until we figured all of the VC were down or gone. We killed five or six, maybe as many as eight, inside of the house. They just piled up like cordwood right in front of us. Then things were quiet in the house.

But things were anything but quiet around us. Now the VC in the buildings nearby were really ticked off and the shooting down into the courtyard increased. Maybe they thought we had been shooting at them. But it didn't matter—we were still in front of that closed gate and unable to get to Maggie.

The whole point now was for us to get into that house and pull out Maggie and whoever else was in there with her. Calling through the locked gate, we told Maggie to come on out to where we were.

When Maggie came running out, Drew immediately asked her where the key to the gate was. So Maggie started searching for the key in this big pile of furniture that must have been five or six feet high. But she knew exactly where to go, into this one little cubical thing that was at the bottom of the pile. Pulling open a drawer, she removed this tiny little key and came up to the gate. Now, with the gate unlocked, I reached up and grabbed her, pulling Maggie out of the line of fire that was spraying all around us.

Of course all of this last action was moot. The comedy of the situation was that we could have blown the lock off that door in about two-tenths of a second. But no, we had to have Maggie get the key and let us in. We were too polite to break into the nurses' house.

But that was how we got Maggie out from under the noses of the VC. Luckily, the other nurses who were living there had gone out on an inland visit, an aid visit, the night before. In reality, I think some Vietnamese friends took those nurses out of the town without telling them what was going to happen. But the other nurses didn't suffer from any of the actions that were taking place in Chau Doc.

Since we had Maggie, that was all we really cared about. After getting her to a safe, secured area, we went back into the city that afternoon. Our mission was ostensibly to try and locate the command center for the Viet Cong forces who had overrun the city. The province chief, who was in fact the military governor of the province, came up to us and asked if we would go back in and try to get his family out.

Frankly, we didn't give a big care about going into town. The province chief's request was just another reason to get into town. We had already broken the enemy "code." We now knew that we could surprise the VC and accomplish a lot without an unreasonable risk to ourselves. We had seen that the VC were not an organized, well-centered, controlled military entity. The VC were instead in sporadic groups that were not in contact with one another. And that meant they could not get fire support from one another except by chance.

Getting into town, we patrolled down the street. There was no enemy activity, but we stayed as sharp as possible. Looking high and low, watching the shadows and corners, doing all the things we would be doing in the jungle, only without the trees; there were houses and buildings instead.

During the patrol, I noticed a wonderful thing. As we were moving into the heart of Chau Doc, all six of us, I noticed that on either side of us, the ARVN troops were now beginning to advance with us. Our SEAL squad had become their leading stick. That was all that they needed, some direction to get moving, and they moved on in with us. I thought that was tremendous. It showed that the ARVNs wanted to take their city back, but they just needed to know how to do it.

Much like the Viet Cong troops, the ARVNs were in little pockets of individuals who had been hiding here and there in the city. They weren't organized, but were beginning to be so as they gathered together around our squad.

Going deeper into the city, we located an area that was supposed to be the VC command area, which was on the way to the province chief's house. The VC command site happened to be in a movie house. In the backyard of this movie theater was a large walled court-yard. And that was the location of the command center. From the out-side, you could see all these radio antennas sticking up into the air.

From our limited elevation, you couldn't shoot or otherwise get through the walls around the courtyard. So we needed to climb. Frank Thornton, Ted Rischer, and I, we all went up on a building nearby. Ted Risher was right behind Frank as we went into a duplex structure about twelve stories high near the movie theater.

We climbed up the shorter building of the duplex, making the entire structure a shield between ourselves and the VC command area. After we reached the roof, we crossed it to the larger building. Now Frank jumped over onto a balcony on the taller of the duplex structures. We had to get to the top of that in order to have a good fir-ing position and be able to shoot down into the command courtyard.

The second guy over was Ted, and then it was my turn. But by the time it was my turn to jump over to the balcony, we had been dis-covered. The local VC had spotted Ted jumping across, so when I tried it, there was no more surprise. As I jumped across, there were a few cracks of gunfire to either side of me. Then I flew off the roof and landed on the balcony.

As soon as I landed, I went flat. There was a low wall around the balcony, of maybe crotch height, that I could hide behind. That wall just started to disintegrate in front of me from all of the incoming fire.

Dropping down, I was now on top of my two Teammates who had

gotten there ahead of me. Now we were on a balcony with a locked door in front of us. But this wasn't going to be as much of a problem as it had been at Maggie's. We knew the procedure now, and we just shot the lock off the door.

Going through the door, we made our way to the rooftop of the taller building. From the roof, we could see down into the courtyard of the theater, and the VC command element who had set up there. The M16s we had with us weren't going to supply the firepower we needed to take out that courtyard. We needed something heavier. Drew, being the PRU adviser, had access to an M18 57mm recoilless rifle, which was not too far away.

We contacted Drew, and he brought the 57 recoilless up to where we were. Having brought a line along with us, we threw it down to Drew and the rest of our squad. With that line, we first pulled up the 57 and then the containers of canister shot rounds. The canister shot round for the 57 mm recoilless rifle fires 133 cylindrical steel slugs to a lethal range of about 175 feet. Effectively, they make the weapon a five-foot-long shotgun. That was a devastating weapon to use against the VC down in that courtyard, which was exactly our plan.

In the process of getting the ammunition up on the roof and setting up to fire, we had some delays. I remember Ted yelling, "Goddammit, hurry up. We're trying to do something up here!"

Well, as soon as he said that, the VC located our position from the rooftop across the street. They started firing at us and down we went. Ted was still standing up and I shouted over to him, "Ted, get down."

As soon as I yelled his name, he dropped as if someone had hit him with a sledgehammer. He had taken a head shot, apparently from a carbine fired from across the street. It wasn't even an aimed shot probably, just one of those things we called a magic BB.

And that was how Ted Risher died, the first SEAL Team Two combat loss of the Vietnam War. He went out like a hero, and I think of him every day.

We had lost another guy earlier. But he hadn't been from SEAL Team Two. He was a West Coast SEAL from Team One who was killed going out on an operation with us.

In that Tet period, action was going on all over the place; there was lots of activity. We were lucky that our own losses were so few.

The month before, on 21 January, Gene Fraley of SEAL Team Two's Seventh Platoon had lost his life while making a boobytrap that detonated prematurely. Just a week earlier, on 18 January, Arthur "Lump-Lump" Williams had been shot while operating with Sixth Platoon. His wound was eventually fatal, but he didn't die until some months later. So 1968 started out kind of hard for SEAL Team Two, and we would lose three more Teammates before the year was out.

But that was the cost of war, and we were good enough that we could keep that cost down. Operations continued. The SEALs were audacious and innovative in the way we operated against the enemy. And we ran into our share of problems, not always from the other side either.

Prior to today's Joint Special Operations Command (JSOC) and USSOCOM (United States Special Operations Command), and the joint services training and operational cross-training, there were interservice problems. It was just that we did things differently in each of the services. What was SOP for one community was taboo for another.

Because of that situation, working with nonnaval SOF units in Vietnam could be very difficult. Regarding the complications that I had working with other services, the first situation that comes to mind was when I was a PRU adviser. Since I was the only American out there in the bush with a bunch of mercenary types, it was up to me to coordinate our support.

For this one PRU operation, I had set up a 105mm howitzer fan along with a number of concentration points. The points were predetermined locations, their coordinates already known to and plotted by the artillery unit. We could reference those points in such a manner—such as "Bravo One" or whatever—that the enemy couldn't tell where we were shooting if he was tapping into our communications net.

On this one operation, I was out in the field with only about eight or twelve of my PRUs with me. We were all out in a hide and could see a large concentration of the enemy coming up in the distance. The enemy saw our location and started charging us. They knew they had a superiority in numbers and were just going to overrun us. So I started calling in artillery fire from that battery of 105s we had on call.

As they were coming in, I was calling in fire over the radio and walking the rounds in to the target. The guys manning the guns were exceptional. Rarely do you get a good artillery battery that follows the forward observer's directions so quickly and accurately. And this was an ARVN battery, with a U.S. Army adviser group in charge. And I was talking to the Army people of course.

The fire was completely covering the area the enemy were in. The rounds were walked in on target and just obliterated the oncoming troops. My PRUs and I were going to make it out of this one, and I had watched the entire scene play out in front of my eyes. That doesn't happen very often, and the power of that artillery at my beck and call raised my excitement level quite a bit. When the enemy forces were gone, in my excitement, I yelled into the radio, "That's enough! That's enough!"

But the incoming fire didn't let up. Those thirty-four-pound projectiles just kept landing on target, their five-pound of high-explosive filler shattering the casings into flying shards of steel. The only thing was, there wasn't anything left of the target. And it just kept coming in, and coming in, and coming in.

"That's enough, goddammit, that's enough," I shouted into the radio.

"Do I understand cease fire, cease fire?" the voice at the other end of the radio link said calmly.

"That's what I'm saying," I still said rather loudly. "That's enough, goddammit!"

The adrenaline had just kind of taken over completely; I was just so excited and out of sorts really that I hadn't been able to think clearly. But the operation was a success, with no losses on our side.

When I got back to the compound, the situation was a little less happy than it had been in the field. The local battery commander came running up to me all kinds of ticked off. He had stood a chance of putting effective rounds downrange on my fire mission. And he hadn't been able to fire to his satisfaction based on my inability to communicate effectively. So he chewed on me for a while about my inability to correctly call in artillery fire support.

The fact was that I was an excellent forward observer (FO). It was just that I'd had a very anxious moment there. But this guy was really getting into my face. "Well, when I said, 'That's enough,' you'd killed them all," I told the red-faced artillery officer. "So I figured that was enough."

Then he chuckled, slapped me on the back, and just walked away.

That little conversation took place while I was working as a PRU adviser with the Phoenix Program. The Phoenix Program was an extensive South Vietnamese nationwide program run in South Vietnam by a major intelligence organization.

The SEALs were chosen to be the advisers of choice for the PRUs in the area where the SEALs operated. That was IV Corps, the Mekong Delta area south of Saigon. The action arm of the program consisted of a province combat team that was known at its inception as a counterterrorist unit. And the philosophy during the early days was that they would counter the terror of the VC with terror of their own.

The personnel who belonged to these units were strictly mercenaries, former ARVNs, probably criminals, and former military types from other Southeast Asian nations including China, Cambodia, and so on. So there was a complete potpourri of nationalities in the unit.

And these units were a very effective way of stopping the infrastructure from doing their terrorist thing during the early stages of the Viet Cong movement. But these units developed a very bad name for themselves as a result of their tactics. As Nietzsche says, "Beware of the dragon slayer, lest you become the dragon." That may have been the case with the early PRUs.

So the program was revamped, and became the provincial reconnaissance units, or PRUs. They became more of a paramilitary, well-trained organization. The men of the PRUs went to a boot camp that was run by Army Special Forces A-Team types. It was only after they went through this training that they were assigned to their PRU.

Each PRU was assigned to a specific province, the South Vietnamese version of our states. Each PRU had the responsibility under the Phoenix Program of collecting intelligence and responding to intelligence. They would enforce what needed to be enforced in the area and forcibly obtain members, or infrastructure types, from the hidden government that was existing or being built in each province by the Viet Cong movement. In essence, we were the secret police that were dedicated to eliminating the political infrastructure, command element, of the Viet Cong. Very rarely did we go after military leaders. The political leaders of the VC were our primary targets.

The PRUs were run, led really, by individual SEALs in the IV Corps area. In the II and III Corps areas, the Army SF types had them; up in I Corps, the Marines had the PRU adviser assignments. So every service had a piece of the Phoenix Program based on the intensity of their particular service's involvement in that corps' theater.

For myself, I had the good fortune to be a PRU adviser for two different provinces, Chau Doc and Phong Dinh. At that time I was an E-5 in military rank. But in the Phoenix Program, no one knew just what I was. That was because we were working in a detached capacity from the military. Instead, we worked directly for the O officer and P officer of the province. These men are the contract guys who are working directly for the company. So in effect, we became company operators, under the O and P officers. Although we still got paid by the Navy, we took our marching orders from the O and the P.

As the adviser of a PRU, you became the company commander of the unit. As an E-5 SEAL, I was running 135 well-trained killers, if you will, all of them excellent Asian military types. They were so good that they managed to get my keister out of the fire when I got hit very badly. They didn't have to do that—they could have left me behind. But they risked their lives to get me out. Those were good troops. And to this day I respect and love them.

The PRU mission was to neutralize the Viet Cong infrastructure, particularly the political infrastructure. The objective was not necessarily to kill, it was to obtain and capture critical members of the infrastructure. To in fact neutralize, and dissuade the building of this hidden government.

The PRUs were extremely efficient in their operations. In IV Corps, very few hard-core Viet Cong units were even operational because of the efficiency of the PRUs and the Phoenix Program.

In spite of stories and exaggerations that have been spread and have grown up regarding the Phoenix Program, it was not a systematic program of assassination at that time. The first phase of what became the PRU program, the counterterrorist-team phase, had

Almost hidden in the deep grass, these SEALs lay down for cover while one calls out on the radio carried on the other SEAL's back.

used assassination as a tool. But it was deemed to be an unsuccessful attempt at accomplishing something that the American public was just not going to accept. At least that's my understanding of it.

The acronym SEAL stands for Sea, Air, And Land. It identifies the three methods we have of operating—by sea, land, or air. The individual who is a SEAL is someone who has been put through probably the most intensive selection process that any military type goes through in the world on a regular basis.

The concept of selection is to drive the individual down to a common denominator of what his inner animal is, devoid of the personality facades and defenses that he has built up in society. He has none of that left and he deals with one thing, his will to survive and continue. If his will is strong enough, and passes that test, then he does continue and becomes a candidate for the balance of the selection process. Once he has completed this process, he becomes trained. That period can extend for several years of constant learning, until he is truly accepted by his Teammates.

After the conclusion of Vietnam, the Navy took a close look at the success of the SEAL program. The military leadership viewed the concept of special warfare much differently than they had before. They eventually saw the value in a small unit that was able to accomplish great things. The situations the smaller units would go into were high risk. But if you lose a small unit, you haven't lost a battleship.

Accomplishing great missions with little risk was considered a good way to go. After an immediate post-Vietnam cutback, the SEALs gradually became larger. This took a number of years but was inevitable, as there was now a recognized use for them.

The missions that followed this buildup included Grenada; where the SEALs were very effective in getting into Governor Scoon's mansion and bringing him out alive. A very dear friend of mine, Duke Leonard, led that mission in. They held the facility for a number of hours longer than they were supposed to. But they did a super job, and one they can easily be proud of.

After Grenada, one of the most publicly known SEALs actions was Panama. That was more of a search, an urban warfare mission, for the special operators, the "six" guys, in the pursuit of Manuel Noriega. Along with about 10,000 other posse members, they chased him all over the city. But they chased him quite effectively and eventually cornered him in the Vatican embassy, I believe. Noriega was finally extracted and arrested and Panama returned to democratic rule.

Desert Storm, the next major conflict, was primarily a conventional war of fire and maneuver. The field commander, General H. Norman Schwarzkopf, was very conventional in his thinking in the use and application of the forces at his command. But he had been a tanker, a tank commander, and Desert Storm was a tank war.

So Schwarzkopf did not use a lot of the SOF (Special Operations Forces) individuals, both Army and Navy. SEALs did conduct a large number of reconnaissance missions along the beaches of Kuwait and Iraq. And the SEALs did excellent diversionary work just prior to the commencement of the ground war. They did exactly what had been done during the Second World War, they swam in to beaches, set off explosives, and created the image that a beach was being opened for major amphibious landings. That trick caused the diversion of at least one division, maybe two divisions, of Iraqis to the beaches to defend against a potential landing that was never going to occur.

There have been many "brushfire" wars around the world that detachments from the SEAL Teams have reacted to. Fairly recently, it has been considered very fashionable to put a 300-man unit on the beach and get somebody politically corrected. The

While on patrol in Vietnam, two SEALs from SEAL Team Two's Sixth Platoon take a short break. Standing, drinking from his canteen, is the Platoon Chief, J. C. Tipton. Keeping watch, armed with an M16A1/XM148 combination rifle/40 mm grenade launcher, is Tipton's Teammate Art Hammond.

U.S. Navy

SEALs, like the other SOF units, are the men who respond to those kinds of missions.

We're headed for a continuing, and greater, use of SOF forces than ever before. The development of JSOC and USSOCOM has created the concept of using the services jointly, or joint service. This is where the best that all of the services have to offer has been brought together in order to conduct precision warfare on the small-unit level.

It would be realistic to say that SOF forces will be used forever in terms of warfare. It just makes sense. The use of electronics is being maximized in the aerial delivery of force. But what a ground force can, and must, do on the target area cannot be replaced. After an air strike had been completed, either large ground forces are sent in, and the lives of many possibly sacrificed. Or a much smaller surgical unit is sent in that is very adept at moving around in a clandestine manner, and they accomplish the same thing as the larger force. Small-unit penetrations can take and hold, or get in and corroborate, the results of other actions.

Dick Marcinko is an extremely controversial fellow SEAL in the community. There are those who love him, and those who hate him. I'm one of those who love him, and for good reason. He has been a brother warrior to me. As a field commander who I operated under, he was excellent. As a fellow E-5 petty officer, he was an excellent shipmate on the beach. And as a fellow older guy, he still is an excellent shipmate on the beach.

In any case, Dick Marcinko is an extremely bright individual. He has a way about him that is disturbing to the status quo. People who want a much more regimented approach to military problem solving have a lot of trouble with his style. However, his technique does work, though I wouldn't recommend it to the entire leadership core.

It is the mental aspect of a SEAL, his personality and drive, that is more important than people realize. The physical aspect of a Navy SEAL is not as great an asset as his mental one. If the mental strength is not there, then the physical is not driven. A case in point is a lot of the students who show up for training.

At BUD/S training, a number of bodybuilders show up, expecting their strength to get them through. Bodybuilders who are very much into themselves but don't give two hoots about anybody else are not Team members. And they probably won't complete training because they just can't put themselves through that much physical, and mental, stress and discomfort. There are some bodybuilders who turn out to be Team members, and they exercise to perfect their physical machine.

But it isn't the physical aspects of a person that gets them into the Teams. It's the drive, that mental aspect, the desire. Guys who have never lifted weights in their lives, never swam, never run before, who have the tenacity to get through. They just won't quit, and it doesn't matter if there's only 150 pounds of individual there. Many men like that have made it through training. Far more than the bulky, strongman types. It's what the mind is all about, not the body.

In terms of intelligence, there's a need for the above average in the Teams today. The concept of the SEALs mission, and the equipment that they are tasked to work with, demand someone who can understand their complexities. The men in the Teams today are given extremely advanced technology to use in support of their own mission or that of other forces.

Today's SEAL is a calculating individual who can take command. If the rest of his unit is knocked out, he can still, if necessary, accomplish the mission by himself. It is that kind of tenacity, the "cannot quit" mentality, that was the heart of a SEAL yesterday and remains the heart today.

One of the results of the selection process, the basic training, of a SEAL is just getting through the program. When you have gone through that, you feel a tremendous amount of self-pride, a strong sense of accomplishment. You have accomplished some extremely difficult stuff. And you have been shown that you could do things you never even dreamed you could do.

As a result of all of that training, you develop a positive attitude. Nothing really seems impossible; the attitude is one of "can do" toward everything. And the Teams are just that, men who work together, are one unit. And they all have that positive attitude. The Teams win.

To accomplish a mission, you conduct your observation first; that's part of the training. What has been observed is processed and understood. With understanding comes the solution to complete the mission successfully.

Our success in our battle against the Viet Cong came about because we looked at how they operated. Our combat experience was very limited prior to Vietnam and there was a lot for us to learn. But we did learn it. We saw how our enemy operated, and we saw how good they were. And we adopted their ways and did what they did. And building on our successes, we developed new techniques, and we became better still.

The Aftermath of Tet

The Tet offensive lasted for weeks. But in spite of the initial successes, the campaign was a stunning defeat for the Communist forces, especially those of the Viet Cong. The U.S. and allied losses included 1,536 killed, 7,764 wounded, and 11 missing. ARVN losses included 2,788 killed, 8,299 wounded, and 587 missing.

Estimated losses among the NVA and VC forces include 45,000 killed, 6,991 prisoners captured, 1,300 crew-served weapons captured or destroyed, and over 7,000 individual weapons captured or destroyed.

The failure of the ARVN forces to defend their country never took place. In spite of early withdrawals, the men of the ARVN forces fought back against the invaders form the north and their own guerrillas from the south. The VC/NVA forces had not been able to bring down the South Vietnamese government. Nor had they been able to hold on to any of the cities, towns, and villages they had captured.

Within a week of the beginning of the Tet offensive, the tide of battle had turned against the VC/NVA. But the north did win the political battle. The American viewing public saw the U.S. embassy in Saigon attacked and breached by VC sappers. A guerrilla force had attacked in a major military engagement, under conditions of almost complete secrecy, something they had not been considered capable of doing.

The Viet Cong never fully recovered from their losses during the Tet offensive of 1968. Whole VC units were almost wiped out to a man. The political and command structure of the Communist forces in the south now changed, with the NVA leadership taking a much greater role. This condition remained until the end of the war.

Chapter 10

HOI CHANHS, PRUS, THE SEALS, AND
THE PHOENIX PROGRAM

Both North and South Vietnam were divided into provinces, administrative units that act as states do here in the United States. Provinces were not large, more the size of an average U.S. county than a state, but they had their own local government and leadership that reported on to the national government in Saigon.

For military purposes, the forty-four provinces of South Vietnam were divided into four military regions or corps. Farthest north was I Corps (pronounced "eye-corpse"). The center of South Vietnam held II Corps, covering the largest land area. III Corps included the Rung Sat Special Zone as part of its area as well as Saigon. And to the south, the Mekong Delta made up IV Corps ("four-corpse").

The Hoi Chanh or "Open Arms" Program operated throughout South Vietnam. Unique to Vietnam, it was initiated by the South Vietnamese at the request of the U.S. government in 1963. As part of the Hoi Chanh Program, Viet Cong or NVA troops in the south could surrender, using leaflets scattered by government forces as safe passes. Paid a bounty for any weapons or major information they might bring over with them, the Hoi Chanhs, as they were known, were given amnesty by the South Vietnamese government. VC and NVA who "Chieu Hoied"—rallied to the Hoi Chanh Program—were also expected to deliver information to the SVN and U.S. authorities. In exchange, local VC would be returned to their homes and families. The program was amazingly successful during the ten years of its existence from 1963 to 1973, and almost 160,000 VC and NVA took advantage of it, according to U.S. records.

The Hoi Chanhs supplied a wealth of intelligence to the South Vietnamese and U.S. forces. Locations of arms and munitions caches, enemy troop movements, and leadership meetings all came out of the Hoi Chanhs. Many of the VC who came over through the program were high-ranking members of the Viet Cong Infrastructure, the VCI. They were the political and military leadership of the Viet Cong in the provinces of the south.

To attack the VCI, the U.S. intelligence community established the provincial reconnaissance units, or PRUs. The action arm of the Phoenix Program, the PRUs were paramilitary organizations made up of local militias, indigenous people, and foreign mercenaries from Cambodia, Laos, and other areas. The PRUs were armed, supplied, trained, and paid by the U.S. intelligence service and military personnel assigned to them. The PRUs came in various sizes, up to an infantry company in number, and were assigned one to a province. The province chief gave the PRUs their directions and they were led by a U.S. military adviser.

In the sixteen provinces of IV Corps, the PRU advisers came from one source almost exclusively. This was Det Bravo, the Navy SEALs. The successes of the PRUs under SEAL leadership were remarkable. Excesses that were known to occur in the Phoenix Program throughout the rest of South Vietnam were a rarity in IV Corps. In some provinces, the Viet Cong ceased to be a functioning entity because of the actions of the PRUs and their SEAL advisers. Many of the men who served in SEAL-led PRUs were ex-VC and NVA fighters and officers who had come over through the Chieu Hoi Program.

Excerpt from SEAL Team Two, Command and Control History 1968
Enclosure (1) to ST-2 Ltr, ser 04 of 7 Feb. '69
Pages 9–10. [DECLASSIFIED from CONFIDENTIAL]
IV. Provincial Reconnaissance Unit (PRU)
This year found certain members of SEAL Team TWO operating not as members of a platoon but as Provincial Reconnaissance Unit Advisers. The program has been found to be more than satisfactory, especially as it provides enlisted men with a great opportunity to develop their leadership qualities.

A detachment from a PRU listen to their American SEAL adviser as they discuss the mission while sweeping through a suspected Viet Cong village. The woven matting and palm frond construction of one of the villages' hooches is detailed to the right of the photo.

Frank Thornton Collection

The PRUs were established to eliminate VC infrastructure in the local provinces, villages, and hamlets, with the emphasis placed upon the gathering of valuable intelligence. The concept is unique in that Hoi Chanhs are employed as guides, intelligence agents, and combatants against their former comrades.

SEAL Team officers and enlisted men are qualified for duty in this program once they have completed a five-week special operations course in California. This course is run under the direction of the Commanding Officer of SEAL Team ONE. After one has completed the course, he is fully prepared to handle all responsibilities and problems associated with isolated duty. The concept, which involves SEAL personnel on attached duty with indigenous, combative personnel, has produced gratifying results and clearly shows SEAL Team TWO's ability to organize, train, and lead friendly foreign forces.

Excerpt from SEAL Team Two, Command and Control History 1969
III. SEAL TEAM TWO COMMAND HISTORY—NARRATIVE
Page 7. [DECLASSIFIED from CONFIDENTIAL]

3. (C) Detachment BRAVO consisted of specially trained enlisted men who advised the Vietnamese Provincial Reconnaissance Units (PRU). The Provincial Reconnaissance Unit was developed to gather intelligence about, and to eliminate the VC infrastructure in the provinces, villages, and hamlets of IV Corps. As advisers to these units, the SEALs of Detachment BRAVO not only assisted in planning and coordinating operations, but also actively led most of the combat missions. The advisers' experience and training, coupled with the aggressiveness of these Vietnamese forces during the past year, continued to produce the high degree of success achieved in previous years. Two advisers lost their lives while leading their PRU in combat missions during 1969. They were GMG1 Harry A. MATTINGLY and AE1 Curtis M. ASHTON.

Excerpt from SEAL Team Two, Command and Control History 1970
III. SEAL TEAM TWO COMMAND HISTORY—NARRATIVE
Page 7. [DECLASSIFIED from CONFIDENTIAL]

3. (C) For the first two months of this year detachment BRAVO was composed of specially trained enlisted men. These men were advisers to the Vietnamese Provincial Reconnaissance Units (PRU). These units were trained to gather intelligence about and to eliminate the VC infrastructure in the various provinces of IV Corps. As advisers to the PRU, the SEALs planned and coordinated operations, but were not permitted to actively participate in the combat missions. The aggressiveness of these Vietnamese forces continued to produce results at a high level.

Excerpt from SEAL Team Two, Command and Control History 1970
Enclosure (2) CHRONOLOGICAL OUTLINE

DATE	EVENT
16 MAY 1970	BM1 RODGER returned from Vietnam, thus ending SEAL Team TWO's commitment to DET "B"

Excerpt from SEAL Team One, Command and Control History 1969
Enclosure (2) (b) BASIC NARRATIVE
OPERATIONS
Pages 1–2. [DECLASSIFIED from SECRET]

b. Detachment BRAVO is under the operational control of the Ministry of the Interior, Republic of Vietnam, and the personnel assigned to it are in direct support of the Provincial Reconnaissance Unit (PRU) Program. During this reporting period [March to December, 1969], with the turnover of control from the Military Assistance Command and the overall Vietnamization of the war effort, this program has decreased from a high of four officers and twenty-four enlisted to its present level of three officers and ten enlisted. This is congruent with the design to completely reduce the SEAL Team commitment to the PRU Program. These personnel are assigned as advisers throughout the IV Corps Tactical Zone, Republic of Vietnam. PRU are armed reconnaissance units of indigenous personnel that have the primary mission of gathering intelligence on key members of the Viet Cong political infrastructure and indicting or eliminating them whenever possible . . . The notable success of the IV Corps PRU Program can be attributed to the professionalism and dedicated leadership and drive of the SEAL advisers.

Excerpt from SEAL Team One, Command and Control History 1969
Enclosure (2) (c) BASIC NARRATIVE
SPECIAL TOPICS—INTELLIGENCE COLLECTED
Page 1. [DECLASSIFIED from SECRET]

2. The significance of the SEAL Team One PRU effort is reflected in the statistics which follow. The success of the PRU Program has often been traced directly to the leadership and professionalism of the officers and enlisted advisers, a small percentage of the total program. The figures listed here are even more significant when one considers that they are the result of targeting the Viet Cong infrastructure, the core of the enemy's command and control structure:

Excerpt from SEAL Team One, Command and Control History 1969
Enclosure (2) (C) BASIC NARRATIVE
SPECIAL TOPICS—SPECIAL TRAINING
Page 5. [DECLASSIFIED from SECRET]

1. Special Operations training, a five-week course for experienced officers and senior petty officers to prepare them to conduct covert and clandestine operations as advisers to indigenous personnel, experienced significant changes both in content and the practical application in an effort to remain current with the world situation and SEAL employment. In the immediate future, it is likely that the basic course will also increase in duration to ten weeks. In addition to the curriculum revision, semipermanent buildings were provided for training at Camp Billy Machen, the Special Operations field training facility at Julian, California.

Leonard "Lenny" Waugh, Senior Electronics Chief, USN (Ret.)

After my first tour in Vietnam with Third Platoon from SEAL Team Two, I didn't return to the States with the rest of the guys when they rotated back in June 1967. Instead, I went over to the PRUs to become one of the first East Coast SEAL advisers to that program.

The PRUs were the provincial reconnaissance units. In South Vietnam, they had provinces, much like the states or counties as we have them here in the United States. The PRUs were assigned one to a province and they went out and conducted reconnaissance missions throughout that area. The PRUs themselves were conceived as paramilitary organizations and were manned with mostly Vietnamese personnel, but also had Humong (Montagnards), Cambodians, some Chinese, and even some repatriated ex–Viet Cong.

The West Coast (SEAL Team One) was running the PRU training program at that time and the question was whether a PRU adviser would work to increase the capabilities of the PRUs. What the adviser would do was plan out a mission for the PRU from intelli-

A group of PRUs move through an open area of grassland while on patrol.

U.S. Navy

gence gathered from different sources. The NILO (Naval Intelligence Liaison Officer) gave us good bits of intel when he came in with something that he thought we would be interested in. The South Vietnamese junk force would also bring us intel. And we also had our own spies out among the population in the field.

All of these sources and more would bring us information that we would kind of hold back "in escrow," and then combine it later with other information. When we had a good picture of a given target or situation, we could plan out an action to take.

Information might come in about somebody being somewhere at eleven o'clock in the evening. And that person might be a target we wanted to get other information from. So we would plan a mission to go out and snatch him up. Sometimes, we would operate with as many as thirty people from the PRU. Other times, we might go out on an op with as few as two people.

Probably the most basic goal of the PRU operations was to capture individuals for interrogation and to gather further intelligence on even higher-level targets. One of our big targets was to capture a VC tax collector. A tax collector would come into a village and force the people to pay him money or goods as VC-levied taxes. He had to know a lot about the province to be able to do his job. And that put him high up in the Viet Cong infrastructure (VCI). That was the higher organizational command and control structure for the Viet Cong.

So capturing a tax collector was a good op. And since he was high up in the infrastructure, we could get good information from him. And that was our basic objective, eliminating the VCI and gathering information on the higher-ups and their operations.

The Phoenix Program was the umbrella organization that the PRUs operated under. But when I was a PRU adviser, I wasn't told that we were under the Phoenix Program. Knowledge about the Phoenix Program was something I learned later.

The VC tax collectors were the big target we went out for a lot while I was a PRU adviser. We really wanted to stop them. This would not only give us a good deal of information, it would also help choke off one source of supply for the VC. But we never passed up other targets if they made themselves known to us. If we found out about a major enemy movement—say, a VC battalion crossing the Mekong at a given point at a certain time—that was something we gave over to the Army or the Navy so that they could handle it.

In my PRU, we weren't equipped for major engagements. What we were set up for was the "sneak and peek" kind of op with five or six people. My PRU could set up and sit at an ambush site and watch the enemy movement. If the enemy forces were small enough, and they usually were, we could try and engage them ourselves. If there were too many of them, we would just watch and come back with the information.

We didn't want to shoot anyone if we didn't have to. In fact, we preferred not even to fire our weapons. Coming back with, say, six prisoners and not a shot fired on our part was a really good op. This was much the same basic philosophy that the SEALs developed in Vietnam. And the adviser program using SEALs and the PRUs was a very successful one, in part because of this approach.

A PRU member proudly pulls a secured Viet Cong prisoner from hiding in a hooch in Vietnam.

Frank Thornton Collection

What we did as advisers was work right with the PRUs, down on their level. We ate with them, drank with them, and went out on operations with them. They were really our kind of people. I trusted my PRUs and they trusted me. By the time I left my assignment as a PRU adviser, my men thought the sun rose and set according to my desires.

One measure of our success as PRU advisers was that the VC put out a bounty on our heads. I had a price on my head that the VC were willing to pay anyone who could take me out. My PRU team leader came back with the priority listing the VC had put out in our province. He was very happy that I was ranked as the number-two most wanted man in the province, and that he was number one, with the larger bounty offered for his head.

If outranking me on the VC most-wanted list made my PRU team leader happy, that was fine with me. The VC wanted him worse than they wanted me. That was good; I could sleep more easily that night.

The price on my head was something like 50,000 piastres. At an exchange rate of roughly 75 piastres to the U.S. dollar, I was worth

The exertion and heat have sweated the camouflage facepaint from this SEAL as he comes in from an operation. The camouflage was a distinctive headgear worn by some SEALs during the Vietnam War.

in the neighborhood of $670 dollars. But the piastre went a lot further in those days. Thankfully, no one managed to collect my bounty, or that of any other SEAL adviser that I ever heard of.

One of the things we tried to do in Vietnam was build up a reputation among the Viet Cong. I'm not talking about any kind of bravado. What we wanted to do was actually make the Viet Cong fear us. When they did that, they would make mistakes. And they might surrender a lot faster, rather than trying to fight things out with us. But the Viet Cong probably didn't know our real designation—SEAL—for a while.

What we did was encourage the rumors about us. When we went out on operations, we cammied up with green, black, and brown face paint. That not only helped us hide in the shadows and among the plants in the jungle, it really made us look a little "unhuman" to the Vietnamese.

The VC took to calling us the "men with green faces." It was just our makeup, but we did make use of the situation. "Watch out for the men with green faces" was a phrase that troubled the sleep of many a VC, we found out later. And that fear was something we wanted out there.

Chapter 11

TO FIGHT A WAR

The SEALs went in to their first deployments in Vietnam fully trained and more than competent to do their job. But the one thing the Teams were lacking was a great deal of experience fighting a jungle, counterguerrilla war of the type found in Vietnam. But the Teams were more than up to the challenge, and they developed new techniques and applications of old tactics continually as they fought.

But no matter how highly trained an individual was, combat left a lasting impression on anyone who went through it. The men of the Teams were no exception. As they gathered the experience that increased their combat efficiency, they also gathered memories of combat, some of which were so vivid, they would last for the rest of their lives.

Excerpt from SEAL Team Two, Command and Control History 1967 Pages 6–7. [DECLASSIFIED from CONFIDENTIAL]
III. Development of Tactics
During the deployment of Detachment "A" to Vietnam, many valuable contributions have been made to the development of operational tactics for small units such as those employed by SEAL Teams in direct action against the Viet Cong. Being unique in topography and climate, the Mekong Delta offers considerable opportunity for imaginative development of small-unit operations. Various methods of ingress, for example, were tried and proved, such as insert by STAB or Boston whaler (thirteen- or sixteen-foot length), launch by PBR and LCM, and insert by helicopter

> during hours of day or night. Successful ingress was also made by swimmers carrying full combat loads under tow. Such tactics as simulated withdrawal by water and then the establishing of a double-back ambush were tried and in many instances found effective. Generally speaking, it was discovered that the effectiveness of a small unit of eight men is limited only by the imaginations of those involved.

Gene E. Peterson

One of the operational techniques we developed in Vietnam was a leave-behind ambush. One of the reasons we developed the technique was that a lot of the time when we did an operation or an ambush we failed to capture a lot of the people at the target. In the sudden confusion, a lot of people disappeared back into the bush. Since we operated a lot at night, it was very hard to follow or track them.

The escaped people could come back on their own to see where we had gone. Or they might come back and bring other VC with them as support. To counter this, we would go in and set up on a place and conduct the ambush as usual. But when we extracted, only half of the troops would be pulled out.

Whether we left the men at the ambush site, or they took up positions around our extraction site, their job was to ambush anyone who followed along our trail. The extraction boat would pull out and travel some distance away from the extraction site. If the leave-behind ambush worked, we would come blasting back in with the boat as soon as we heard the shooting. If it turned out to be a "dry hole," we circled around and came back to pick up the leave-behind troops after a short time had passed.

This kind of creative operation worked very well for us sometimes. One of the times that I remember us using this technique was right after we had hit an ammo dump. Once we blew up the dump, everyone in the area knew we had been there. After the blast, the rest of the platoon pulled out, and five of us stayed behind.

There was a kind of little mud ditch, maybe two or three feet deep and about four feet wide, running alongside our target area. The bottom of the ditch was filled with a soft, gooey mud that we sank into when we hid in the ditch. Once we had settled in, the mud was well up on my chest as I lay there.

Once you have situated yourself in a muddy site like that, you really can't move much. Any movement on your part will send waves through the mud, sloshing it around and making enough noise to alert anyone coming up. So we stayed silent and still in that mud for about ten or fifteen minutes.

Somebody started coming into the target area from up in the bushes behind us. We really couldn't see him at all clearly, but we could hear him moving through the jungle. The first thought going through our heads was that maybe we had been compromised. If someone had detected our position, they could be setting up to ambush us.

As we watched what was going on, suddenly this man disappeared. And then all hell broke loose.

Apparently, a company of North Vietnamese had set up across the river from us. The water was only about forty feet wide and they must have detected our position. Instead of us ambushing someone coming into the destroyed ammo dump, we ourselves were now the targets for someone else.

The situation almost didn't seem real; it was almost like watching a movie. That was kind of funny for me; I had been in Vietnam long enough to have experienced my share of firefights. But this time I was watching and could actually see the bullet hit the mud in front of me.

It was sort of like slow motion when you saw the bullet hit the mud. There would be the hit and the mud seemed to slowly spurt up. Then it would settle back down again and the dimple in the surface would collapse. Then another one would hit and the same thing would happen. This was like watching TV, only the bullets were real.

It absolutely fascinated me for a moment. I may even have said out loud, "Wow, it looks just like TV." Suddenly the realization hit me. Damn, this wasn't TV, it was real.

Sinking down, I settled into the mud about as far as I could go and still be able to breathe. Hanging on, I got on the radio and called for our boat to come in and pick us up.

As soon as I called for the extraction boat, it seemed that you could hear their engines fire up, even though they were a mile or more away. They were coming to get us with their throttles wide open.

It was night, the normal time for us to operate in the Teams, and the extraction boat might have a hard time finding us. One of the unusual pieces of ordnance we had with us was a special grenade with luminous material inside it. When one of these grenades went off, it spread this material that glowed with a blue-green light all over its burst radius. That light would be the signal that marked our spot to an overhead Seawolf helicopter. Hopefully, the Seawolves would see the light and not shoot at us.

All you had to do was take the grenade and toss it. When it fired it spread this chemical all over the tops of the foliage above us. The glow was much like you see on the dial of a watch. Not enough to really see by, but hopefully enough to alert the incoming Seawolves.

The choppers started coming in to our position as I began to hear the boat roaring down the river in our direction. The rockets from the Seawolves were being fired right over our heads—you could see them being fired and feel the heat blast from their exhausts, the Seawolves were that close. As the rockets were blasting through the trees over our heads, limbs the diameter of your legs were being broken off and dropping down on us. But that wasn't anything in comparison to those same rockets going through the trees and detonating on the other side of the river.

These Seawolf gunships were also armed with miniguns, mounted outside of their rocket pods. The minigun is a multibarreled machine gun that spins its six barrels as it fires 7.62mm ammunition at high rates of speed, on the order of 3,000 rounds per minute for those mounted on the Seawolves.

While the Seawolf was firing over our heads, and the rockets were blasting out, the miniguns were firing. The bullets came out of the front of those weapons like a steel spray. But the fired ammunition casings were also pouring out from the sides of the guns. Those hot brass casings rained down on us, literally like metal raindrops. But it was a hot metal. Just like the bullets hitting

A port-side helicopter mounted outboard minigun rains fire down on the Viet Cong below. The heavy blast of muzzle gases appears as a huge, white cloud of flame a few feet in front of the weapon.

the mud earlier, the fired minigun casing would smack into the mud, and then there was an audible sizzle as the metal cooled suddenly.

It was kind of exciting.

As the Seawolves poured fire into the NVA positions, our extraction boat was coming up the river and getting closer and closer. I could hear the .50-caliber machine guns mounted along the side of the boat chopping up the countryside. And the bursting 40mm grenades being put out by the grenade launchers on the boat made a constant string of explosions. And over it all was the deep thrumming roar of the 7.62mm minigun near the bow of the boat, pouring out its ammunition at several thousand rounds a minute.

As the boat came closer, I started getting worried that they would take our position under fire as well. In the excitement of the fight, they might forget where our position was. So at just the last second, as the boat approached, I started shouting into the radio for them to stop shooting.

Just as it seemed as if our own people would destroy us, the guns on the boat stopped firing. The boat turned into the bank and headed right for our location. As soon as it touched the bank, we pulled ourselves up out of the mud we were lying in and clambered aboard.

Just as the last man climbed aboard, the coxswain slipped the engines into reverse and pulled away from the bank. Now the guns were firing again as we left the area. But we all got out okay. No one was hit, and no one was hurt, except for the bangs and bruises we got from landing in the boat.

Later we learned that a whole company of North Vietnamese had set up on the bank of the river, directly across from us. There had been at least forty or fifty guys over there, dumping fire into our position. But they were badly chewed up by the rocket fire from the Seawolves overhead, and the heavy gunfire of our own support boat.

The men who crewed our support boats have my respect for the job they were doing. First of all, they had to pull away from where they had inserted us, and then move some distance upriver. Once they were a safe average distance away so as not to compromise our insertion, they would quietly nose into the bank. Then they just sat there and waited for our call for extraction or support.

The fortitude of those men was amazing to me—to just silently sit there, being still and quiet, just waiting for us. And then whenever they actually had to come in and get us out of a hot situation, they immediately jumped into action. Forgetting about their own safety or anything else that was going on, they came and got us.

I don't know how the boat drivers were doing what they did. It was pitch-dark out there on the river in the middle of the night. And they couldn't use a light without making a target of themselves. The drivers would just tuck their faces up against the rubber hoods on the radar scopes and watch the glowing green traces of the river-bank on either side of them. With these as a guide, they would race their boats at top speed to get to us.

They never spoke about the jeopardy they were putting themselves in. Those boats and crews were there to help and support us, and that is what they did.

Without them, we couldn't have done many of the things we

have been credited with. And a lot fewer of us would have come home intact or lived to operate another day. Those boats and crews helped make the difference for us countless times.

The Seawolves are another unit we owe a lot to. You would get into a situation on an op where you needed air support, and you needed it right now! And on some of the occasions when we called in Army helicopters, they were ten or fifteen minutes away. That can be more than enough time for even a unit of SEALs to be over-run, wiped out, and the enemy long gone before the helicopters show up.

But when we did an op with the Seawolves on call, they knew where we would be and when. If we called for air support, they were just right there. I don't know where they came from or how they got off the ground that fast. But it seemed like as soon as we made the radio call for the Seawolves, they were right there overhead within three of four minutes.

And those Seawolf pilots and crews weren't afraid to do what we needed. They would come right in and actually touch the tops of the trees to make sure that they protected us. The crews would drop ropes to pick us up if there was no other way out for us.

How the Seawolves got into the position they did with their birds, and flew they way they had to, I don't know. But the support that we received from the Seawolves brought a lot of men home to the Teams who otherwise wouldn't have made it. They were unbelievable.

■ Chapter 12

TO SAVE A LIFE, THE CORPSMEN

In the Teams, one experience is shared by all, and that experience is training. It is while undergoing BUD/S, or the earlier UDTR, that a man demonstrates that he has that drive, determination, and heart to make it through some of the hardest military training in the world. Teammates share training stories with each other all of the time. Everyone has a favorite.

But some individuals served in the Teams who never went through UDTR or BUD/S. They simply were not allowed to do so because of an interpretation of the regulations and international agreements of war. But every SEAL or UDT operator who served with these men considers them full-fledged Teammates.

A hospital corpsman is an enlisted man trained to give first aid and basic medical treatment, particularly while under combat conditions. The U.S. Navy Hospital Corps is the only enlisted corps in the Navy, and has a history of service and valor dating back to the corps' founding on 17 June 1898. This valor is well illustrated by the fact that hospital corpsmen have received over half of the Medals of Honor awarded to enlisted men in the Navy.

When the SEALs were first commissioned, a number of hospital corpsmen were among the plankowners of both Teams. But by the time the SEALs were sending direct-action platoons into combat in Vietnam, corpsmen were no longer allowed to go through UDTR training. This had to do with the fact that corpsman going through training had to work with demolitions as well as small arms.

The 1949 Geneva Convention allows Navy hospital corpsmen to be classified as noncombatants. This allows them to be armed for their own defense and that of their patients. But they are not allowed to carry weapons for any other reason. With these restrictions came protections, centering on corpsmen's treatment if they are taken prisoner, among other things. But the corpsmen of the Teams relinquish any protections given them by the Geneva Convention in order to serve fully with their Teammates.

After receiving their full training to qualify as hospital corpsmen, those men who also volunteered to join the SEAL Teams underwent a special course of training before they were allowed to enter the Teams. The special-operations-technician course made the corpsmen who went through it fully qualified divers and parachutists. When they arrived at their respective SEAL Teams, pre-deployment training with their platoons also made the corpsmen proficient with weapons and able to move on patrol effectively.

Each deployed SEAL platoon going to Vietnam was to have a hospital corpsman assigned to it. Corpsmen are most often called simply "Doc" in the Navy or Marine Corps. But in the Teams, they were also called something even more significant—they were called "Teammate."

Jack Salts, Senior Chief Hospital Corpsman, USN (Ret.)

In January 1978, I retired from the Navy after twenty-one years, four months, and seven days of active duty. And during that time, I had the privilege of serving as a hospital corpsman in the Teams.

In 1960, I was a Navy hospital corpsman going though the X-ray technicians' school at a naval hospital. While at the hospital, I met a lady who eventually married Delmar "Freddie" Fredrickson. Sometime later, while I was going through an advanced hospital corpsman school on the West Coast, I again ran into her, and through her, met Freddie.

The stories Freddie told me about life in the Teams made them sound like something I really wanted to be part of. But the Navy had other plans for me at that moment and I was soon stationed in Seattle, Washington. I volunteered for UDT training, but was quickly turned down.

As a corpsman at that time—the mid-1960s—I was not allowed to go through BUD/S training. There had been a window of opportunity back in the early 1960s when corpsmen were allowed to go through UDTR training and join with the UDTs or SEAL Teams. But that was stopped after it was determined that the Geneva Convention prevented hospital corpsmen from being allowed to handle demolitions. Or at least that's how I remember the reasoning.

But I knew the Teams had to have hospital corpsmen, especially since they were getting ready to go to Vietnam and see active combat. Corpsmen are the field medical personnel of the Navy. We go out into the combat area to help the wounded. We're right there where the bullets are flying, trying to save the lives and ease the pain of the wounded.

There were some people I knew who were plankowners of SEAL Team One and still in the Team in Coronado. I had spent three years in Seattle, working in the hospital and trying to get into the Teams. All my requests were denied, so finally I just called down to SEAL

Team One and contacted Freddie Fredrickson directly. He told me he would talk to Lieutenant Del Giudice, who was the CO of SEAL Team One at the time, about the situation.

That was about all I could expect. But when Freddie called me back, his news wasn't what I wanted to hear. "Jack, I'm sorry," Fred told me. "There's no way that you can do it. The only way you can get to the Teams is by becoming deep-sea-diver [hardhat] qualified, completing jump school, and underwater swimmer school."

"So," I asked back, "how do you do that?"

"You apply for special operations technician."

If that was the only way I could go to get into the Teams, so be it. So I did that, and my first stop was deep-sea divers' school at the Washington Navy Yard in Washington, D.C. Six months later I was a qualified hardhat diver.

There was a two-week break between my graduation from deep-sea-divers' school and the beginning of my jump school. During the break, I was assigned to UDT 22 in Little Creek. So that gave me a very short taste of life at a UDT, but I still had the balance of my training to complete.

My short stay at UDT 22 was followed by three weeks at Fort Benning, Georgia, and the Army jump school there. Then came eight weeks of underwater swimmer school in Key West, Florida.

All of this training resulted in my being assigned back to Underwater Demolition Team 22 at Little Creek, Virginia, as one of their hospital corpsmen. It was January 1966. This was the long way around, but at least I had finally made it to the Teams.

Lieutenant Commander David Schaible was the CO of UDT 22 during the beginning of my time there. Getting to a SEAL Team was what I really wanted to do, but Commander Schaible told me that he had a working agreement with the Navy detailers up in Washington regarding hospital corpsmen. The detailers were the men who assigned people to posts throughout the Navy, and what they said was pretty much the last word on assignments.

What Commander Schaible told me was that he would receive all of the hospital corpsmen when they graduated deep-sea divers' school. Once the corpsmen were assigned to UDT 22 and arrived in

Little Creek, he'd put us through some pretraining and physical conditioning to prepare us for jump school.

The conditioning and training I remember well. But what I didn't know was that Commander Schaible was also picking out the people he wanted to have in his UDT. So even though I had asked to be assigned to SEAL Team One so that I could be with my friend Freddie, I ended up on Commander Schaible's want list and was assigned to UDT 22.

Maybe being in the UDT first would be a good thing, I thought. Spending time in the UDT would teach me the ropes better and I could then move over to a SEAL Team. That worked out, eventually. But it took me three years to get to a SEAL Team.

But life in UDT 22 had its adventures as well. In 1968, I was part of a crew that was sent from Little Creek, on the shores of the Atlantic Ocean, to a demolition job at Midway Island, half a world away in the middle of the Pacific. On the way back from that job, we landed in San Diego for a stopover.

It just so happened that the day we arrived in San Diego was the same day that Commander Schaible was relieving Commander Anderson as the CO of SEAL Team One. I was there at the ceremony and right afterward, while they were cutting the cake, I looked up to see this big guy just spreading the crowd apart as he approached me.

"Doc," he said when he saw I was looking, "come here."

This didn't look like the kind of guy I would say no to. So I walked over to him and he just said, "Come with me."

I followed the man to his office; inside, Commander Anderson was changing into civilian clothes. Then he picked up the phone and called Washington. He was talking to some officer there, but I could only hear part of the conversation. The part I could hear involved him asking about a corpsman in UDT 22 and how he would like to have him in his unit.

Looking over at me, Commander Anderson asked, "What's your rank and horsepower?"

"I'm a second class hospital corpsman," I told him. And then I told him my Social Security number and other pertinent data.

He chitchatted with the man at the other end of the phone for a while and then hung up. Turning to me, he asked, "How much leave do you have built up?"

"A week," I answered.

"Well, when you get back to UDT 22," he told me, "your orders will be there."

And when I got back to UDT 22, my orders were there, along with a little surprise. The minute I walked into the office at UDT 22 to turn in my leave papers, the yeoman there told me that the XO wanted to see me immediately.

So I walked in to see John Ferruggiaro, who was our XO at the time. He let me into his office, shut the door, sat down, and put his feet up on the desk.

"Mister," Ferrugario said to me, "I don't know who you think you are, jumping the chain of command, going behind everybody's back, and getting yourself a set of orders to SEAL Team One. But I'm here to tell you, don't unpack your bags."

"Why's that, sir?" I asked, more than a bit puzzled.

"The day after tomorrow, you're going to the Med [Mediterranean]," he told me. "I've got an operational hold on you."

So he had the last say-so. I made a Med cruise for UDT 22. After I got back, I transferred to SEAL Team One and the West Coast.

Even though I had wanted to get to a SEAL Team for so long, initially I was a little reticent about operating as a corpsman with them. There was always that feeling I had, and maybe it was an unfounded one, about not having gone through BUD/S training; even though I'd had to go through a much longer period of training to get to the Teams, there was that question of was I good enough? Could I measure up?

But I think people realized that most of the other corpsmen who were in the Teams and hadn't gone through BUD/S were pretty good at their jobs. We worked hard at what we were supposed to do. And over time, virtually every one of us was accepted as a Teammate.

The big test for a Team corpsman came when he was deployed to a combat tour in Vietnam. My first deployment to Vietnam was in January 1970. It was an exciting time, to say the least.

While building up for the deployment, during the weeks of pre-deployment training, you got to know everyone in your platoon. You actually reached a point where you could tell what any of your Teammates in the platoon would do in almost any given circumstance. The camaraderie that was built up during that time is something that we will live with forever. It just can't be taken away from us. It is uniquely ours.

Actually being a hospital corpsman in combat was unlike anything I had experienced before. I'd think back to all of the movies I'd seen as a teenager, before joining the service. Those films, following the Korean War and WWII, showed a corpsman as someone who wore a red cross on his arm and on his helmet. They made you wonder if you would just be a big target when you finally became a corpsman.

But it wasn't that way at all in Vietnam. We didn't wear the big red crosses. Instead, we wore what everyone else wore. And in the Teams, we did what everyone else did. When you were operating in a platoon of two officers and twelve enlisted men, or when they were split into squads of one officer and six enlisted, everyone had a number of jobs to do. The radioman handled the radio and maintained communications. But he was also a rifleman, grenadier, or automatic-weapons man.

A hospital corpsman, if there was nobody to patch up, had to add his firepower to that of his unit; he had to do his share. And he could carry any weapon that he was familiar with and confident about handling. Generally, the corpsman not only carried his own medical kit, but each member of the platoon also carried some medical supplies with them. That way, if I was working on someone who was hurt over here, someone else could be tending to another injured person over there.

Every member of the platoon was trained in some lifesaving skills. Each platoon went through some formal medical training. Nothing as sophisticated as what a hospital corpsman had to go through. But each man knew enough that he could jump in and help when he was needed during a lifesaving situation. And if the corpsman got hit, then there was somebody to help work on him. So our guys were pretty well trained.

Just being there and going out on a patrol, making contact with

---

the enemy, and everyone doing just what they were supposed to—that came from all of our training. Whether a man would jump to the right, or to the left, and what the corpsman would do in a given situation, that had all been covered long before. And being able to come out of the fight later made all those long hours of training worth it.

But that first time in combat is never quite like training. The first thing that went through my head when the bullets started to fly was for me not to let my Teammates down. The second thing that went through my head was to get back home alive myself; I had a couple of sons and a family back there waiting for me.

I was scared, but I don't think I acted scared. Instead, I just did my job alongside my Teammates. Fortunately, we all got out in good fashion. My platoon never lost anyone in combat. Though one person was badly wounded—by accident of all things.

We had captured a village chief or some kind of important VCI character. Taking our prisoner away in a sampan, we had the chief secured with plastic riot cuffs in the boat as we were paddling away. The village chief managed to break loose of his handcuffs, which were secured behind his back. And he tried to make a break for it over the side of the sampan.

As the village chief suddenly went over the side, the Teammate who was assigned to keep the prisoner covered swung his weapon around onto him. But as the prisoner went over the side, the light sampan rocked violently from side to side. Our Teammate went rolling over onto his back, his feet rising into the air, as he tried to fire. And he managed to nail himself right in the foot.

So that was the worst injury of our deployment. While the rest of the guys dealt with the prisoner, I treated our wounded Teammate. Though his wound probably wasn't nearly as bad as the razzing he would be getting for some time to come.

There was never any conflict for me personally in my being both an operating SEAL and a corpsman. When it was time to fight, I could use my weapon to kill. When there was a need for my other skills, I would work hard to help heal.

Periodically, we would have what we called downtime. That was when we would get in out of the field and not have any operations scheduled for a while. During this time, I had three or four guys within the platoon who just loved going out with me to the surrounding villages on what were called "Medcaps." During a Medcap visit, we would do whatever we could for the children, the women, whoever needed medical attention.

Illnesses and diseases didn't care that there was a shooting war going on, and we would treat these maladies as best we could. That work was rewarding as well.

On one particular Medcap, up one of the canals in IV Corps, we pulled into a little village and started taking out the candy we had brought for the kids. The villagers began coming out, and through one of the Team interpreters we had brought with us, we explained what we were trying to do. All we did was tell them we were there to help in any way that we could. Anyone in need of medication or treatments for sores, or anything else, would get it.

The villagers liked what we were offering, and the people just started swarming around like they were coming out of the woodwork. They needed what we had and we were glad to give it. That work was just something we could thoroughly enjoy.

What we didn't know was that there was someone in that village passing information along to the VC. This enemy informer would tell them just what we were doing and who we were doing it for. After we left, there would be retributions against the village as a whole and also specifically against some of the people we had treated.

All we had been trying to do was help the local people, just do a job that didn't cost anyone anything. And here there was someone who would rat on them and just make their lives that much more miserable. And things were done and said to make us look like the bad guys to the villagers. And instead of good, we would bring down more harm on those people we were trying to help.

The situation was a perplexing one, and we were caught in the middle. The question was whether we should continue conducting our Medcaps or just wash our hands of it. What finally came about was that we had to be a lot more selective as to how we medically treated the locals.

In my opinion, the Vietnamese people were really under a gun, literally, during that war. They didn't know who they could turn to for help. If they turned to the Americans, they would be persecuted by the Viet Cong and the North Vietnamese. And if they turned to them, we wouldn't be getting any assistance from them and they'd just make a target of themselves from our side. There just wasn't any simple answer for them.

I'm sure that there are some misconceptions about just who the Navy SEALs were back in the Vietnam days, and what our job was about. None of the men I worked with during my thirteen years in the Teams appeared like the Rambo of the movies. In fact, there was no standard kind of SEAL. Everybody was different.

There were times when everybody would have the macho, get-up-and-go attitude of taking the war to the enemy. And there were also times when these same men could hold a baby in their arms with obvious tenderness. These men who could sit in a swamp silently for days also loved going out on a picnic with a bunch of their kids. SEALs are human, and no different from anyone else in all that being human means.

A man in the Teams has just been trained to do a particular, and difficult, job. And we do that job to the best of our abilities. When it's over, we go back to being family men.

A SEAL Team is effective because it's a close-knit group. When it comes time to do a job, there may be differences between the men of a platoon or team. But those differences are put aside for the greater good. The job gets done, and you don't often hear of a job that was given to a SEAL platoon or SEAL Team that doesn't get done. When I think of the Teams, that's the word that comes to mind first—"team." There's no one person in the SEALs; there's a group of people working together. "Team" is a big word, and it's a big group of individuals who come together to make us a SEAL Team. We can work as individuals on an assignment, but we can also come together as a cohesive unit and accomplish anything.

Greg McPartlin, Hospital Corpsman, Second Class

My enlistment in the Navy began in June 1967, when I started boot camp at the Great Lakes Naval Training Center just north of Chicago.

SEAL Team One, Alfa Platoon prior to deploying to Vietnam. Kneeling on the far right in the front row is Greg McPartlin, the platoon's corpsman.

Greg McPartlin Collection

It was interesting just how I settled on the Navy as the service I would be in. My brother Fred was an A4 pilot in the Marine Corps and had already seen action in Chu Lai, Vietnam. Originally, I was going to play football for Notre Dame, but when my scholarship was turned in to Parsegian by Terry Brennan, it was just lost in the shuffle when a large influx of players came in from the South Side of Chicago.

Since I was already classified 1A by the draft board, I figured I would go ahead and rush up to the Marine Corps recruiter in Waukegan, go over to Vietnam as a Marine, and take care of my brother's ass. But when I drove up to the recruiting center in an ambulance, the recruiter had other ideas.

At the time I was earning my living as an ambulance driver in Lake Forest, Illinois. The recruiter asked me just why I was there to join the Marines. When I told him I wanted to be with my brother, he told me there was a real need for hospital corpsmen. Okay, I'll be a Marine hospital corpsman, I told him.

Then he floored me a bit. Pointing across the room, the recruiter told me I had to talk to another recruiter in the office. When I saw who he was pointing at, my immediate comment was "But that guy's a squid!"

But the Marine recruiter promised me that it would be in my enlistment contract that I would go directly to the Marine Corps from hospital corpsman school. He said they would put it in writing, so I believed him.

The Navy supplied the corpsmen for the Marine Corps, so I soon found myself in the Navy, now a squid myself. And just like it said in my contract, after I finished corps school, I went right on to field med school and then was assigned to the Third Marine Force Recon at Camp Lejeune. Arriving in time to be sent over to Vietnam for the Tet offensive of 1968. During the heavy fighting, most of my platoon was either hospitalized or killed. So we were rotated back to the States early.

When I was being interviewed about a new assignment, my detailer asked me if I could swim. Not knowing where the man was going with his question, but having had my fill of Marine Corps life, I told the man that I could walk on water if it would get me out of the Marines. And I quickly found myself volunteering for a new assignment.

The powers that be put me in a new program called special operations technician. It was for hospital corpsmen and was in Key West, Florida, where we would be trained to be SEAL operators. Back during the Vietnam era—at least the early part of it—corpsmen were still considered noncombatants. That was kind of a holdover from World War II and Korea, where the corpsman only carried a sidearm for his own and his patient's protection. Those corpsmen never operated as straight infantry types.

The rules in force at the time that I was serving precluded any corpsmen from attending UDTR because of the demolitions and weapons phases of training. So the Teams had to get their corpsmen from the fleet, and that wasn't too appealing to the operators in the UDT and SEAL community, since they wanted men with a little more specialized training. So the program in Florida was started as an addition to the underwater swimmers' school in order to give corpsmen the necessary additional training.

The program in Florida consisted of a lot of physical-fitness training, a lot of diving and underwater swimming, and small-unit work. After the rest of the UDT trainees from the East Coast left—they had been there for the underwater-swimmer-school portion of the training—the rest of us continued with instruction in diving medicine and field medicine.

Getting to the special operations technicians' school wasn't just a matter of my volunteering for it. I had to take a number of tests to qualify. The training was tough; nineteen corpsmen began the program and only four of us graduated. And this was where I learned about the UDTs, how they picked up the Mercury and Gemini space capsules as well as conducted the same missions as they did during World War II. The SEAL Teams were completely unknown to me; their operations were still listed as secret.

After we finished special operations technicians' training in Key West, we were sent up to Lakehurst, New Jersey, for parachute training at the Navy school there. Now I was a corpsman, underwater swimmer, and jump-qualified. Finally, they assigned me to UDT 21 in Little Creek, Virginia, late in 1968. The UDTs were also short of corpsmen, so I ended up operating with both UDT 21 and UDT 22 out of Little Creek. This meant that I pulled two deployments in a row, both of them UDT winter deployments to Roosevelt Roads, Puerto Rico.

By the time I returned from Puerto Rico, it was May 1969. One of my counterpart corpsmen with the West Coast Teams had been killed just the month before in Vietnam. My XO at the time, Fred Kochey, called me in to his office and told me that I was going over to the SEAL Team. I told him that wasn't a problem and I would go and get my gear. Then he told me that the Team I would be going to was SEAL Team One.

"What?" I said. "SEAL Team One, Hollywood UDT? You're going to send me over to those guys?"

Apparently he was. There was a pretty good rivalry between the East Coast and the West Coast Teams. But I wasn't going to be able to change anything. They transferred me to Coronado, California, in May 1969.

Arriving in Coronado was kind of interesting. First of all, I was a numerical replacement for Alfa Platoon, which was already in pre-deployment training. Dick Wolfe, a corpsman who was later killed in Vietnam, met me at the SEAL Team One headquarters and said, "Gosh, Greg, you're so lucky. You get to deploy in September. In fact, your platoon's out in Niland right now undergoing training."

It was all of late June, so in a few months I was going back to Vietnam. But Coronado had their Fourth of July parade coming up, and since I was free-fall-qualified, I was going to be part of the demonstration team for the show. This resulted in my going out to the platoon with there only being a little over a month of predeployment training left.

When I arrived at the platoon, what I hadn't expected was the cold-shoulder routine I received from the guys. They thought I was just some guy coming right off a ship. It was about 114 degrees out at Niland, the SEAL Team One training area out in the California desert near the Salton Sea. Sitting there in my greens, holding my orders, I was sweating from the heat. The lieutenant finally reached over and took my orders from me. As he was reading over my records, he called over the platoon's leading chief petty officer.

The lieutenant proceeded to explain to the LCPO that I had already been to Vietnam, that I spoke the language, and had more than just the experience they would expect someone straight from the fleet to bring with them.

So the situation improved a bit right there. Within a month Alfa Platoon was ready to go, and I had adapted fine. There was some minor question about outfitting me properly as a SEAL corpsman. The platoon found out that my shooting skills weren't up to their level. And it didn't look like I was going to improve a whole lot really quickly. They issued me a Stoner light machine gun. I think they wanted to be sure that I would remain a good corpsman and be surgically correct on all of my shots.

Basically, they didn't want to trust me with any less firepower. With a Stoner, I could put out a whole lot of rounds very quickly. The fact that I missed every few rounds didn't matter much when I could put out a few hundred rounds at a time.

They didn't even hold my having been a Marine against me. In fact, they thought it might have been some good training.

Since I was already familiar with being in-country in Vietnam, going over with Alfa Platoon held no real surprises for me. It had only been about a year and a half since I had been on the soggy shores of Vietnam. Now I was a seasoned combat veteran, an old man with all of twenty years of living behind me.

When I arrived in Saigon, the first thing that hit me was the smell. No matter how many movies they come out with, they will never duplicate that smell of rice paddies, muddy river water, and the ocean. All of it overlaid with the odors of the jungle and decaying organic matter.

We settled down in a little base in IV Corps, right there on the water, a floating base on the river called SEAFLOAT. Our platoon saw action right away, beginning with our first operation. That proved to be a forerunner for the other SEAL platoons that would be following us. We had both good ops and bad ones. Some people were lost and we raised a lot of havoc with the enemy's troops.

One of the things I tried to teach everyone in both of Alfa's squads was enough first aid to keep me alive in case I was hit. If someone else was hit, it was okay as long as I was there to help them. Most of the guys were always very cool and very calm. My previous experience in Vietnam had made me used to the situations that arise in combat. Most of the rest of the platoon had a combat tour behind them and they operated with a tremendous amount of poise and presence of mind.

If somebody was wounded and went down, the platoon immediately set up a perimeter around the wounded man and me. Then a medevac would be called up for an immediate extraction of the wounded. My job was to take care of the casualty, and I concentrated on that while my Teammates did their jobs.

Fortunately, in Alfa Platoon, not one of us was ever seriously hurt. There was an incident in October '69 where another SEAL platoon walked into our ambush. Their officer, Lieutenant (j.g) David Nicholas, was killed along with their scouts.

That terrible day was Alfa Platoon's breaking-in op for the deployment. Lieutenant Nicholas stood up to try and stop the firing when his platoon walked into our ambush site, and it cost him his life. I worked on him for forty-five minutes, until I almost passed out from heat exhaustion myself. But there was nothing that could be done.

A squad of SEALs move ashore from their insertion boat. They are operating in Kien Hoa Province, fifty miles southwest of Saigon.

The incident was investigated and no one was found to be at fault. The loss was chalked up to the fog of war that takes place so often in combat. But the loss did shatter the morale of both platoons. Captain Dave Schaible came over to SEAFLOAT and we all went through extensive debreifings. From that incident, we learned that you don't separate units in the field and have them walk toward each other; the chances of killing your own man are just too great. The technique is called a hammer-and-anvil ambush, and it immediately fell out of favor in the Teams.

But not everything we did involved carrying a weapon and dropping the bad guys. Part of the old cliché—that we were over there to win the hearts and minds of the peasants—was something I helped work on directly. We would go into villages that were controlled by the Viet Cong. You always knew they were Viet Cong villages because by the time you went in there, there would be no men around, just the elderly, women, and children.

Unarmed, I would go in wearing just a plain green uniform, no cammies. A couple of boat-unit guys would usually be with me for my security. The area we were in was south of the U-Minh Forest. Usually, the old folks would come up to us first and start talking in French. These people hadn't seen a round-eye since the French were there back in the 1950s.

With my stethoscope around my neck, and a tongue depressor in my pocket, I would be called Bac Si, *Vietnamese for "Doctor," by the villagers. We came bearing gifts for the children—candy, small toys, that kind of thing.*

Besides treating the locals for whatever ailments and injuries they had, we also gathered information. We could ask a child where their father was, what he was doing, who or what they might be afraid of, things like that. And the answers could tell us a lot about VC activity in the area.

After a few trips into the same area, the kids would get all excited about our showing up as soon as they saw the boat. And the best intel you could get came from little children; they didn't know how to lie about politics and the war.

The villagers would receive Phisohex [antibacterial] soap, vaccinations, bandages, and antibiotics. A lot of my time was spent with the midwives in an area. Whenever they were having a problem with a birth, they would send a message up to SEAFLOAT and I would come down to help. In my two tours, I probably assisted in 150 births. During one incident, I even performed a C-section to save the life of the child and the mother. I may be the only Navy corpsman to have performed that operation during the Vietnam War.

That woman had been in labor almost thirty-six hours. I had asked for permission to bring her back to SEAFLOAT, but the "black-shoe" [regular Navy] officer at the time said that I couldn't bring her aboard. Instead, he wanted me to send her to the nearest Vietnamese hospital, a three-day journey by sampan. Both the woman and the child would have been dead long before they ever got to the local hospital.

So I went into the village during the early evening. That was when the VC were operating, so a squad of SEALs went along with me. The operation was satisfactory, the baby and the mother were saved, and my CO congratulated me in the morning for delivering a new VC. I think I received a Navy Commendation for that.

Several days later I was on an ambush where I was in a position to fire on three VC who were moving in on us. I gave them a chance to surrender, but they weren't having any of that. So I ended up killing all three. Later I received the Bronze Star for my part in that operation. The joke among my Teammates was that I received a Bronze Star for killing three VC and a Navy Comp for saving one.

So when Admiral King was giving out the awards after we were back from that tour, I spoke up about the incident. Captain Schaible knew I was going to do it, but when I received my Navy Commendation medal, I didn't say anything. But when Admiral King pinned the Bronze Star on me, I spoke up asking if that medal meant I was up one and down three, or down one and up three. He never got the joke, and Schaible just shook his head at the whole thing.

Corpsmen did a lot of humanitarian actions, both during Vietnam and elsewhere. Only in the Teams you did your actions usually with a weapon in your hands. The SEAL Teams consist of many different rates [jobs] from the ranks of the Navy. The only man in his rate who is certain to work in that job is the hospital corpsman. Boatswain's mates, gunner's mates, enginemen—they all work as an operator in a platoon.

A hospital corpsman is going to be called on to use all of the skills he has been taught. A good corpsman will be a preacher, mortician, and savior. But in the Teams, a corpsman is also going to be a fighter.

Separating these two jobs—that of a fighter and that of a healer—is not real easy. But much of the ability to do this comes from the basic philosophy of the men of the Teams. SEALs do not fight for their country; we fight for each other. We don't care what the politicians back in Saigon or Washington might have been saying. When you were in the field and the bullets were flying, it didn't matter what Nixon might have been saying—you fought for the man on either side of you. And that was all that mattered to me.

When a Teammate was hurt, then it was the corpsman's job to get him out. But the corpsman is also responsible to see to it that he doesn't get killed getting that wounded man out of danger. No corpsman did anyone any good by being a hero and running out into the middle of a fire-fight to save a man only to be killed before he got two steps. That's no help to anyone.

For myself, I always tried to assess the situation. And that was also why I carried a big gun. I could go out and lay down a base of fire and do what was necessary to get to my patient. And if that meant I had to let him bleed while I helped the squad suppress the incoming fire, that was just how it was.

We operated in very small units. In a big fire-fight, every weapon counted. Of course our hope every day was that each one of us would

Greg McPartlin (upper left) prepares to sling his Stoner Mk 23 machine gun as he and his Teammates move through the tall grass to approach an extraction helicopter. Greg was struck moments later by a single enemy bullet.

Greg McPartlin Collection

make it back from an op. And during that six-month tour, we all did get out alive, and we still got our job done. Though we did get dinged once or twice.

The only trouble with being a hospital corpsman in the SEALs is when you're hit and call out "Doc!" Then nobody knows what to do and all of your Teammates forget all of their medical training.

During one operation, I took a hit in the arm. It wasn't a bad wound at all; it wasn't even worth the Purple Heart they gave me. But it did hurt like hell, and I still have the scar to remind me. After I was hit, suddenly I had two guys wanting to give me morphine, and one guy trying to start an IV in my arm.

Here I was, already with a wounded man in my arms, holding an IV in my teeth leading down to the patient, and I take a bullet in the

Wearing a SEAL/UDT blue and gold T-shirt, Greg McPartlin poses for the camera while holding an M3A1 submachine gun. The bandage on his upper right arm covers the wound he received during an extraction.

Greg McPartlin Collection

upper arm. There was just this trickle of blood down my right arm as we headed for the medevac bird.

By the time we got on the bird, three guys were trying to give me morphine and two were setting up IVs. And a third was trying to strap a tourniquet onto my right arm and damned near twisted it down to the bone. As he twisted the tourniquet tight with his knife, I started losing the feeling in my right hand. The medevac took me to the hospital, where they put in some forty stitches to seal up my wound, and it got me away from my Teammates before they turned me into a one-armed morphine addict swollen up from too many IV drips.

It was just that my Teammates liked me so much. The good thing about being the corpsman in the SEAL Team was that it made you a cumshaw artist. A good corpsman can get his hands on anything, and everything, he needs. Like in the movie The Green Berets, the medic got everything. We had control of the shot records, the brandy, the pills. So we were usually pretty well respected by everyone in the platoon. Not even a big tough SEAL likes to have his shot [inoculation] records mishandled and end up having to go through all those needle sticks again.

But as a SEAL corpsman, I also had a Stoner light machine gun. The hardware the Teams have today, as I have seen on static dis-

A fully camouflaged SEAL demonstrates the weapons used by the Teams in Vietnam. On the table in front of him are (from left to right) a China Lake modified Ithaca shotgun with an extended magazine and duck-bill choke. Then there is an M79 grenade launcher, an M166A1 rifle, a bolt action heavy barrel sniper rifle, and a pump-action 4-shot 40mm grenade launcher. In front of the SEAL is an M60 light machine gun and he is holding up an M16A1 rifle with an XM148 40mm grenade launcher mounted underneath the barrel. The SEAL has slid the barrel of the XM1448 launcher forward for loading as part of his demonstration.

U.S. Navy

plays, is light-years ahead of what we worked with then. But there's still nothing that they've come up with that's better than the Stoner, in my opinion.

The Stoner Mark 23 light machine gun was the deadliest weapon that you could have in a close firefight—up to maybe 100 to 200 meters' range. That's true if you kept it clean and it was used properly. The Stoner fell out of favor as they became worn and the guys played around with them. Pulling off the stock and putting on a short barrel does not make it a pistol, but guys would try and handle it like one.

My point man would take his stockless Stoner and try to hit a target, and end up shooting up the sky. Then my platoon leader would call out, "Doc, get 'em," and I would track in on my target while it was crossing a rice paddy. You just took aim and the Stoner made targets go away. The bullets would just walk in on a target and make a big shield in front of you. The rounds from a Stoner were absolutely lethal.

A Stoner could fire at a rate of up to 1,000 rounds per minute and held a box of 100 or 150 rounds underneath it. You could change a box of ammo in about fifteen seconds. A Stoner would just scare the dickens out of anybody.

One time, when we were coming in on a helo, we started taking some ground fire. A Navy lieutenant was on board the bird carrying some orders from Ben Thuy. As we flew along, I saw these green tracers start coming up from the ground. The lieutenant was sitting on the door gunner's flak jacket, while I was just wearing my blue-and-gold T-shirt, swim trunks, and coral shoes.

As those tracers started to rise, I pulled up my Stoner and cocked back the bolt. As I looked out the side of the bird, the door gunner pointed out the spot where the tracers were coming from. So I pointed down with my Stoner and pulled the trigger. The lieutenant managed to be just in the spot where my weapon was ejecting its hot, empty brass.

Then we were past the target and out of danger. The pilot refused to go back to let me shoot some more. The lieutenant, his nice, starched and pressed uniform a bit sweat-soaked now, didn't want to go. When I told him that it was the enemy shooting at us and we could shoot back, he said his orders had to go through. So that ended my Stoner fun for that trip.

We didn't always treat officers with such a lack of discipline; sometimes we were worse.

There was one time when carrying a Stoner didn't play to my advantage very well. Admiral Elmo Zumwalt was the COMNAVFORV (Commander, Naval Forces, Vietnam) in 1969 and he paid a visit to SEAFLOAT. He had with him a reporter, who has since become a big-time anchorman, and a small entourage of news types. According to our base security, this group of reporters basically had carte blanche to go anywhere they wanted.

A group of us were coming off an all-night ambush where we had made contact. It had been a long night, as our boat crew had been shot up pretty badly. For myself, I smelled pretty bad, had already been doing CPR on one of our guys, and one of our three prisoners was seriously wounded. So things were kind of in disarray. Needless to say, we were all hungry, tired, cold, and dirty.

When we entered the mess hall, there were tablecloths laid out on everything. Guys with gold braid up and down their arms were running all around. Salutes were being given and returned. Not at all what our normal SOP looked like on SEAFLOAT. Gold braid and salutes can mark you as a target big time in a combat zone.

We were all coming back and just beginning to wrap up what we had to do. I had just finished securing a prisoner in the SEAL Team area when I left the compartment and ran right into a cameraman. When he asked me what I was doing, I told him that I was just putting some prisoners away and that he wasn't supposed to be in that area.

Like so many other reporters, he continued with his questions. He asked me if I was a SEAL, then asked me my rate. I told him my rank instead and he insisted on knowing what my rate was. When I finally told him I was a hospital corpsman, he just lost all expression in his face.

Then he asked me what it was I was carrying slung from my shoulder. Continuing my "dumb little me" routine, I told him it was my first-aid kit. He wanted to know what was on my other shoulder, so I told him it was my Stoner, my machine gun.

"Isn't it against the Geneva Convention for a medic to carry a weapon?" he asked. "Shouldn't you have a helmet with a red cross?"

With that last stupid line from him, all the fun went out of the situation and I just about lost my temper. Stepping right up into his face, I told him in some graphic detail just what he could do with his Aqua Velva–smelling fat ass and that he should immediately leave our area before he saw what a Stoner could really do.

Just about then, one of Admiral Zumwalt's aides came around and saved that reporter. I was also told that I probably wouldn't be the PR man for the SEALs anymore. And I didn't have much of a problem with that.

All of us tried to answer questions about our rates, or anything else really, as little as possible. There were people out and about who didn't know who we were, and we liked to keep it that way. And there were some who were quite jealous of us when they did know who we were.

At that time in Vietnam, the SEALs had pretty much all of the good deals. My mom never had to send me canned turkey for Christmas or Thanksgiving. We never went without steak, beer, or cigarettes when we wanted them. Even that day I ran into the reporter, we had our steaks.

Coming in from an operation, we cleaned our weapons before we cleaned up ourselves. The day that I ran into the reporter, we followed our usual procedure, but something got between us and our postoperation showers.

We could smell these steaks cooking, and being as hungry as we were, the smell was very tempting. Going up to the back door of the chow hall, we asked if we could get something to eat. The cook had no problem with that and we tramped into the chow hall, dirty camouflage uniforms, muddy boots, general aroma of the swamp, and all.

Some clown came up and asked if we would mind waiting until the officers came in and ate first. That didn't go over very well. Dave Langlois, one of the guys in our squad, had a few choice words with the gentleman who wanted us to wait. And with that, the individual left the chow hall to tell the aide, who in turn passed the message on to the admiral that the SEALs were in the chow hall.

The thing was, Admiral Zumwalt loved the SEALs. So he came into the chow hall and went around introducing himself to everyone. Things were pretty jovial and relaxed. The guys all shook his hand and said hello, but we were all a lot more interested in the food right then. We hadn't eaten in a day and the smells had raised our appetites quite a bit.

Then Admiral Zumwalt, COMNAVFORV, the boss of every U.S. naval asset in Vietnam, met Dave Langlois.

"Hello," Admiral Zumwalt said to Dave. "What's your name?"

"Dave," Langlois replied. "What's yours?"

Not taken aback a bit, Admiral Zumwalt answered, "Elmo."

"Hey," Dave said, shaking the admiral's hand, "how yah doing, Elmo? You gonna eat with us?"

With that invitation, Admiral Elmo Zumwalt sat down and ate

---

lunch with the SEALs he thought so much of. And his aides waited nervously, hovering about the chow hall while we had our steaks.

Admiral Zumwalt's son was one of the boat drivers at SEAFLOAT. So the admiral made periodic visits down to our neck of the woods. Some years later Admiral Zumwalt felt personally responsible for losing his son to cancer. Our operational area around SEAFLOAT was heavily defoliated with Agent Orange and that later cost Elmo Jr. his life.

But Admiral Zumwalt has kept in touch with us over the years. And he still remembers eating lunch with that "colorful" bunch of SEALs at SEAFLOAT.

The camaraderie of the Teams then just can't be duplicated today. It's a solid example of the fact that you just can't go home again, things change. Back in 1969, 1970, the Teams were small, not much more than a few hundred of us total in the whole Navy. Each man knew almost every member of his Team. And we all took it very personally when we lost one of our own. And we celebrated with such zeal that we became famous for some of our antics.

Unfortunately, that reputation for hard partying has cost the SEAL community on occasion. Out at Niland, in the desert east of San Diego, we had our training camp. This training camp wasn't quite completed in 1970–71. We had a warrant officer by the name of Jess Tolison who was in charge of the camp. As one of Tolison's instructors, I would spend two weeks out at the camp and one week back in Coronado.

In the fall of 1971, we were ordered to build a pop-up range out at the Niland camp. Pop-up targets can react to bullet impacts and they can be electronically held down only to pop up again when a button is pushed. This lets classes run small-unit tactics and react to targets, knocking them down, as they patrol along.

Doctors back then had a different way of dealing with the high heat of the desert than we do now. Instead of the hydration that is done today, we dealt with the heat by taking salt tablets to replace the minerals lost through sweat. Instead, we should have been replacing the water lost. But the tablets were what was prescribed at that time.

One day, we had been working on the pop-up range for some twelve or fourteen hours. It was hot, sweaty work. Going into a small *local town, we had dinner after work. Myself, Frank Bomar, Jess Tolison, and a number of other instructors were just relaxing a bit.*

After dinner, Mr. Tolison said he was going to drive out to the camp and pick up several of the students who were still straggling along out there. Chief Bomar said he and I would go out in my car and meet up with Mr. Tolison later. About fifteen minutes later Frank Bomar and I had finished off the pitcher of beer we were sharing and headed out along the twisting road to camp.

We came around the curve near the camp and spotted the camp's six-by truck up ahead of us lying upside down. I grabbed up my medical kit and a flashlight and went up to the truck. There were no students in the back of the vehicle, but Mr. Tolison was trapped in the front cab, and he was severely injured.

Frank went back to get help. Mr. Tolison's injuries were so severe that just seeing them made me sick to my stomach. Because I vomited by the side of the road, some beer was left on the ground. When the state highway patrol came out and saw Mr. Tolison and the state of the car, and then got a whiff of the smell, they immediately jumped to the wrong conclusion.

They thought we had been partying pretty hard that night. And I couldn't convince them that we had just been coming back from dinner where a bunch of us had drunk nothing more than a few beers. And they wouldn't believe that Mr. Tolison hadn't had anything to drink at all.

Jess Tolison had been killed when that truck rolled over on the curve. The state police put in their report that the accident was alcohol-related. That was never the case that day. When I got back to the Team area, I told Captain Frank Kaine that the accident had certainly not been alcohol-related. But the state police even used a picture of the truck from that accident to illustrate how alcohol could kill.

That situation sent me a little bit ballistic. Our commanding officer at the time was not giving me a lot of support. The situation had left the hands of the SEAL community and others were making their own statements about it. But Mr. Tolison's friends and family should know that he never did anything wrong that day. Jess Tolison was a highly decorated SEAL with some five tours to Vietnam to his credit.

My CO got upset with my stance on that situation. And I pretty much just told him where to go. And he had the last word—he was going to send me out of the SEAL Team. But serving in the SEALs was strictly voluntary, so I told him that I was done. There wasn't a lot of time before my enlistment was up anyway, so I went over to UDT 13 for the few days it took to put my paperwork through.

Though we did party hearty, Mr. Tolison did not lose his life in an alcohol-related incident. The loyalties that built up during service with a SEAL Team did not come lightly. There wasn't one of us who wouldn't have laid his life down for his Teammate. And we might face a life and death situation every day. There is no "I" in SEAL Team; we were all members of the same family, the same Team.

That camaraderie is what makes the reunions and associations of the older SEALs so important for the SEAL Teams of today to see and experience. In today's Navy, there are thousands of SEALs. A member of the Teams today just doesn't have the opportunity to meet and know everyone today as he might have in the past.

And this is where McP's Irish Pub in Coronado comes into play a bit. This is a place where everyone in the Teams has a chance to meet Teammates from the past and the present, East Coast and West Coast.

In 1982, I was tired of the real estate business and I bought a bar in Coronado—now McP's Irish Pub and Grill at 1107 Orange Avenue. When the place opened in 1982, it was not the "kinder and gentler" military people speak of now. We had the Marines coming in from one base, and the SEALs coming in from another area, and the regular black-shoe Navy guys coming in from all over.

Boys being boys, the mix at McP's turned into a scuffle now and then. So I put up a Trident on the wall and told everyone that I was a former SEAL. More and more of the old Team guys came in. Gradually, we've become world famous as a watering hole of the SEALs in Coronado. From the time they're done with training until they retire as an admiral, you'll find SEALs dropping in at McP's. But the instructors won't let the students come up to my place until after they graduate.

A Navy SEAL today is probably the smartest, strongest of mind and fittest of body, young man who's ever come out of high school or college. Back when I became a Navy SEAL, the joke was that we were the ones who forgot and just stood there while everyone else stepped back when the call went out for volunteers. The SEAL of the 1960s is different from the SEALs of today, with two exceptions, and those are the physical fitness and the endurance.

But it doesn't matter whether you were a Navy SEAL, UDT operator, Marine Recon, or Army Special Forces, from then or now, we all put our pants on one leg at a time. There's a fair amount of teasing and good-natured ribbing between the services, and even among the SEALs of the different coasts, but there is an inherent camaraderie as well.

Back when the SEALs were first starting, they received a lot of their training from the U.S. Army Special Forces. And the SEALs gave a lot of the initial swimming training to the Marine Force Recon outfits. Today, the missions overlap so much that the lines between the units can get pretty blurred. We are all fellow warriors.

The men I served with in the Teams are probably the finest individuals I have ever known in my entire life. Unfortunately, after serving in the Teams, we all went our separate ways. The reunions help us catch up, but we sometimes don't stay as close as we should. But the guys I worked with are never far from my mind.

We gather sometimes just by chance, which is one of the great advantages I have in owning McP's. And then we'll rehash the old stories. And I'm sure some of the new kids are tired of hearing the same old lines from the dinosaurs of the Teams.

But the history of the SEALs is important if only for one reason. And that is to try and set straight some of the myths about the rootin'-tootin', rape and pillaging snake eaters of the Teams. These men are intelligent and hardworking. The men of the Teams today are doing one heck of a job of putting themselves in harm's way every day.

Far from what can ever be shown in books or on television, these guys are doing stuff around the world that just isn't for us to know about. They are out there on the sharp end, and talking about what they do, even generally, could increase the danger they face.

Popular fiction, TV shows, and movies portray a SEAL that isn't like the men I knew in the past or see today in the Teams. The term "Rambo" has been thrown around for years and refers to a loaner, a man who accomplishes anything by himself. That's just something that's made up; it's a fantasy. There is no such thing as a Rambo in the Teams, and there never will be. There just isn't a place for someone who will not make himself part of the Teams and work together with his Teammates.

There are some men from all the branches of the military who served during the Vietnam era who didn't fare well in civilian life. From what I've seen, most of the SEALs were just the opposite. The men of the Teams were not "Saigon cowboys." They saw things and did things that were very fierce and more than a little scary. But you don't see them sitting on a street homeless, crying their eyes out. Most of them have done very well on the outside. Partly because you never completely leave the Teams behind. They become a part of you.

As a corpsman, I could be in the middle of a firefight and suddenly have a man down. Once I knew my other guys had me covered, the perimeter was secured, and they had a base of fire laid down, then I was in on the wounded man. I just wouldn't see or hear anything else; I didn't have to. If a bad guy was to come up and kill me, it would be because my other Teammates didn't protect me, and that just wouldn't happen while they were alive.

All I was concerned with was getting the wounded man stable and assessing his situation. The combat would be taken care of. It's scary at first when you look back on it. But when your adrenaline gets flowing, just your job becomes important. I could see and hear my patient, and nothing else.

When I operated with my Teammates, my level of confidence was so high that I thought I was a neurosurgeon and all of my Teammates were Superman. There's was nothing I wouldn't do to save a life in that situation. Sometimes, I may have screwed up a bit, but I always gave it my best. My Teammates deserved no less.

There was nothing I was ever scared of when I had my other guys around me.

The stigma a corpsman has to overcome right away is that he's not as good as everyone else because he doesn't have a BUD/S-class number. I graduated as a special operations technician at the same time that Class 45 did. We were trained to be operators; we couldn't have functioned in the field otherwise. The only thing we were lacking in our training was a formal Hell Week, and they *really made up for that in Key West, during the demolition phase of training.*

Honestly, if I had had to go through regular BUD/S training, I don't know if I'd have graduated or not. I don't know if I'd have had that desire to continue that you just have to feel. I had already been to Vietnam with the Marines before I joined the Teams. But I do know that I was a good operator and I was a hell of a good corpsman for the Teams.

As a corpsman, I felt capable of doing anything my three books would have allowed me to do. Those books are the PDR [Physician's Desk Reference], the Merck Manual, *and* Current Therapy. *Even for a doctor, if it isn't in those three books, chances are you don't need to do it.*

■ Chapter 13

TO BRING THEM HOME: BRIGHT LIGHT AND THE POWS

The SEALs in Vietnam were in a unique position to take immediate advantage of any intelligence that came their way. Using their own intelligence networks, as well as information brought to them from other sources, the SEALs could quickly put together as complete a picture as possible of a given target. And with their experience, organization, and support, the SEALs could react to a sudden target faster than any other U.S. military organization.

Within hours of confirming a target, a SEAL leader could assemble his operating unit, support, transportation, and communications. Authorization for an operation was often not needed for some of the SEALs' operational areas. This let the SEALs react to some of the hardest, and to some the most important, targets of the Vietnam War—the rescue of POWs.

Though no U.S. POWs were ever successfully rescued from enemy

In a haunting illustration of the Vietnam War, this exhibit was set up in the Pentagon. Depicted is the environment of a North Vietnamese prison cell where 178 Navy men spent up to eight and one-half years in captivity. Thirty-six of these men died while imprisoned, and almost all of the POWs suffered regular torture. The small oval lumps are roaches, the larger one to the left is a rat.

U.S. Navy

hands during the war, the SEALs conducted a number of operations that released South Vietnamese prisoners, some of whom had been held in horrible conditions for extended lengths of time.

The small size of the SEALs' operational units gave them the speed to act on fragile, time-sensitive information. Any SEAL in Vietnam would drop everything in order to go on a POW op. The power of the desire to release fellow soldiers held by the VC or NVA is something only someone who has been in combat can completely understand.

On several occasions, the SEALs put together swift yet complex operations to liberate POWs. The U.S. military considered the POW issue so important that they eventually gave the POW liberation missions their own code name—BRIGHT LIGHT.

In addition to operating in very small, independent units, the SEALs and the UDTs worked as part of much larger operations. One of these missions was the rescue of American POWs held in North Vietnam. It was a huge and involved operation, cloaked in secrecy. But every effort was worth the cost as far as the men on the ground were concerned, the Teams among them.

Philip L. "Moki" Martin, Lieutenant, USN (Ret.)

When I was about five or six years old, growing up in Hawaii, I remember seeing the UDTs training off of Maui, blowing up the old concrete obstacles. There were several men I got to know just briefly who told me that if I was ever to join the Navy, the job they did was what I would want to do.

My entire life has been spent in the water. I began scuba diving after only five minutes of instruction and enjoyed it right away. It was the Richard Widmark movie The Frogmen that pretty much sealed up my adult life. I was only about ten or twelve years old, but after seeing that movie, I knew that being a Frogman was what I wanted to do.

A few years later my plan was to enlist in the Navy right after graduating from high school. Once in the Navy, I would volunteer for the UDT, and that was exactly what happened, though it took a little longer than I would have liked. I enlisted in the Navy in 1960, and it took me about four years before I received orders for UDT Replacement training (UDTR). I was assigned to Class 35, and we began training in January 1965.

My sole intention in volunteering for the Teams back then was to join the UDTs. The SEAL Teams were new at the time and very little was known about them. There had been some very brief articles about them in the Navy's All Hands magazine and almost nowhere else. The SEALs were kind of a super-secret thing, and supposedly they carried guns and crawled around in the mud. That wasn't what I wanted to do. I wanted to be a Frogman. That had been my goal and my dream for a long time.

UDTR training was fairly easy for me—in the water. Having practically grown up in the sea, I was a very good and powerful swimmer. Handling the surf was nothing new; I had been surfing for years. And being from Hawaii, I hated the cold water. So I became a much faster swimmer than I had been, just to stay warm.

It was my dislike of the cold water that made me the fastest swimmer in the class. Moving hard and fast just helped keep me warm. But there were a couple of times when I outdistanced my swim buddies, swam off and left them behind. That wasn't something that was allowed in the Teams, and the instructors had ways of dealing with it.

Barry Enoch was one of Class 35's instructors. And when I left my swim buddy behind on one swim, he dealt with my transgression. He had a rope, a really heavy one, that was about five feet long and had loops at each end. Instructor Enoch looped one end of the rope around my neck, and the other end around my swim buddy's neck. Now if I wanted to outswim my swim buddy, I would have to tow him along. And if he wanted to lag behind, he would have to put up with strangling. But I still remained a good swimmer.

There was some trouble in the water for me during my first cast-and-recovery training. The trick, they told us, was to kick real hard with your fins as the pickup boat was approaching and try to get up to where your waist was out of the water. I was trying so hard in the kicking that I forgot that you were also supposed to lock your arm and shoulder into one position so that the rubber loop [snare] wouldn't give you too strong a jerk when it went over your upraised arm.

Well, I forgot, and the loop jerked, and it just about ripped my arm out of its socket. But since we had to do cast and recoveries eight or ten times that day, I kept going. In fact, I was surprised that no one dislocated their shoulders during that evolution.

But once we got the hang of it, cast and recovery was really fun to do. This was something only the UDT did. It was straight out of the Widmark movie, and the UDTs had been doing it consistently since WWII. For me, being a part of that was kind of the culmination of a dream. Now I was really connected to those UDT men who had gone before me. And propably they had also thought it monotonous to do after having done it ten or twelve times in one day.

What I did have trouble with was the runs. Running had never been my sport. And PT, the physical training part, got tougher and tougher as UDTR went along. But I just kept hanging in there, sometimes making it through on just pure guts alone.

The hardest parts of training for me were the long field operations during the last phase of training. These were training evolutions that went on for several days. They just seemed to go on and on, and caused tremendous physical breakdown. But you just had to keep going.

The long field operations didn't take place until after we had already completed twenty weeks of training. Now we were doing these final exercises and they just seemed to go on forever. Those last three weeks of training were, for me at least, actually worse than Hell Week.

We were operating from a ship off San Clemente Island, and there was never enough rest. It was just go, go, go . . . constantly, without stop.

But that last day of training, when we all stood on the grinder during graduation, that was worth all of our work. That feeling of accomplishment was unlike anything else. Even though I was only twenty-two years old at the time, and including everything that has happened to me since, there has been nothing to compare to it. While still a young man, I had accomplished the dream of my life, I was a member of the UDT, I was a Frogman.

After graduation, I went on to UDT 12. It wasn't long before I was making deployments to Vietnam. At that time, in 1965, Vietnam was really just starting. The West Coast UDTs were sending just some short detachments, operating from Subic Bay in the Philippines to Da Nang and to ships working off the coast of South Vietnam.

But off of Vietnam, we were able to do all of the things that I had been trained to do as a UDT operator. We did hydrographic recons up and down the Vietnamese coast. We were even assigned to do two underwater demolition jobs. Those were kind of rare in UDT at the time; most of our jobs involved doing surveys of beaches and rivers all over the place. But we actually had a chance to go in and blow up some rocks and other obstacles to clear the way for some U.S. Marine landings.

In April 1967, I joined SEAL Team One after I had completed several deployments to Vietnam with UDT 12. My entire platoon from UDT 12 was transferred over to SEAL Team One to become a SEAL platoon and augment the Team. As I remember, this happened three or four times during that period of the war. SEAL Team One had the major commitment of manpower to the Vietnam War and they needed to build up the SEAL Team fairly quickly. Transferring over an *entire UDT platoon allowed the platoon to maintain its cohesion as a unit and also helped to speed up its training as a SEAL platoon.*

The only integration done with the UDT platoon was to add to our number a few—maybe three or more—SEALs who already had Vietnam combat experience behind them. Those experienced SEALs helped season the UDT platoon and provide them with additional leadership. Then the UDT platoon went through SEAL basic indoctrination training— what was called cadre training back then.

The eight-and-a-half-to-nine-week-long cadre training program had the entire platoon working together on everything

On the coast of South Vietnam, two UDT operators hold flag poles so swimmers off-shore can align with the beach. They are conducting beach surveys for likely landing beaches for U.S. forces. These surveys were conducted well before the U.S. committed large numbers of ground troops to the Vietnam War. The men are armed against possible Viet Cong attack.

U.S. Navy

from communications to insertions and extractions. We also received a lot of weapons training and some "kitchen" [improvised] demolitions. But most of the training cycle concentrated on small-unit tactics.

For small-unit tactics, we worked together initially as a whole platoon of fourteen men. Then we would break down into smaller six- and seven-man squads. This was where we learned the SEAL methods of operating in Vietnam—how to conduct patrols, ambushes, and other operations.

My first SEAL deployment to Vietnam was in August 1967 with Alfa Platoon. Our platoon commanders were then Lieutenant Joe DeFloria and Lieutenant (j.g) Tom Nelson. Tommy Nelson and I had been in the same UDTR training class and Joe DeFloria had been in the class right after mine. Besides those two officers, everyone else in the platoon had either been in my training class or was from the classes of that era, 1965–1966.

Alfa Platoon deployed straight to Nha Be, a little Navy base about fifteen miles or so south of Saigon, on the Long Tau River just above the Rung Sat Special Zone. Most of our operations in the Rung Sat were ambushes. We ran a lot of ambushes against waterborne traffic to try and interdict the VC chains of communication and supply in the Rung Sat.

For our first combat operation in Vietnam, Alfa Platoon was taken out on an ambush, led by one member of the SEAL Team platoon we were relieving. I believe the SEAL Team One operator leading us that op was Chief Ted Kassa. Chief Kassa stayed with us for several operations. Kind of "getting our feet wet" and becoming a little used to the operating area.

That system of introduction to an operating area was very well done, I thought. It got everyone in the right frame of mind and gave us a lot of confidence in operating as a platoon and smaller squads or fire teams.

Doing the work I had trained for was something I enjoyed. The platoon had trained on all different kinds of ops before leaving for Vietnam. But the ambush was the one we had spent the most time on. So when we did our first combat ambush, I thought, This is it! I'm getting to do what I was trained to do.

Little did I realize that just sitting in ambush and shooting at the enemy was really not my idea of SEAL Team work. After a while I thought there were a lot of other kinds of operations that we should be doing—more intelligence gathering, for example. Of course a good ambush could result in gathering hot intelligence on an area. But it was the sneak-and-peek kind of thing that I really wanted to be doing.

There are a number of operations from that first combat tour that stand out in my memory. Mostly, they're the ones where we went out on a straight patrol looking for things. On one such op, we not only found some ammunition caches, we uncovered a whole ammunition factory.

We had been just patrolling through the jungle, looking to confirm some of the things that our intelligence people had told us were happening in that area. Moving from point to point to point though the jungle, we just kept checking things out. Eventually we reached a place where it got really muddy and we just couldn't move any farther.

The mud ended up being our biggest enemy in the Rung Sat. The whole area was a big tidal zone, and for several hours every day when the tides were out, you would find large areas of mud stretching out all over. Almost all of our travel in the Rung Sat was in the mud. Most of the time it was only about waist-deep. But on this particular op, the mud was up to our chests, and we just couldn't move anymore.

We tried to bring some equipment from the ammunition factory back out with us. But we were already so loaded down with weapons and ammunition, we couldn't add any more weight to our loads. The patrol had already gone 2,000 maybe 3,000 yards into the Rung Sat. To get to where we needed to be to extract by boat would have taken another 2,000 or 3,000 yards of travel. It had taken us half a day to get to where we were; it would have been well into the night before we could have gotten out on foot.

The mud training we had all received during UDTR really helped. We learned to kind of slide across the top of the stuff rather than actually walk through it. But you could only do that for so long before you were completely exhausted. And in the Rung Sat, you also had to contend with the nipa palms and the mangrove swamp. The plants all kind of grow together and you can't really go across that kind of terrain, you just have to go around it.

It was during the daylight hours on that patrol when we finally bogged down in the mud and had to call for extraction. There wasn't anywhere the extraction helicopter could set down to pick us up, so we used the McGuire rig in combat for the first time.

The McGuire rig was named after the Army Special Forces sergeant major who designed it, Charles McGuire. It was a 100-foot rope with a loop on the end and a padded canvas seat. You sat in the seat and rode it like a child's swing. The extraction bird we had come in only had three rigs—or "strings," as they were called—and only one guy could ride on a rig at one time.

The trip on a McGuire rig was a wild one. The helicopter would drop the lines, you'd get in the seat, and it would lift you up like a giant elevator. But the rigs couldn't be drawn into the helicopter. So you stayed in the seat until the bird could set you down someplace safe. And that seat would be moving through the air at something like ninty knots, hundreds of feet above the jungle canopy.

It was kind of neat to have that happen, but it was kind of hairy at the same time. Since the helicopter only had three McGuire rigs, it could only pull three people out at one time. As we had nine people in the patrol, that meant three trips. When it got down to just the platoon leader, the radioman, and myself, the ten or fifteen minutes it took the extraction bird to leave and come back seemed to go one for an eternity. In spite of our working in small groups, we weren't used to being just three SEALs alone in the jungle, right in the middle of VC territory. Especially not in broad daylight.

I did three tours of duty in Vietnam with UDT 12, all of them operating out of Subic Bay in the Philippines. Then I went back for three more tours with SEAL Team One, the last one being from the submarine Grayback for Operation THUNDERHEAD.

Along with a number of the older SEALs who had been operating in the Rung Sat and the Mekong Delta, I had always thought that the intelligence-gathering missions were of primary importance. The ambush really wasn't the best way to gather intelligence; we should have been working more along the lines of abduction of key enemy personnel. It was when you snatched up a target that you could interrogate him at length and learn a lot more than you could learn from just a body. And so eventually the Viet Cong infrastructure, the VCI, did become the primary target of a number of SEAL operations.

As we started our first tours in Vietnam, the SEALs did a lot of mud sloshing, walking around and setting ambushes up. Occasionally, we hit a tax collector or somebody who was kind of low in the Viet Cong infrastructure. But as we continued to operate, we got smarter and smarter and learned how to fight that war. In the latter part of 1967 and onward, we started hitting more intelligence-rich targets. These were things that had more to do with the coordination of VC operations, the leaders who knew more about what went on in a province than just an average VC would. And this intelligence could lead to bigger and better targets, even the location of active Viet Cong POW camps where American prisoners were being held. That was the big target for a lot of us.

I was with Delta Platoon on my second tour in-country; we were based out of Cam Ranh Bay and operating in the area of Nah Trang Harbor on the shore of the South China Sea. Specifically, we were looking for VCI leaders, high-level Viet Cong. And we had a working relationship with the Army Special Forces in the area that gave us an excellent intelligence net. So we tried to target specific individuals we had heard about, catch them alive while they were on the move or holed up in what they thought were safe areas.

Right about the time when we had the operations going, my fire team, the first squad of Delta Platoon, moved down to the Nam Can area, the very southern tip of South Vietnam. We set up a little operating base with the help of an Army MAT (Mobile Advisory Team). The operations we conducted in the area were in preparation for the Navy's setting up SEAFLOAT and then, later, SOLID ANCHOR.

While we were down in the Nam Can, the rest of our platoon, under the direction of our platoon leader, Lieutenant (j.g.) Joseph "Bob" Kerrey, continued the operations out of Nha Trang. On 14 March 1969, Delta Platoon conducted an operation that was kind of a culmination of all the little intel-gather ops up until then. Delta Platoon—Second Squad really—had built up a tracking record of sorts for this one VCI's movements. Now they had a chance to target this one individual for capture.

Final intel for the op showed up late at night, and the squad had to hustle to get the operation under way in time. The SEALs just dropped what they were doing and headed for Hon Toi Island in Nha Trang Harbor.

The VC on the island, we later learned, were setting up to conduct a limpeteer attack [a swimmer attack using limpit mines] against U.S. shipping in the area. But that wasn't what the SEALs were going in for. The VC were assembling a really high-level VCI and NVA meeting for that night, and that was the SEAL target. Delta was in the right place at the right time, but things didn't go well for them when they hit the VC group.

The island wasn't much more than a very large rock sticking up from the water. When the SEALs inserted into the island, Lieutenant Kerrey took the team up and over the main rock cliff that made up the island. The squad broke up into fire teams for the attack. While they were sneaking around the VC base on the island, some noise alerted the base and all hell broke loose.

Lieutenant Kerrey rallied his men and they were pouring in fire on the VC when a grenade went off near him. The blast just about destroyed his leg. In spite of his wounds and pain, he directed everyone to set up a perimeter and secure a helicopter landing zone. The team extracted after raising real havoc with the VC.

Later Kerrey was medevaced back to the U.S. But the next day, when they went back in to check the VC camp, they found a bunch of limpet mines, made in either China or North Vietnam. So that was how we learned that they were getting ready for a major limpeteer attack against our shipping. There was also a bunch of intel picked up during the fight and the next day that showed the SEALs had broken up a really high-level meeting.

If that limpeteer attack had gone through, it would have been a big surprise operation against our forces. Nha Trang and Cam Ranh Bay were located in relatively calm areas, so a swimmer limpeteer attack would have done some real damage. And it was prevented because the SEALs were going in on another target on the island.

Delta Platoon returned to Coronado in July 1969. As the war was winding down in the early 1970s, the SEAL platoons were slowly being moved out of Vietnam. Some platoons were stationed aboard ships and others were sent to Okinawa as their base of operations. For my third tour to Vietnam, in 1972, I was sent to Okinawa as a member of Alfa Platoon. We were the Naval Special Warfare Western Pacific Detachment (WESTPAC), a SEAL detachment placed at the disposal of the Navy's Third Fleet.

In San Francisco Bay, California, the LPSS-574 *Grayback* moves out to sea. Traveling on the surface, the two rounded hangar doors on her bulging bow are in plain sight in this picture.

U.S. Navy

We were just in Okinawa as a contingency platoon, just to be ready in case something came up. So we trained out of Okinawa and Subic Bay in the Philippines. We also spent some time doing cold-water training in Korea. But it was down in Subic Bay that our most interesting operation came about.

Station at Subic Bay was the LPSS 315 Grayback, originally commissioned as the SSG 574 back in 1958. The Grayback was a conventionally powered diesel-electric submarine that had originally been intended to carry the Regulus nuclear missile. Up on the bow of the Grayback were two large hangars, intended to house that missile.

Back in the 1950s, the Grayback would have had to surface to fire her missiles. Once the deck was out of the water, the clamshell doors on the hangar would open and the Regulus missiles could be taken out on their launch trolleys. The Regulus missile wasn't a rocket; it was more of a winged cruise missile. So the wings had to be unfolded before the missile could be launched. Once the Regulus was off the deck, the hangar doors could be closed and the Grayback could dive back under the surface.

In the 1960s, the two bow hangars on the Grayback were converted to lockout chambers for the SDVs, the four-man Mark VI, Mod II

Though much lighter when under water, these SDVs have to be manhandled along the deck of the *Grayback* while being loaded. The size of the hangars and their massive doors is illustrated by the UDT operators walking through the open hatchway.

swimmer delivery vehicles used in the Teams at that time. These SDVs, known as the Two Boats, were wet-type underwater vehicles that could carry a crew of two men and two passengers much farther than the men could swim. Because they were wet-type vehicles, the passengers and crew were exposed to the water that flooded the hull, and had to wear breathing equipment during their trip.

The Grayback's bow hangars had two parts, what was called a wet side—it was from here that they launched the boats—and a dry side. The SEALs lived on the dry side of the bulkhead. On the other side of the bulkhead, on the wet side, where you had access to the hangars up on the deck, lived the UDT platoon that crewed the SDVs with drivers and technicians.

As far as we knew, we were just going to be the SEAL contingency platoon assigned to the Grayback. We would be available if an operation came up that called for our skills. As it turned out, an

An artist's rendition of the USS *Grayback* releasing SDVs while underwater.

operation had been in the planning stages, but we knew nothing about that when we went aboard the Grayback at Subic.

As the others were planning the operation, we were working with the UDT platoon and their SDVs, mostly just riding as passengers aboard the Two Boats. The SDVs would leave the Grayback while the mother submarine was still underwater. They would carry us to a certain point, we would get out, and the SDVs would then leave. Returning later, the SDVs would rendezvous with us for the return trip. We then got aboard and returned to the Grayback.

What we were training for was Operation THUNDERHEAD. The mission was basically to liberate some U.S. prisoners out of North Vietnam. Intelligence gathered by U.S. aircraft and other means had indicated that some Americans were going to escape from the Hanoi Hilton. The escaping POWs were to travel down the river to the Gulf of Tonkin. Once there, the men would signal anyone who could pick them up.

During our briefing on the operation, we were told that the Grayback would be going in close to some islands that were offshore from certain rivers. The submarine would just sit there offshore while we went in to the island to try and spot the escaping POWs.

The SDVs and their UDT crews were going to transit from the Grayback to this one island. Once the SDVs reached the island, the two SEAL passengers were to get out and insert onto the island while the SDV returned to the Grayback. On the island, the SEALs would set up an observation post where they could observe the mouth of the river off on the mainland.

The SEALs were just to sit there on the island for one or two days and then get relieved by another pair of SEALs from the Grayback. The object was to watch for a signal from the escaped POWs and render them all assistance possible. The specific signal we would be watching for would be a series of red lights set up in a certain configuration at night. During the day, the signal would be red flags.

We would hardly be the only people on the lookout for these signals. The U.S. Fleet had helicopters flying up and down the shoreline of North Vietnam, as close as they dared to come to the NVA anti-aircraft defenses. But the island where we were going to set up our observation post had the best view of the mouth of the target river.

The day the prisoners were supposed to escape was known, and we went in to the island a day or so ahead of that. That way, we'd be in position well before the escaping POWs should be able to arrive on scene.

We had no real idea as to the size of this mission. Our part was well known to us and we had been thoroughly briefed. What we didn't know was that there was a large chunk of the U.S. Fleet also offshore watching for these POWs to come out. We didn't know if there was going to be just one POW or more. Later I learned that between two and five POWs were supposed to be in on the breakout. But we were prepared to get out as many as we could.

Our job was to secure the POWs and get them back to the Grayback or call in one of the helicopters to extract them. We would do anything we had to in order to get the men out before the NVA knew what had happened.

But no prisoners escaped from North Vietnam during Operation

THUNDERHEAD. And the operation proved very costly to us. We lost our platoon commander on a helicopter insertion on the day after we started the first operation.

On the first underwater insertion, we lost an SDV. The vehicle had bad problems negotiating the tremendous current coming out of the target river. At the time we were using all of our newest systems to try and get us to a certain point. What the systems told us was that we were fighting this heavy current.

We had to get to the blind side of the island, where the helicopters couldn't go. That was where we were going to set up our op. But the SDV ran out of battery power and ended up dead in the water. All of us from the SDV were picked up by a search-and-rescue helicopter and returned to the U.S. Fleet. Most of the ships offshore didn't even know the Grayback was in the area, so our appearance came as a surprise to some people.

That night, we were going to cast off from a helicopter to get back to the Grayback and kind of rethink our insertion plans for the island. It was during the helicopter insertion in the vicinity of the Grayback that we lost Lieutenant Dry.

The platoon commander for Alfa Platoon in 1972 was Lieutenant Melvin S. "Spence" Dry. He ended up being the last SEAL loss of the Vietnam War. During our helicopter insertion, we jumped from the bird into the water and Lieutenant Dry broke his neck when he impacted on some flotsam in the water. Because of the heavy secrecy regarding Operation THUNDERHEAD, his loss wasn't reported as being due to a combat operation. Instead, his family was told he was lost in a training accident.

It has only been in the last several years that I've been able to speak openly about what happened to Lieutenant Dry, how he actually died. All of us in the platoon were disappointed that more wasn't made public about Operation THUNDERHEAD. Even though no POWs were ever rescued during that op—much, much later it came out that the POWs never made it out of the prison in the first place—we felt it was a tremendous effort.

I've always believed that a lot of the success of the SEALs in Vietnam and elsewhere was due to their methods of insertion and extraction from a target. They would go in where no one would expect anyone to be able to go. And they went in quietly, and came out just as quietly.

The insertion on the night that Spence Dry died, a lot of things happened that we, as SEALs, would not have done if it had been left entirely up to us. The helicopter insertion, even at night, was something we had done before. But the height and speed of the bird was questionable. And this isn't just my opinion; everyone who exited the bird that night had the same thought. We learn from our mistakes, but in the Teams, those mistakes can be very costly.

The Navy SEALs are not perfect; we make mistakes. I've never thought of the SEALs as a perfect specimen of a weapons system or a group of individuals. We were probably the best-trained men available to do that kind of work—basically, unconventional warfare, as it was first called; now it's referred to as special warfare.

As we saw in Vietnam, the SEALs had more of their own destiny within their control than most other units. The young platoon officers were almost totally in charge of an operation. If they ran across something that was not in the original plan or patrol order, they had the option to make the decision right there in the field to take care of the bigger or better target.

It was very important that the officers could do that. And keeping that "can-do" tradition of the Frogman and the SEALs alive helps them make the decision to take on the bigger target.

A Frogman is now a state of mind; it is someone who has volunteered to do anything—to go anywhere and do anything they have to do in order to get the mission done. And they will get the mission done before anyone expects them to. Our shared training in BUD/S helps give us all a base experience to build on. And the brotherhood of the Teams supports each man doing his best in support of his Teammates.

The hierarchy in the Teams is different from any other place in the Navy, or even in most of the military. Officers and enlisted men all go through training together, and that makes us all the same as far as being an operator in the Teams goes. But we're still in the

Navy, so there has to be a distinction between the officers and the enlisted men.

But my experience in the Teams has shown me the neat thing about the officers in the UDT and the SEALs is how they always asked the opinion of the men they led. Everyone, from the old, grizzled, experienced chief to the young, shaved-headed, new seaman, was asked at one time or another how they thought something would work, or what they thought of a situation.

The officer always made the final decision about how something would be done. But officers were never above learning from their men.

What I came away with from the SEAL Teams was the belief that I can go on, in spite of things like a disabling injury. During my basic UDT training class, and while serving in the UDT and SEAL platoons, I learned that the toughest thing to face is adverse conditions. Whether it is in your job, or your family, or in your life outside of the Teams, once you have been in the Teams, you learn how to reach down inside yourself and get through the toughest times.

You can't stay in the Team your entire life. But I love the guys who are serving today just as I do the men I served with so long ago. It is a great organization, and a great place to learn, both about the world and about yourself.

Today, I work in a field very separated from what I did in the Teams, and that's art, painting. And I think it's neat that I can look at art today from another set of eyes, those of an operator from the UDTs and the SEAL Team. And it was my experience in the Teams that gave me the ability to do that.

We worked on the sharp end, faced dangers and overcame them in the Teams. Vietnam was the ultimate test of the fighting ability and spirit of the Teams, and some of us reveled in it. It was where we served best, in combat. I've known SEALs who had just come off the plane from Vietnam and they immediately went over to the platoon officer of the next deploying platoon back to Southeast Asia. All they wanted to know was if there was any way they could join that platoon, trade with somebody, in order to go back over.

Chapter 14

THE LAST DETACHMENT

SEAL detachments had been in Vietnam since their earliest deployments. Detachment ECHO had been part of the SEALs program of instruction to South Vietnamese unconventional warfare units. The men trained by the SEALs from this detachment were some of the Vietnamese individuals who conducted the maritime operations of OP-34A.

Excerpt from SEAL Team One, Command and Control History 1969
Enclosure (2) (b) BASIC NARRATIVE
OPERATIONS
Page 2. [DECLASSIFIED from SECRET]
  c. Detachment ECHO is under the operational control of Commander U.S. Military Assistance Command, Vietnam. SEAL Detachment ECHO presently [December 1969] consisting of two enlisted personnel acts in the capacity of advising indigenous personnel in the conduct of special warfare in a counterinsurgency environment. This present manning level of two enlisted was reduced from one officer and five enlisted as a result of the Vietnamization program . . .

But Det Echo ended along with a number of other SEALs detachments as the conduct of the war was turned over to the South Vietnamese in the early 1970s. The training and advising of the LDNN—a brother unit of warriors who also worked in a maritime environment—had been part of the SEALs mission.

Originally, LDNN stood for Lien Doc Nguoi Nhai, meaning "soldiers who fight under the sea." Later, though the initials didn't change, LDNN stood for Lien Doi Nguoi Nhai, and later still, it was changed to Lien Doan Nguoi Nhai. *Doi* means "team" and ***doan*** means "group"; the name change reflected the growth of the LDNNs, the South Vietnamese SEALs, during the war.

The final full detachment for the SEALs, Det Sierra, was an advisory group for the LDNNs.

Excerpt from SEAL Team One, Command and Control History 1970
Enclosure (2) (b) BASIC NARRATIVE
OPERATIONS
Page 2. [DECLASSIFIED from CONFIDENTIAL]

d. Detachment SIERRA is under the Administrative Command and Operational Command of Officer-in-Charge, Naval Special Warfare Group, Vietnam. Detachment SIERRA personnel are tasked with training and advising Vietnamese SEAL Team personnel (LDNN) as part of the Vietnamization Program. Detachment SIERRA personnel serve as both instructors at the LDNN training center at Cam Ranh Bay, RVN, and as field advisers with the operational LDNN platoons. Detachment SIERRA at present [1970] consists of two officers and eleven enlisted .

With the disestablishing of MACV-SOG in April 1972, the Strategic Technical Directorate Assistance Team (STDAT) 158 was commissioned to replace it. The last SEALs from Det Sierra went over to STDAT 158 when Sierra was ended. The mission of STDAT 158 was to assist and advise the Vietnamese. It was as a member of STDAT 158 that Lieutenant Tom Norris conducted his behind-the-lines operation to rescue downed pilots.

With this final assignment, the SEALs were again working with their Vietnamese brothers, the LDNN, as they had at the beginning.

There is some difficulty with describing the Navy SEALs and some of the individuals who have performed their actions so well. The term "hero" is not used in the Teams; in fact, it is considered a very serious insult in some situations. To the men of the Teams, a hero is someone who goes out of his way for his own glory, not for the betterment of his fellow warriors. In doing so, a "hero" can put the rest of his unit in jeopardy because he isn't concentrating on doing his job.

In the SEALs and the UDTs, the Team is everything. Whether it is your squad, platoon, Team, or just your swim buddy, the individual does what is best for the whole. An operator serves the greater good, not himself.

A Teammate is someone you trust with your life, just as he trusts you with his.

Michael Thornton, Lieutenant, USN (Ret.)

Back in the 1950s, I saw the movie The Frogmen *starring Richard Widmark. This was where I first learned about the UDTs. Since I already loved the water, that movie helped me decide that I wanted to be a Navy Frogman. The reason I wanted to be in the Navy was that I had seen the movie about the five Sullivan brothers who were all assigned to the same ship during World War II.*

Those five Sullivan brothers all drowned while trying to save one another after their ship was hit. I've always been a tight-knit-family type of person and that story helped make the Navy appeal to me. And being a Frogman looked like it would be the best job in the Navy.

I didn't know anything about the SEAL Teams when I enlisted in the Navy; no one did. They were still so secret that very little real information had come out about them. And I still had to go through the regular Navy channels to get to the UDTs.

When I first came into the Navy, you had to spend some time in the fleet before you could volunteer for UDTR. But I was kind of lucky in that my ship was decommissioned after I'd been on her only a few months. Since I had already passed the UDT screening tests, I went straight to Coronado.

So in 1968, I became a member of Class 49, West Coast. That was a cold winter class; in fact, it snowed in San Diego that year. Training for me was hell. Our instructors were people like Vince Olivera, Terry Moy, and Dick Allen. These were just super guys. You could tell these men had a lot of power in them just by looking at them, and a tremendous amount of knowledge. You might not have loved these instructors while you were going through training, but there was no way you couldn't respect them.

Everyone tends to remember some specific incidents about when they went through training. For me, that incident was when we were coming back from the mud flats during Hell Week. One four-man boat crew had called some girls up and told them where we would be and when. They came down in a flatbed truck and picked us up along with our IBS.

Engineman First Class Michael E. Thornton, the last SEAL Medal of Honor recipient of the Vietnam War.

U.S. Navy

We were driving back down the Strand from the mud flats, more than covered in mud ourselves. While all of our classmates were paddling along in that cold ocean, we were riding in the back of that truck drinking hot coffee. That didn't last too damned long though. Vince Olivera and Terry Moy pulled up behind us in an ambulance. That was when all hell broke loose. It pays to be a winner; it does not pay to get caught pulling a fast one.

It was probably my own fear of failure that got me through Hell Week. For myself, I had always tried to set goals in my life. Before going to UDTR, the goals I had set were always smaller ones, set one at a time, and I had never pushed out there too far. But UDTR pushed you to your personal limits, and far beyond that. Passing that training was a huge goal I had set for myself. But I knew I could do it, and I wanted to prove to myself that I could indeed complete it. I didn't want to fail, to quit.

As far as I'm concerned, everyone thinks about quitting during training. Anyone who says they never thought about quitting is either lying, or they've just forgotten about it. The time I really wanted to quit, Vince Olivera had a water hose down my throat and I couldn't say that I wanted to quit. I just couldn't speak; if I did, I would have drowned. And I have to thank Vince Olivera for getting me past that moment of weakness.

Graduation was a great day of accomplishment for me and my fellow classmates. Class 49 had started with 129 guys, and we graduated with only 16 of us standing there that day. I think there was a great feeling of satisfaction in our whole group. There was a strong feeling of togetherness, brotherhood, a kind of family atmosphere in the knowledge that we had reached that day, that goal, through all of our efforts.

There was the additional plus for me in that I knew I had been selected to go to SEAL Team One. A lot of the instructors during our training had been in SEAL Team. So they spoke about the SEALs to us. Everyone was saying the SEALs were kind of the elite of the elite, so naturally that was where I wanted to go. But there were a lot of guys in my class who still wanted to go to the UDT; they wanted to be Frogmen. But I felt very comfortable on land, just as I did in the water. So the SEALs held a great deal of appeal to me.

A number of us arrived at SEAL Team One and immediately left for jump school. When we returned, it was time for SEAL indoctrination training. Little time was wasted between my arrival at the SEAL Team and my being ready to be sent over to Vietnam with a platoon.

Once we had it together as far as general training went, we got it together as a platoon. A number of the guys from my training class were in Charlie Platoon, and we had leadership in the form of men like our leading petty officer (LPO), Barry Enoch, and Lieutenant Tom Boyhan.

The bulk of Charlie Platoon was made up of men from either my UDTR class or the class that had graduated just behind ours. This group included one of my best friends, Hal Kuykendall. So we started working as a platoon, and a family basically. Then we deployed to Vietnam.

Deploying to combat was frightening in some ways. But I've always said that fear is good for you in some ways. You can use fear in a positive manner, taking the fear and using it to make you more up on the situation around you, and sharper about everything else. It can make you more aware of your fellowman, those on both sides of the fight. You have to learn to use fear, because it will be there. If you're not afraid about going into combat, then you're not quite right in the head.

During my first combat operation, I was scared to death. It was supposed to be a simple breaking-in op. Something we were taken out on to show us the area and teach us some of the local ways of operating. The only thing was that we stumbled in on a district-level meeting of some serious Viet Cong leaders. And when we showed up, all hell broke loose. The simple patrol turned into a serious firefight.

None of our guys were injured, but I think we ended up with something like a seventeen body count on the enemy. All of our guys were pretty well psyched up after that, but it was a strange way of introducing ourselves into that type of situation.

Being a big guy, I carried a big gun and was assigned as an M60 gunner in the platoon. And I carried a lot of ammunition to feed that big gun. On an op, I would pack anywhere from 1,200 to 1,800 rounds in belts to feed my M60. I never wanted to run out of ammo, which I had seen happen to other guys. It wouldn't be too much fun to be out on an op and discover that your weapon had turned into not much more than a twenty-three-pound club.

Out at Ben Luc, where we were operating at the time, we always had fire support. But later, when we moved down south to Dung Island and to other places, we didn't have the fire support we would have liked. And in that situation, you never want to run out of ammunition.

Carrying 23 pounds of machine gun, between 78 and 117 pounds of ammunition, and the rest of my web gear and clothes, I didn't float very well at all. I don't know why I even bothered to carry one of the small inflatable life jackets we had; it wouldn't have held me up very long at all. Maybe I just wanted to have a pillow along, is all.

But the tour went well, and I never sank out of sight at least. After we returned to the States, I only remained at Coronado for *about a month. Inside of thirty days, a detachment of us were sent to Thailand to train their Frogmen in SEAL tactics and techniques. Then we went up on the border between Thailand and Laos and Cambodia. There was a lot of unconventional warfare taking place on the border against Communist infiltrators.*

We were a small detachment. There was Al Huey, Captain (then Lieutenant, j.g.) Dick Flanagan, Doc Schroder, and myself. Just the four of us were training this foreign unit. A petty officer such as myself running operations just wasn't unusual in the SEALs. We had junior petty officers and a lot of Navy chiefs running operations as PRU advisers during Vietnam. If you were capable of doing the job, and had proven yourself during a deployment, the Teams would use you. It was just that simple. And our ability to do that allowed small detachments such as the one I was on in Thailand to accomplish all that we did.

In the Teams, if you could do the job, you were given the job. "Cannot do" shouldn't even have been in a Teammate's vocabulary. If it was, you'd be going into a situation with a negative working against you right from the start. You always had to look at the positive side of a situation. No matter how dim or how bad a situation gets, always look at the positive side. You were still alive, still moving, and you could always affect your situation.

After I returned from Thailand, I still had more deployments to Vietnam ahead of me. When I returned to Vietnam with another platoon, some of us were broken off into smaller units and sent off to work with other groups. I was sent to work with the KCS, the Kit Carson Scouts, along with several other SEALs. Then I worked with Al Huey and the PRUs down in My Tho for a while. So we were always moving around. If someone got hurt in one of the other platoons, or in another area of operations, we always went and supported them in any way we could.

That moving around made my second tour to Vietnam a very interesting one. I had worked with a wide variety of men in the different units. But the Vietnam War was winding down for us; the U.S. involvement in the war and combat operations was becoming less and less as more of the fighting was turned over to the South Vietnamese. By 1972, it was very hard to get in on a deployment to Vietnam, and I was part of one of the last SEAL platoons to go over there.

By September 6, 1972, nearly all of the U.S. combat troops had been pulled out of Vietnam. The only U.S. servicemen still out in the field were advisers. The SEALs I was working with weren't down in the south of Vietnam, with IV Corps, south of Saigon, our old stomping grounds. Instead, we were working in I Corps, operating in Quang Tri province, way up northeast of Hue City. Our base was actually in a place called Tuy Not, which was on the ocean.

Primarily, we were working with different units of the South Vietnamese LDNNs. We were providing them with advisers as well as whatever support we could bring to bear. We were basically doing recons and other intelligence-gathering missions. The NVA was crossing the thirty-eighth parallel at the time and we were providing some eyes-on intelligence on their movements.

We were still trying to break up the infrastructure and intel-gathering means of the NVA forces as well as collect information on them. So we ran quite a few different operations, either eliminating enemy personnel or outright capturing them. And the information we gathered helped us set up bigger operations as well as developed targets for bombing missions, which were really running heavily at that time.

By the fall of 1972, we were trying to see just how far south the infiltration of the NVA had reached in Quang Tre province. In the areas that we reconned, we found abandoned American tanks that had been given to the South Vietnamese. These tanks were still full of fuel and ammunition, fully capable of running and fighting. And they had just been left on the sides of the roads and trails. The NVA force that was sweeping down from the south was just overwhelming the South Vietnamese units in the field.

Higher command had planned a reconnaissance operation to come in by sea on a specific target area, the Cua Viet River base up in Quang Tre province. Our job was to do a reconnaissance of the base and gather all the intelligence we possibly could.

Based on our information, an amphibious unit would come in to try and cut off logistical support to the rest of the NVA forces down south. With a stranglehold on the fastest NVA supply route to the south, Command and the South Vietnamese government were hoping to force a treaty onto the North Vietnamese and get our guys out of Hanoi, to free our POWs and bring them home.

Ryan McCombie and William "Woody" Woodruff had originally been tapped to conduct the recon operation up on the Cua Viet. But everyone kind of got shuffled about when Dave Schaible picked Tommy Norris to go on the op. As the most senior and combat-experienced man immediately available, Tommy chose me to go along with him. Give the way things turned out, he's since said he was very glad he picked me.

This operation was taking place in one of the lowest morale times of the war for us. There was still a lot of SEALs in-country and everyone was eager to operate. But there just weren't very many operations available. So a rotation system was set up to try and give everyone a chance to go out on missions.

There were three officers in our group—Tommy Norris, Doug Huth, and Ryan McCombie. So whenever an operation came up, a different officer went out on it and picked a different enlisted man to accompany him. At the end of October 1972, an operation came up, but Tommy jumped the rotation a bit since he was scheduled to go back to the States in a few weeks and was running short of time.

So Tommy Norris pulled rank on Ryan McCombie, who was up for that op, according to the rotation. Then Tommy chose me to go with him instead of Woody Woodruff, who was the next enlisted man up for an op. But Woody went with us and stayed on the insertion boat. And I thank God that he was there, because if it wasn't for Woody, we'd all still be out there floating around, or shark meat.

On the operation, we were inserting from a Vietnamese junk. Two U.S. Navy destroyers were supposed to be vectoring us in, directing us as they saw us on their radar screens. Something went wrong, though—a destroyer was off-line on his vector or whatever—and when we took the vectors in to the beach, it was obvious we had missed the target.

The bunch of us going in on the op hit the water and went in to the beach, leaving the insertion junk behind us. When we landed on the beach, we were supposed to be able to see the mouth of the Cua Viet River. But there was no river in sight.

I told Tommy that we were in the wrong place. But the skipper of the Vietnamese junk that had brought us in said he was sure we were in the right place. That skipper ran his boat all up and down the shore in that area, so Tommy decided to go ahead on the op.

Tommy's decision was for us to go ahead and patrol along the beach a bit and see just what we had gotten into. It turned out the junk had just about put us into North Vietnam. We were far north of where we were supposed to be.

As we patrolled along the beach, we were passing huge bunkers that had obviously taken some time to build. The situation was unbelievable. There were campfires everywhere and we could hear people talking, laughing, and walking around. We were right in the middle of a North Vietnamese Army unit.

So we had myself, Tommy, and three Vietnamese LDNNs. Tommy was the right size—he could pass for a Vietnamese at a distance. And of course the three LDNNs wouldn't stand out. But I make a pretty big Chinaman. So I stayed bent over, trying to keep a low profile.

We continued patrolling; since we were already there, we thought we might as well gather as much intelligence as we could. Then we would move out to the beach and find an area to hide for the evening and call for an extraction later that night. We didn't have the slightest idea where we were. So we figured we would move up and make comms [communications] and then extract later that evening. Then we'd be reinserted and try the op again in the right place.

Things pretty much happened that way. We got to the beach and patrolled out. There were tanks there, and heavy artillery guns, fire support—all of the materials of a standard army. Pulling out to the beach, we moved along to a better tactical position, one where we had a swamp on one flank. Now we had a position where we had the ocean on one side and a big swamp and waterway on the other. So with both our flanks covered by natural obstacles, we only had to worry about our north and south flanks.

So I was placed out on point with one of the LDNNs. We set up a perimeter and Tommy got on the radio. He was trying to make comms with the destroyer lying offshore. It turned out the admiral of the Seventh Fleet was riding on that very destroyer at the time. His normal flagship, the Newport News, had damage to one of her gun turrets and was going to return to the Philippines for repairs. So the admiral had just moved his command flag to one of the

The strain of long days operating show on the SEAL's face as he waits for action during training. In his left hand, he holds a Mark 79 Mod 0 pencil flare kit for signaling.

U.S. Navy

destroyers a short time earlier.

We got comms with the destroyer finally, but they didn't know where we were any better than we did. And there was no way to really find out exactly where we were located along the shore.

During that period of time, two North Vietnamese came moving down along the beach toward our position. They were looking for a number of things all at the same time. One of the ways the VC and NVA in the south resupplied themselves was from packages tossed into the water offshore. The surf brought the packages to shore, where they could be found on the beach.

The NVA patrol was also looking for any signs of infiltration, footprints along the sand or anything like that. One of the pair was walking right along the waterline, about 100 yards in front of the other guy. The other guy was walking up and down through the sand dunes, the same dunes where we were hiding farther down the beach.

So it was obvious that our hiding place was about to be compromised. A plan was quickly put together where I would take care of the one NVA guy who was moving through the sand dunes. The young LDNN officer who was with us was given a hush puppy, and he would use the suppressed pistol to eliminate the man walking along the waterline.

In order to maintain complete silence, I was to take out the man in the sand dunes with my hands. And then the LDNN officer would have his chance to take out the beach walker with a suppressed gunshot. The NVA walking among the sand dunes came around one dune and I took up the CAR-15 I was armed with and struck him with the butt. He fell to the ground unconscious.

When I had taken care of my man, I gave the high sign to the LDNN officer so he could take out his target. That young officer walked out from where he was hiding and spoke up, demanding that the beach walker surrender!

That LDNN officer was armed with just a pistol pointing at the NVA soldier. He wasn't supposed to threaten the guy with it—he was supposed to shoot him. The NVA soldier was carrying an AK-47, and when the LDNN told him to surrender, he just giggled, swung around with his own weapon, and opened fire.

The LDNN officer jumped behind a sand dune and took cover. I grabbed up my weapon and started chasing the NVA guy down the beach. Hopefully, the noise wouldn't give away our position, especially since I was armed with the same kind of weapon the NVA were carrying. If I could eliminate that NVA soldier, he couldn't tell anyone where we were or how many of us there were. Then we could pull out and move back into the swamp or something.

I chased that guy up the beach, down along the tree line, and almost to a village we had spotted earlier. Finally, I ended up shooting the guy, but by then it was too late. An NVA quick-reaction team of about seventy-five guys had started coming to his rescue.

So now I had this NVA team shooting at me while I was running back out of the tree line to where Tommy and the others were. Now Tommy started getting us supporting fire from the ships offshore. We set the perimeter up again, and I was put up on point. Tommy was back in the sand dunes, where he could watch the flank where the swamp was.

There were two LDNN enlisted men with us who had been with me on two previous tours. I had handpicked those men, and I was glad I did. One of them was with Tommy at the radio. The other was down on my left flank, up behind me.

While I had been chasing that escaping NVA up the beach, the others had gathered up the man I had knocked down with my weapon and started interrogating him. They found out that he was able to point out on a map exactly where we were. While I was trying to hold the NVA elements down, Tommy had gotten back in touch with the destroyers and given them our position. That was when they came in to give us gunfire support.

As those destroyers came in on the target, they started drawing fire from the NVA artillery we had spotted along the shore. The heavy NVA guns actually outranged the five-inch guns of the destroyers. So as the ships came in, they took on fragments as one of the destroyers was hit.

The firefight that we were involved in with the quick-reaction force got very hot and heavy. The NVA soldiers were trying to encircle us, and they came into very close range during the fight. At one point I was on one side of a sand dune while an NVA soldier was on the other side. I would shoot from one area, roll over, and come up and shoot from another area. Then I would roll again and move before shooting. You didn't want to come up in the same spot twice.

The NVA didn't quite operate like that. I would see a guy come up, and as soon as I saw his head, I took aim at that area. When I finally saw the top of his head, I just shot right through the sand. The high-speed CAR-15 bullets would zip through the few inches of crest on the sand dune and nail that NVA in the head. But before I saw that happen, I was already rolling to another shooting position.

The NVA had moved up on both sides of our flanks. I was on the sand dunes ahead of my guys while Tommy was farther up on the sand dunes. We had brought several M72A2 LAW rockets with us, and Tommy had already put one of them into the tree line. The explosion of the rocket warheads seemed like incoming artillery fire and helped keep the NVA from moving forward.

The blast from the LAW stopped the NVA advance, but they were already too close. A grenade came flying over the dune to land near me. I grabbed it up and threw it back. Then that same grenade came over the dune again, and I threw it back—again.

It was one of those lousy Chicom [Chinese Communist] grenades with a fuse that was anything but dependable. Which turned out to be a good thing for me. The fifth time it came over the dune, I just knew it was going to blow. I crouched down and tried to make

*myself small as the grenade came back over the dune and deto-
nated behind me.*

*Seven fragments hit me in the back. I yelled, and I guess that
NVA thought I had been killed. When he came over the top of the
sand dune, he saw where I was lying on my back at the base of the
dune. Then the last thing he saw was the muzzle flashes of my CAR.*

*After I flattened that NVA, Tommy yelled over and asked if I was
all right. I called back that I was okay. Then he asked if I had been
hit and I told him I had been, but that it was nothing major.*

*Almost 500 yards behind us, was a sand dune all by itself. In
front of us were a bunch of sand dunes where the NVA troops were
doing fire-and-maneuver. The NVA would get behind one sand dune,
then fire in our direction as another group moved up. Then the other
group would cover the first group's advance.*

*By that time I figured we had already killed anywhere from
twenty to twenty-five NVA. But there was still plenty of them left to
take us out. But then they just stopped advancing in on us. They
weren't moving forward anymore; they had just stopped and were
holding their ground.*

*We found out later that at that moment an NVA company, the
288th, had moved in to the area and were surrounding us. It was
at that point that Tommy made the decision that we would all fall
back to that one solitary sand dune. He had made contact with the
Newport News who was still offshore. The Newport News was a
Salem-class heavy cruiser that mounted eight- and five-inch guns.*

*Tommy had called in gunfire support from the Newport News
right in on our own position. We only had a few minutes before the
260-pound, eight-inch and fifty-five-pound, five-inch shells started
making our section of beach cease to exist. So I took myself, Quon,
one of the LDNN enlisted men, and Tai, the young LDNN officer,
back to that solitary sand dune while Tommy gave us covering fire.*

*Once at the sand dune, we turned to give covering fire to Tommy
and Dang, the last LDNN. But then Dang came back by himself. He
looked at me and just said, "Mike, da-uy's [dah-whee's] dead, da-
uy's dead."*

*I wouldn't take that as an answer, I looked at him and said, "Are
you sure?"*

"Yes, Mike," he answered back. "He was shot in the head."

I took no time to consider the situation. Actually, I didn't give any thought to anything but one course of action. You never leave your friends behind, even less so a Teammate. I had to make the decision to go back for Tommy, knowing that he was dead. When I got to him, I thought he was dead, but I still had to recover his body. What the NVA would have done to him in the way of mutilating his body—that I couldn't have lived with. It didn't matter if I died; I couldn't have lived with myself if I had left him.

I looked up and could see that the NVA were close to overrunning the position where Tommy was. I jumped up and ran over to Tommy's last known position. As I approached the area, several of the NVA were already starting to overrun the dune. I opened fire and killed several of them coming over the dune. Then several more were around the dune and I shot them down, too.

Tommy was lying on the side of the sand dune, crumpled down in the sea grass. He had been hit in the left side of the head and the wound was terrible. So I grabbed him up and threw him over my shoulders and started running back with him.

These NVA troops saw me running and started chasing me. If they had any RPGs or heavy machine guns with them, it would all have been over. Instead, they just had their small arms, and sand was kicking up all around Tommy and me as the bullets impacted nearby. Then the first of the eight-inch rounds from the Newport News hit the ground. Ka-boom.

The concussion from the shell picked me up and threw me about twenty feet. As I was flying through the air, I could see Tommy actually leaving my shoulders. Then he fell and hit the ground. God almighty, I thought as I climbed up from where I had hit. Shaking off the effects of the concussion, I struggled over to where Tommy lay and grabbed him up again.

And he looked up at me and said, "Mike, buddy."

Tommy had spoken to me. The son of a bitch was alive! That made me happy. And at least if we were going to die now, we would be going together. But I didn't want us to go just yet.

Tommy blacked out again. So I picked him back up onto my shoulders and again started running back with him. Other rounds from the Newport News *started landing all around us. I was glad I had gotten up and run that little distance I had at first because those incoming rounds were dead on target, exactly where Tommy had called them in. Both of us would have been dead from our own side's rounds if we hadn't gotten away from those dunes.*

The Newport News *was bombarding the beach as I ran on to the rest of our people back at the sand dune. The LDNN were looking to me to tell them what to do, and I just told them that we would swim for it. Whenever a SEAL or Frog looked for a means of escape, we always turned to the water. And that was what I did now.*

I had Tommy's AK-47 with me; I had picked it up back when I grabbed him up at the dunes. I knew we had been running low on ammunition. The whole time of the firefight, Tommy had been on the radio keeping our communications channels open and getting our fire support on target, so his magazine pouches and weapon were still pretty much full.

So, like I said, I picked Tommy up and put him on my shoulder again. He hadn't said anything since that one line back after the explosion. With Tommy solidly in my grasp, I said "go!" and we all started running.

At just about that time the incoming barrage ceased. The Newport News *had started taking fire and pulled off the firing line. They had lost contact with us when Tommy was hit, and all they could see through their big eyes [binoculars] was NVA troops running around on the beach. The* Newport News *also wasn't supposed to be that far north, so when they figured we were lost, they moved back farther offshore.*

When the Newport News *pulled out, they also called back on the radio to Da Nang. The report that went out to Ryan McCombie and all of the rest of our guys was that we had all been killed. The message was garbled a bit—the story was that Tommy was dead, but had gotten back to the ship, the LDNNs were all dead, and I was supposed to be missing in action. That wasn't quite the actual situation.*

As we were running to the shoreline, the NVA moved in as soon as they saw us moving. The enemy was coming in from both sides now. They had surrounded us; some of them had come up and around the intercoastal waterway and were moving in from our south. The origi-

nal troops that had been coming in were closing from the north and west. That only left the open sea to our east as an avenue of escape.

We jumped into the water and started swimming out to sea. I had fired off every round of ammunition I had for my CAR-15 and Tommy's AK. I was swimming out with Tommy in front of me, pushing him ahead of me. Quan, who was just a little guy, not much more than four foot nine or ten, had been shot in the butt, losing almost his whole cheek. So he wasn't in any shape to swim.

Slinging the AK-47 across my shoulders, I took my life jacket and put it over Tommy's head. For some reason, that dumb SEAL Team Two guy had put his jacket around his right ankle or something—however they do it on the East Coast. Maybe he wanted to float upside down or something; it never did make any damned sense to me. At any rate, I couldn't find it and I was a little too busy to look around for it.

So I inflated my life jacket around Tommy and pulled the H-harness over my head as well. That secured Tommy across my back with his head above water. Then I put Quan in front of me and just started breaststroking out to sea.

In the movies, you see bullets just flying through the water, splashing up all around the target. Well, that's what the water looked like around me. And I was praying that they wouldn't hit me now, because if they did, we would all be going down.

So we swam out of their range of fire and the bullets slacked off completely. Then we could see the Newport News floating away, heading south and out of the area. But we had swum well out of the range of the shore fire, and the guys on shore were just jumping up and down.

I never could understand why those NVA didn't call in for support craft or something to come out on the water and get to us. Or maybe they did and the craft didn't show up until later. Because we didn't hang around to find out. I started swimming south with Tommy on my back and Quan in front of me. And the other two LDNNs just came right along.

After we got out of the surf area and beyond the range of the NVA's small arms, I had stopped and attended to Tommy. He had been coming in and out of consciousness and I had to attend to his wound as best I could. The swells were lifting us up and down and we would probably have been very hard to see from shore. Maybe the NVA thought we had drowned. But at least they were leaving us alone for the moment.

Taking two four-by-four-inch battle dressings, I stuffed one into the wound on Tommy's head and wrapped the other one over the top of it. The injury was so big that the dressings still didn't cover it. It was a devastating wound; an AK-47 slug had entered just under his left eye and exited out the left side of his head. I could feel him shivering as he started slipping into shock, and I thought we were going to lose him for sure.

But there wasn't anything more I could do. When one of the LDNNs asked me what we were going to do, I told him we were just going to keep on swimming. So that's what we did, just kept swimming . . . and swimming . . . and swimming . . . and swimming.

Sometimes you just have to continue on; it's instinct that keeps you going. Could I have easily just stopped and died right there? Yes, I could have. But that wasn't the way I lived, never has been. I had a wife and kids back home, and I wanted to see them again. And I had friends I wanted to see again as well. So I just kept going.

Finally, I saw a junk off in the distance. Pulling off my AK, I started firing rounds into the air. When I started shooting, I couldn't tell for sure if that junk was one of ours or theirs. But we were all pretty close to total exhaustion. And Tommy had to get some real medical attention. And when that junk heard my fire, it started to approach us, and I could see it was one of ours.

It was one of the junks that had brought us in for the op. Woody Woodruff hadn't given up on us. After talking to the Newport News over the radio, he had spent the night searching up and down the coast, forcing both junks to remain in the area. And they had found us.

The junk picked us up from the water we had been in for hours. Woody had picked up Tai, the young LDNN officer, earlier. Tai had left our position when I had run up to get Tommy. He had moved out to sea on his own while the other two LDNNs, Dang and Quan, had held their position to give us covering fire.

But we had gotten out to the boats at last. We got Tommy up on deck, and then I helped get Quan and Dang on board. But I was now *just so exhausted I couldn't pull myself up into the boat. There were three Vietnamese trying to pull my fat ass out of the water and it just wasn't going to work. So I told them to just throw a hawser over the side, which they did. I twisted a bow into the line, stepped in it, stood up, and kind of rolled myself over and into the junk.*

As quickly as I could, I got to the radio and called Woody to tell him that we were all alive. And I told him we had all been hit. Tommy was the worst by far, but little Quan had lost the whole right cheek of his ass; even Dang, the radioman, had been hit right in his back-pack radio and he had fragments all over his back. And I had seven grenade fragments all over my back.

The next message went out to the Newport News *and told them the situation. They had a doctor aboard and would get back to us as quickly as they could. The CO of that ship had them turn around and head for us at full speed.*

When the Newport News *came alongside, we climbed aboard. I carried Tommy down to medical, where the doctor looked at him and told me he didn't have a chance to live. They called in for a medevac bird and got Tommy back to Da Nang, where Ryan McCombie was on hand waiting for them.*

There wasn't a U.S. brain surgeon in Vietnam then; all of them had already been sent back to the States. A C-141 with a full medical team on board left Clark Air Force Base in the Philippines, headed for Da Nang. They picked Tommy up and flew him back to the hospital.

Tommy's first operation lasted eighteen and a half hours, and they didn't expect him to live. The Navy flew his mom and dad over as well as his brothers. But Tommy didn't know how to quit. He went through operations for two and a half years, and he's still alive today.

We finally flew back home just a few months later. Then the POWs were released by North Vietnam. That was also one of the greatest days of my life. We brought all of our guys home; there were just no more operations to do. Ryan and a couple of the others had gone out on a few ops after that Halloween [1972], but the SEALs' involvement in Vietnam was pretty much over.

Sometime later, after I was back in Coronado, I received a phone call with some startling news. I was told that I had been put in for the Congressional Medal of Honor. My answer was a little brusque;

actually I think I just called it a bunch of BS, and I just blew off the whole thing. But the person on the phone kept trying to convince me that I had been put in for the Medal.

That operation and long swim had taken place on Halloween eve, October 31, 1972. The next year, October 15, I was expected to be in the White House, receiving the Medal from President Richard Nixon. Tommy was in the D.C. area. He was up in Maryland, in the military hospital in Bethesda. The people in charge there wouldn't let him go. So I went up to Bethesda and kidnapped him, and took him to the White House with me.

The greatest honor I have ever had was when they hung that Medal around my neck and Tommy was standing right at my shoulder. That Medal was half his. And it belongs to all of the men and women who have ever supported our country. It doesn't belong to Mike Thornton.

SEAL Team One was my home again for a while. We did a lot of traveling, going up north to Fort Greeley, Alaska, to open up our new arctic training center. Later I went over to BUD/S, where I became an instructor under Captain Anderson. At BUD/S, my philosophy of training was to put the students under every mental stress that we possibly could. There wasn't much question that physically, the students would be in shape to handle whatever came their way. But I wanted to know what mental capability they had, just how much they could handle.

In our job, if you can't handle the mental problems, the fear, the anguish, you're no good to us. So I was more on the mental side, that kind of toughness, than on the physical end. But the students probably just thought I was an asshole, or at least that's what everybody tells me.

But the students who were going to graduate from my classes would be as good as, if not better than, any that had graduated before. I was very proud to be a part of the family of the Teams. Terry Moy, Dick Allen, Vince Olivera, they had all done their jobs in helping to make me a SEAL. The other guys in SEAL Team One, who had given me my training, they, too, had made me proud to have been a part of their group.

It was an honor to have been part of that group, that family. There really isn't any other way to put it—it was a family. We lived together, we died together. We loved, and we cried—we did it all together.

My natural family all lived closer to the East Coast than to Coronado. And I finally wanted to be closer to them after a few years. My father was getting older and I liked the idea of being able to spend some time with him. So I transferred to Little Creek, Virginia, and SEAL Team Two.

I spent about a year there. It didn't seem to matter what I had done, or what my qualifications were, when I arrived at SEAL Team Two, I was a West Coast puke. The men who were there—the likes of Bob Gallagher, Rudy Boesch, and Mikey Boynton—they just figured you had finally decided to get over to where the real work was done. They never did tell me why they put their UDT life jackets in their pants cargo pocket while on patrol, though.

After spending time at SEAL Team Two, I moved even farther east. As part of an exchange program, I went over to England and spent a tour with the British SBS (Special Boat Service) while they sent one of their men to take my place at SEAL Team Two. That was a lot of fun. And the tour gave you a whole different outlook on how British techniques worked as compared to our operational techniques. It was a very enjoyable tour.

And as far as I'm concerned, the quality of the SBS is excellent, really outstanding. I think they are the best special warfare unit in Great Britain. We went against the SAS (Special Air Service) several times. And we seemed to win what I called the "shoot-outs" every time.

Back at Little Creek, I was going up the ladder in the enlisted ranks. My goal of making chief was reached, and then I was made E-8 (senior chief). Later I knew was going to be selected for E-9 (master chief). I had to decide just how long I was going to stay in the Teams. I could stay for twenty or thirty years, and I already had fifteen years in when I had to make a choice.

Master chief is just about as high as you can rise in the enlisted ranks. But I could rise further still as an officer. So I went for my commission and the Navy declared me an officer and a gentleman.

Under the tutelage of Dick Marcinko, I became a plankowner of SEAL Team Six in 1980. Six had the mission of conducting counterterrorism actions for the Navy. And that was a great bunch of

The crowded conditions aboard an LSSC as a SEAL squad settles aboard. The fact that the SEALs were given a lot of leeway in what they wore as a uniform is shown in this picture. The rounded bulge below the radio on the one SEAL's back in the center of the picture is an inflated flotation bladder. The bladder, originally intended to float demolition charges, will also help keep this SEAL's radio afloat if he slips into the water.

U.S. Navy

guys and a great tour of duty. The men Dick Marcinko started that organization with were some of the best Navy guys I ever worked with in my life. I was proud to have been a part of it.

The new enemy for Six was a scary one. The SEALs fought unconventional war in Vietnam; antiterrorism is even more unconventional. What one terrorist can do with a single bomb is unbelievable. And he will give up his life to complete his mission, use his own body as the delivery system for a bomb. This is something that everyone has to be aware of in this country, that such terrorists exist, even among our own people.

But there are units of men, such as SEAL Team Six, whose mission is to protect the people from terrorists and their actions. And they do their jobs very well.

To the young men who might want to take the challenge of becoming a SEAL, I would like to say, Never give up! Always look forward

Lieutenant Thomas R. Norris, the second SEAL Medal of Honor recipient of the Vietnam War. This photograph was taken after Norris suffered his severe wounds while operating on the mission that resulted in Michael Thornton receiving the last SEAL Medal of Honor awarded from the Vietnam War.

U.S. Navy

because the past is gone behind you. And don't be afraid to make decisions.

Tommy Norris is one hell of a man, a workaholic, but also a very brilliant, loving, and caring individual. And he continued to serve his country after he left the Teams. In spite of his injury, he went on to make a great second career for himself in the FBI. There, he's made some of the biggest undercover hits anyone has ever done. And he is also a true friend; we're closer than brothers. And I know the feelings are mutual.

Under all of the training, the equipment, the ammunition, under all of that high-tech material of today's warrior, there's flesh, a body, a soul. Just like all men, SEALs are people who care, who feel. That ridiculous Hollywood image of a SEAL as a fighting machine couldn't be further from the truth. The men of the Teams are men who want to be remembered by one another.

In Vietnam, we were literally facing death every day. So we wanted to fulfill our lives. We lived large and partied hard; that's where a lot of the stories of excesses of the SEALs came from. Maybe we reached too far sometimes; I don't know. But deep down inside, we knew each day might be our last.

And sometimes, it was the last day for some of our Teammates. Before we shipped out to Vietnam, we all threw some money into a *kitty. If you lost it on that tour, the rest of the platoon would take that money and go down to the Tradewinds, our hangout at that time. There, we would drink all of the beer we could consume on our Team-mate's money. And we would celebrate his life.*

It wasn't a sad thing, though we felt some sadness. Instead, we just tried to celebrate him as we had known him. We had lived with him, known him, and knew just what type of person he had been. We had known a Teammate during the best times of his life, and that life had been cut short young. So that was how we saluted a lost Team-mate, how we demonstrated the honor we felt in having known him.

The kind of man who becomes a Navy SEAL, or UDT man before him, is an individual who wants to be there. That's the only thing that's the same in every one in the Teams. We have people from all walks of life in the Teams—small men, big men, it doesn't matter what they are on the outside, it's what's on the inside that counts in the Teams more than anything else. You had to want to be a SEAL, and you had to want it hard. Otherwise, you would just never make it through training.

And when I was an instructor, I made sure of that. And that's the same feeling the instructors at BUD/S have today.

■ Chapter 15

WAR'S END: THE AFTERMATH OF VIETNAM IN THE TEAMS

The Secretary of the Navy takes pleasure in presenting the NAVY
   UNIT COMMENDATION to
THE NAVAL ADVISORY GROUP, Vietnam

and

THE MARINE CORPS ADVISORY UNIT, Vietnam
for service as set forth in the following
CITATION:

For exceptionally meritorious service from 10 May 1965 to 28 March 1973 in connection with combat operations against enemy forces in the Republic of Vietnam. During this period, advisors from the Naval Advisory Group and the Marine Corps Advisory Unit, attached to Commander United States Military Assistance Command, Vietnam, provided guidance and assistance to the Vietnamese Navy and Vietnamese Marine Corps throughout the Republic of Vietnam. These advisory teams successfully achieved the transition of the Vietnamese Navy from a fledgling force of 8,000 men to a strong, dynamic, and aggressive force of 42,000 men; concurrently the Vietnamese Marine Corps was reorganized into a first-class combat force. Participating in hundreds of combat, psychological and pacification operations, U.S. Navy and Marine Corps advisors contributed to the high state of training and readiness of the Vietnamese Navy and Marine Corps and their notable record of achievement. Through a concerted effort, the ACTOV (Accelerated Turnover to Vietnamese) Program was completed and all logistic and intermediate support bases were turned over to the Vietnamese Navy. The courage and devotion to duty displayed by the U.S. Navy and Marine Corps advisors throughout this period reflected great credit upon themselves and were in keeping with the highest traditions of the Marine Corps and the United States Naval Service.

John W. Warner
Secretary of the Navy

With the end of the Naval Advisory Group, Vietnam, the last major U.S. Navy commitment to Vietnam was over. The Navy SEALs and the last UDT detachments had left Vietnam much earlier. During the peak of their deployments, only a few years earlier, nine SEAL direct-action platoons of 2 officers and twelve enlisted men had been in Vietnam at any one time. This didn't include the number of SEALs and UDT men assigned to other detachments. All told, there were almost 200 SEALs in-country at one time.

This huge number of SEALs in combat dramatically shows the growth of the SEAL Teams from their initial allotment of 60 men each. SEAL Team One had the greatest share of the Vietnam commitment, and also saw the largest growth in manning allotments. At its peak in 1971, SEAL Team One had over 350 officers and men in its ranks. SEAL Team Two also saw a time of rapid growth, but not on the same scale.

With the end of the war came the end of the need for such large manning levels in the SEAL Teams. SEAL Team Two reduced its levels through normal attrition. A number of SEALs from Team Two decided to retire from the Navy after the Vietnam War.

SEAL Team One comprised a younger population. This made retirement and normal attrition insufficient to meet the Navy's demands for a smaller postwar Team. Setting up their own criteria, SEAL Team One and its Command released a number of men from the ranks back into the Navy fleet. One result of this reduction was that a number of younger SEALs did not extend their enlistments and left the Team when their service commitment expired.

MANNING—PERSONNEL ALLOWANCES/COMPLEMENTS

SEAL TEAM ONE—INITIAL MANNING (1962) 5 OFFICERS / 50 ENLISTED

1966	1967	1968	1969	1970	1971	1972	1973
25/97	29/155	29/182	37/225	53/225	52/310	39/274	25/170 to 25/178

DETACHMENT GOLF—PLATOONS DEPLOYED TO VIETNAM

1966	1967	1968	1969	1970	1971 (End 7 December 1971)
2	3	3	5	6	6

SEAL TEAM TWO—INITIAL MANNING (1962) 10 OFFICERS / 50 ENLISTED

1966	1967	1968	1969	1970	1971	1972	1973
20/100	23/115	27/116	23/115	23/115	23/103	20/123	20/128*

DETACHMENT ALFA—PLATOONS DEPLOYED TO VIETNAM

1966	1967	1968	1969	1970	1971 (End 14 June 1971)
0	3	3	3	3	3

*Organized as 7 Platoons, HQ Platoon (3/13) Training Platoon, 5 operating platoons (2/12)

James Janos, Storekeeper, Third Class (Governor Jesse Ventura)

*Even though he told me not to, I followed my brother Jan somewhat
in my decision to first join the Navy. I'd had a swimming scholarship
to the University of Northern Illinois and it fell through because of
some of its rules and regulations. Being an ex–competitive swimmer, I joined the Navy to become a Frogman, a member of the UDT,
just like my brother was. So the decision was, in part, an extension
of my swimming.*

*There isn't such a thing as a professional swimming career. Being
an ex–competitive swimmer, you can do nothing to become a professional one. The closest thing there is are the Teams in the Navy. Since
I was all of eighteen years old, and not sure of what to do with my life,
enlisting in the Navy just seemed like the right thing to do at the time.*

My brother Jan had graduated high school in 1966; I graduated in 1969. I think it was about 1968 or so that Jan decided to enlist in the Navy. He had worked a couple of years after school and then enlisted with the intention of becoming a Frogman because both of us had been scuba divers as kids. We had spent a lot of time scuba diving as teenagers and we were both qualified sport divers.

Since Jan wanted to be a Frogman, and he was the older of us, he went through training first. When I followed a few years later, I probably had as much insight about what it took to get into the Teams as an outsider could have in those days. But, training was, and is still, a lot more than anyone ever tells you.

The hardest part of training for me was running. I had always hated running but was a natural swimmer. So when there were swimming evolutions, I enjoyed those a lot more because I excelled at them. But thinking about the things I didn't like about training, I think duckwalking, with your knees bent and your body down low, while carrying the rubber boat on your head—that wasn't something I cared much for either.

That kind of thing was always tough for me because I'm six-foot-four. So when I carried an IBS, there was no way I didn't get the full weight of the boat on my neck. And it always seemed that I had these little shits up front, guys five-foot-three, who had six inches between the IBS and the top of their heads. Then they would tell me later how tired they were carrying the raft, and it never touched their heads to begin with. I'm probably bald today because of those rubber rafts pounding on my head.

But it was the running I didn't like that much. And you run at BUD/S a lot. For years and years after I got out of the Navy, I didn't run. But I've taken it back up now.

My class was Class 58 and I think we started June 22, 1970. I arrived in Coronado for training on Friday, and class started Monday. So I didn't have the benefit of any pretraining whatsoever. When I got there, I was given my gear and a rack, and started with the class right away. I had never run the obstacle course before, and that was what I did for the first time on Tuesday.

Generally, after you've gotten good at running the O-course, you can do the course in about ten minutes. Some guys were faster; we had Ray Holly in the class and he ran it in about six minutes. For a tall guy like me, nine or ten minutes would be a respectable time after you had experience at the course. For me that Tuesday, the first time I ran it took me forty-three minutes. And it was forty-three minutes of pure hell because the instructors would make you do things over and over again, whether you did them right the first time or not.

The part that sticks out to me about that particular ordeal was finishing up that day. Since I didn't have any pretraining, my hands weren't ready for the demands that I put on them. The skin hadn't toughened up. So I had four big flapping loose bits of skin on each hand from blisters that had formed and broken open. They were bleeding around the sand that had been driven into them. Infection was starting in fast, so they were kind of a mess.

Terry "Mother" Moy, my first-phase instructor, came out at the end of the day and set up a table with a first-aid kit on it. Moy asked if any of the trainees had flappers, and I was dumb enough to volunteer the information. "I do, Instructor Moy," I said.

"Come on up here, boy," Moy said in his most pleasant growl.

So I ran on up there and Instructor Moy asked me if I was right- or left-handed. When I told him I was right-handed, he told me to hold that hand out.

When I held my hand out, I figured that he was just going to pour the Mercurochrome on it. But when I held out my hand, he grabbed each flap of skin and just ripped them off.

Then, when he was done doing that, he told me the reason he asked me which hand I used. "Now you do the other hand," he said.

There wasn't much point to arguing with an instructor—Moy the least of them—when I was going through BUD/S. So I had to stand out in front of the class and tear off all of the loose, hanging skin on my left hand.

"Now get back in line, you big dummy," Moy growled.

As I scurried back into line, I realized the training lesson of that little incident. Never volunteer for anything. Be as inconspicuous as you can be, blend in with the group, and don't bring any undue attention to yourself. That is a lesson that stands out clearly in my memories of training.

But going through BUD/S is more than just training you, and testing you, to go into the Teams. That training also helps prepare *you for life. No matter what you do later in life, no matter how tough it is, or how depressed you may get, or how sorry you start feeling for yourself, you will always think back to BUD/S. That will help carry you through. It's something you'll always take with you. Once you've become a Team member, you're always one. It never leaves you.*

That course of training helps create a benchmark in your life. It gives you a barometer, a gauge, or a level, which you can measure everything else against. There has been nothing that I've encountered in life that has been worse than that training. And I passed that; I completed it. That makes it the benchmark. No matter how tough my pro wrestling and all of that stuff could be, it was never as tough as BUD/S. No matter what you do in life, you can match it up to BUD/S, and you will prevail.

It seems to take an eccentric person to join the Teams. Maybe someone who is off-the-wall a little. But it's people with an inner strength who get through the training. You'll see a lot of people who come to training, and they look like Arnold Schwarzenegger. And then you'll see some scrawny guy standing next to them, and you'll wonder what that guy is even doing here. He doesn't look like anything.

Then, twenty-two weeks later, the guy who looked like Arnold Schwarzenegger is long gone and you can't even remember who he was or even his name. And that little guy will be standing there, soaking wet and covered with mud and sand and salt water and wanting more. He will be your Teammate.

So you learn very quickly to never judge the book by its cover. It's what the guy carries inside of him that makes him what he is, not the muscles and looks on the outside.

We have a term—Banana—we use to describe someone who's soft on the outside and soft on the inside. Well, sometimes you'll see people who're soft on the outside, but they're rock hard on the inside. And I think in the Teams we're people who are very motivated, very focused, and who don't accept the word "can't."

All of this made the day you graduated from training one of tremendous import to your life. You felt what can only be described as the pride of the Teams. It was an accomplishment built over the twenty-two weeks of the most rigorous training that

BUD/S trainees crawl through the mud during training. This experience served the men of the Teams well during their missions in the swamps and mud of Vietnam.

anyone can imagine. And a feeling of gratification comes over you at graduation.

But then, in good Team fashion, during graduation, I was also thinking about my Teammate Platt. His two cousins had come down for the graduation. They were really good-looking babes and we were all heading down to Tijuana that night, someplace we weren't supposed to go. So in good Team spirit, I was already a pirate who was going to break the rules. And I hadn't even been assigned to a Team yet. My instructors had taught me well.

The only thing was, the instructors turned out to be right about going down to TJ. Platt ended up being tossed in jail down there and we had to pass the hat back at the barracks to bail him out. And the instructors had told us specifically that after graduation, we weren't supposed to go to Tijuana to celebrate.

In spite of our can-do attitude, there were some things we just weren't supposed to do. The ocean could teach you very quickly that you couldn't take her on and expect to win. But we operated in the ocean almost every day.

During my first deployment to the Philippines, I had the opportunity to work off the Grayback, a very special submarine used by the Teams. The Grayback was the only submarine of her kind, adapted for the special uses of the UDTs and SEAL Teams. She had these two large hangars on her bow, each one waterproof, with a hatch leading into the front compartments of the sub. You could flood the hangar compartments and lock out a minisub [SDV], IBS, or about eighteen combat swimmers at a time.

The big hangar chambers each had a single huge domed clamshell door, hinged at the top. The big doors could open or close while the Grayback was underwater. We were under the water one night, having completed our operation for the evening. Everyone was switching off from their own breathing rigs to the "hooka" units that were hanging from both sides of the hangar. The hooka rigs let you breathe off of boat air from the submarine. But once you were on one, you could only move the short length of the air hose.

The patrol leader had communications with the crew inside the submarine and they were the ones who opened and closed the big doors. For whatever reason, the big doors couldn't be stopped once they had started to open or close. At least that was the situation then.

This wasn't any big deal for us; we were all inside the hangar, breathing off of the boat air, and the patrol leader had them start to close the door. As the big door started its downward travel, all of a sudden there was about a nine-or ten-foot shark, certainly big enough to get your attention, up on the deck of the Grayback. And he was swimming right toward us.

The hatch was closing, and the shark was heading right toward the compartment. I didn't know sharks very well, but I didn't think he would like being closed in with us very much. That pointy nose of his just headed straight toward us as the big hatch was still on its way down. And at the very last moment, the shark turned away and went on with his business.

Looking down and forward from the bridge on the sail of the *Grayback* can be seen the two huge doors sealing the forward hangars. The tracks along the deck outside of the doors are used to move the SDV cradles during launching and recovery operations.

U.S. Navy

The hatch closed, without any uninvited guests coming in. But that wasn't going to be the last time we had a run-in with a shark.

We were doing a 212-foot bounce dive off of the coast of Point Loma, right outside of San Diego. A bounce dive is where you go down for a minimum amount of bottom time so that you don't have to decompress. We didn't have more than thirty seconds or so of bottom time, so most of the dive was just going up and down in the water.

All ten or twelve swim pairs were done with the dive. The IBS had just been pulled in from where it had been tied to the side of the PL [patrol launch]. A couple of the guys were lighting up cigarettes when up from the stern of the PL came an eighteen-to-twenty-foot-long great white shark. The dorsal fin seemed to be sticking up a couple of feet from the water.

This was long before the movie Jaws had been released. So we hadn't seen Quint, or the shark, or anything like that. That huge shark just cruised on by the PL, not more then ten feet or so from the side of the boat. We just looked at him and thought, Boy, he's big. That shark was almost the length of the boat. And we hadn't been out of the water, the last swimmer pair, maybe forty-five seconds to a minute. I wouldn't have cared to have been in the water with him; it was his chunk of ocean right there.

Back in our training, someone asked Instructor Moy what we should do in case of a shark attack. And Moy just told us to make sure that our swim buddy was smaller than we were. That way we could pull him in front of the shark.

He didn't mean it really, and there has never been a known shark attack on a Frogman or SEAL during a combat or training swim. But there are things that tell SEALs and Frogs that they're only visitors to the sea.

But in spite of the work and the risks you accept in order to be in the Teams, it's all more than worth it. Many have said that you never leave the Teams. Even after you get out of the Navy, you're still a Team member. You hear the word "hoo yah" from anyone, and right away, your ears perk up. You never completely lose track of the people you served with.

You might go on with your life. But whenever you come back and are reunited with your Teammates, it's like time has stood still. Even though many of us are more than a little gray now, and maybe a bit overweight as well, and we can't run four miles like we used to, we're still the same people inside.

Many of us have families now, and children of our own. I have a son who's three inches taller than I am. But when I meet with my Teammates, all of the other people in my life go away for just a little while. It's kind of like stepping into the Twilight Zone. You're back with the men you spent the greatest part of your lives with.

When you get among three or four, or maybe just one or two, of your old Teammates, you go back to being who and what you were then. Sometimes, it can be a little embarrassing, when you're in your late forties, to be acting like you did at nineteen or twenty. But it's a very good time.

The new guys going into the Teams today are phenomenal to me. They're probably a lot better athletes than we were. Today, they also incorporate sports medicine into training a lot. And the instructors work hard at keeping the students from becoming injured during the evolutions and activities they have to complete.

But some things have never changed. You still have to have the heart to get through training. That remains the same from the first day, so many years ago, until today. And, God willing, it'll stay that way in the Teams for a long time to come.

You can leave the Navy, but you can never really leave the Teams.

If there was one person in the Teams who I look to as my sea daddy, the man who showed me what it meant to be in the Teams, it's Frank Perry. We called him Superman. He was between forty-one and forty-four years old when I served with him at UDT 12. He was actually with the first UDT 12 detachment that went into Vietnam. And Frank was the epitome of physical strength, and yet the most quiet, well-balanced, and fair man there could possibly be.

Frank Perry kept those of us in his platoon in great physical condition; I was in as good a condition in the Teams as I had been at the end of BUD/S. Frank had been a former BUD/S instructor. And he didn't harass anyone; he just did the normal PT as he worked out for himself. And the rest of us tried to keep up.

This guy was remarkable, even among a large group of remarkable men. He was one of the few guys who could climb up this hanging rope that was near the grinder, with a pair of twin-ninety air tanks on his back. And he did the climb with only his arms. Just a wiry-built guy, and among us, he was the one called Superman. The softer the sand got for a run, the faster Frank became. Or at least it seemed that way. Running on the hard pack, Frank would be great. But once he got down in the soft sand, he would pass even other runners. He was probably one of the top five runners in the entire Team, and that was running against some twenty-year-olds.

And those were the kind of men I served with. People like that are just some of the reasons you can never really leave the Teams.

And I would like to thank the older guys who let me be a part of the greatest military fraternity in the world. And to the young guys today, I would say, "Welcome. You've got big shoes to fill. No matter what you've done, there's a Teammate who's done it before you."

If you make it into the Teams, you have entered a fraternity of *people who you can be very proud of—for what they have done, and for the path they have laid out for you new guys to follow. And it's for the new guys to go beyond that path, to go farther. That's the nature of things and that's the way it will always be.*

■ Chapter 16

A NEW REBUILDING

By the middle of the 1970s, the manning levels of the SEAL Teams were no longer being lowered. The number of qualified SEALs who left the Teams had been a pool of experience and knowledge that had been taken away from the Teams. In 1974, a reorganization of the Navy resulted in an opportunity for the SEALs who had left the Teams.

Reserve SEAL Teams were developed as part of the Navy Reserves in 1975. The idea of SEALs in the Navy Reserves was to augment the active Teams in case of national emergency or war. Originally under the command of the director of the Navy Reserves, the SEALs in the new units trained once a month for two days over a weekend and for two weeks during the year.

Old Teammates who had left the SEALs came streaming back. Men who had gone on to very successful civilian careers would travel for hundreds of miles to be part of their Teams again. Doctors, lawyers, police officers, schoolteachers—all leaped at the chance to once again run, shoot, jump from planes, dive, and blow things up. They were an invaluable resource in the form of highly qualified, experienced, and capable Teammates.

John Sarber, Captain, U.S. Navy Reserve (Ret.)

For four years of active Navy service, I was a member of the Navy Special Warfare community. Once I left the active service, I didn't leave Special Warfare, as I joined the Navy Reserve. As so many oth-

---

ers had done, I found being a member of the Navy Reserve SEAL Team a classic excuse to spend one weekend a month and two weeks a year falling out of airplanes, diving, and blowing things up.

To qualify to do all of this, I first had to pass training, which I had done no more than a few years earlier with Class 13, West Coast, a nice, cold winter class.

In someone's infinite wisdom regarding my training class, it was decided that we would benefit from receiving some basic infantry skills in addition to UDTR. So about 130 Navy students went up to Camp Pendleton for a week of training with the Marine Corps.

Those instructors ran us all over that base, up and down the hills, with M1 Garand rifles and tin hats [M1 steel helmets]. The swimming-pool training was a bit brisk in the cold weather. It was so cold that one night the water in our canteens froze. So it was decided to only expose us to one more day of the Camp Pendleton training, but since the surf was up and crashing so nicely on shore, that was where our training took place.

We put the class in eight or nine rubber boats and all of us entered the surf zone. And not one of the boats came back. Instead, we were all flipped over from the surf action and washed on down shore. When we finally came ashore, it certainly wasn't where the instructors wanted us to be.

It may have been decided that it was just a bit too cold for our training at Camp Pendleton. Not because the instructors were that worried about us, but because out of the 130 students who had started that week, sixty or seventy had quit by the next day.

So the remainder of the class was sent to another training unit, this one in Hawaii. They loaded us on board an LST and we traveled to the islands. But the Hawaiian Islands were anything but a sunny place for relaxation for Class 13. Once there, we had to begin training all over again, including going through the whole of Hell Week. And we had already completed three days of Hell Week back in California.

It was during training that we all developed the fraternity that existed in the Teams. That feeling came from every man knowing that another man, no matter whether he had trained in 1950, '70, or '90, had gone through the same experiences. Details are different. But each man had to reach deep down within himself and find what was necessary to get him through. For myself, I just decided that the instructors would have to kill me to make me quit. And I think that I was hardly the only one to think this over the years. Men like that I think a great deal of.

As a by-product of this attitude, those of us who completed the ordeals of training don't hold a lot of sympathy for those who quit along the way. Even while Class 13 was still undergoing training, we held that view. When we all reached Hawaii, the instructors talked about bringing back those who had quit during the frigid days at Pendleton. And the rest of us didn't want to see that done.

The day we were told that we had completed training became something of a high point in my life, and I'm sure that's true for a number of others. Nothing else I had ever done took as much work to achieve, and I really appreciated the accomplishment.

From graduation, the group of us walked across the street and reported in at UDT 12. For us, it was a great big deal. For the men who were already at the UDT, well, they had been there before. Besides, it's always fun to mess with the new guys.

When we reported in, the officer, the commanding officer, and executive officer just looked up from their desks and said, "Here we go again." Myself and the other handful of officers from Class 13 received our assignments and out we went into the UDT.

It seemed that serving in the UDT, and later the SEALs, wasn't like even being in the Navy. We were always in some sort of uniform, not quite the same as the rest of the service. For us, blue-and-golds (T-shirts) and swim trunks were a normal uniform of the day. So was a wet suit or just the swimming trunks. We just didn't have the typical shipboard regime found in the rest of the Navy.

Each day was something new in the UDT. We could be sitting in a bar in Coronado on Saturday afternoon when the phone would ring with the skipper or XO at the other end of the line. I could be told that my platoon and I were needed in Anchorage, Alaska, by Monday morning. Back to the base and a quick grab of a prepacked war bag and then a group of Frogmen would be on their way to a northbound flight. By Monday afternoon, the bunch of us would be swimming under the arctic ice.

It was intriguing, it was hard work, and it was fun. We had to go

---

here, or we had to go there. The whole of the world's oceans were the operating theater of the UDT. And the jobs could sometimes be very difficult, and dangerous. The ocean does not easily allow men to operate under her waves. But the Navy saw to it that we all received some extra money for our hazardous duties.

The arctic is a good example of the kind of missions we were asked to perform. Just getting there was kind of a high for me my first time, because it took us fourteen days just to get up to Fairbanks. From Fairbanks, a plywood-bodied bush airplane flew the bunch of us farther north.

Sitting in the right seat, I could look out the window. Behind me were a number of my guys all crammed into the back of the plane. In the left seat was the pilot, a missionary to the native tribes living in the north. Looking out the window and seeing oil spewing from the engine, or the wings flapping up and down as the air took them, I could see why the bush pilot was a man of God. Religion can come quickly to you when you are in that kind of situation.

There were no radios or tower instructions. Instead, we found ourselves lifting off and flying out over the tundra, trees, and snow. Then came a landing out on an iceberg somewhere with a tractor or some other vehicle appearing out of the white to meet us.

It was interesting work, and we had a job to do that involved demolitions, underwater surveys, and other water work. At one point I was fortunate enough to travel from Point Barrow across the arctic to Cambridge Bay. For a while I was flying along just south of the North Pole before moving down to points farther south. For four months, I and my men moved throughout the arctic, a cold adventure but a rewarding one.

After ten years of good time in the Navy, which included my time in the Teams, flight training, and some of my college, I decided to leave the active service. The Navy Reserves required one drill weekend a month in a regular Navy environment. But for my two-week active-duty requirement, I was able to go back to Coronado and requalify with the Teams in parachuting, diving, and things like that. On top of the qualifications, I was able to spend time with my friends who were still in the active-duty Teams.

That was the start of my Special Warfare reserve career. But just going back to the Teams for those two weeks a year wasn't enough. More could have been done to create a reserve component of the Teams, something that just didn't exist. Several of us who had been in the Teams started politicking with the Navy, both in San Diego and in Washington, D.C., in order to start a reserve SEAL Team. In February 1974, our efforts were rewarded and an authorization was issued to form a reserve UDT.

That was great news for a lot of us. This now meant that we would have our own reserve unit and do our monthly drills as a unit. We put the word out mostly to the eight Western states about the formation of the new unit. The Western states were chosen because they were the most likely to have enough men who were close enough to Coronado to gather there for the monthly drills.

The first meeting ended up with around ten officers and fifty enlisted men, an unheard-of number of civilians coming back into a reserve unit. There were doctors, bankers, attorneys, police officers, cinematographers, producers, and others, all wanting back into a Special Warfare environment.

These were men who had made a success of their careers out-side of the Navy. But the lure of the Teams was always there for them. In a reserve Team, they could exercise that desire to be back in the Teams, and not have to give up a lucrative career outside of the Navy.

Now we were able to gather once a month, for a weekend, and do all of the things that we had been so used to during our active time in the Teams. As the commanding officer of the reserve Team, I found it very difficult to combine the civilian aspects of my reservists with the discipline and basic requirements of the Navy.

For one example, I had three police officers who worked under-cover duties in their full-time careers. That meant they had long hair, considerably past the Navy's grooming standards. The unit had to pass inspections, but these men were not in a position to cut off their hair to meet regulations. And some of the people who inspected us, such as Captain Schaible or Admiral LeMoyne, just didn't like the long hair very much at all.

But a lot of fast footwork, and the introduction of wigs, hats, and hair grease, got the grooming problem down to a manageable level. At least we were able to pass the required inspections.

Most of the guys didn't have a set of dress blues for the inspections. Even in the active Teams, you rarely wore that traditional Navy uniform. So our being able to conduct our inspection in standard camouflage uniforms came as a relief to the men under my command.

But though they didn't wear dress uniforms much, the men in that reserve unit had a lot of materials to go on their uniforms in the way of decorations. A large number of Bronze Stars and Purple Hearts were scattered among that first group. That was a fact that I was always proud of.

But the active-duty and reserve forces of the Navy didn't really know what to do with us for some time. Here we were, a group of veterans with a lot of experience in-country both in Vietnam and elsewhere, a valuable resource to the Navy. In the active Teams, and even in the Navy as a whole, men with combat experience were something in short supply.

But after they spent some time getting used to us, the Teams learned to use our combat experience to their advantage. Our guys would come in on their own time, even their vacation time, to serve with the active-duty Teams. They were involved with exercises all over the world. Korea and other theaters saw reservist personnel operating right alongside their active-duty counterparts. And that helped keep their skills up-to-date, and their experience added to the overall quality of the Team.

There wasn't really any friction between the active-duty Special Warfare community and the reserve Team. But there were some initial teething problems with incorporating my unit with the rest of the reserves.

Here I was with 100-plus guys, all qualified Special Warfare operators, and the reserve command wanted us to spend our drill weekends with the regular reserve forces. What that meant at the time was spending a weekend in classrooms at the San Diego Naval Training Center. This was not something that would go over big with men who were used to operating in all the environments of the world, the outside environments.

Classroom drills were something that didn't happen. Instead, we moved in with the active Teams in Coronado for our drills. First, I went over and met with the command staff for the UDTs and asked them how we might be able to move my unit onto the base to use the UDT facilities. Besides the portable gear we needed to use for our drills, such as diving gear, weapons, and such like, we also needed to have easy access to the unmovable items, such as the obstacle course, the surf, and the beach.

The Navy wanted to issue my unit funds for it to operate, and of course we accepted them. So when I went over to the active-duty community, I was able to make some offers to them. Instead of us just using and putting wear and tear on their aqualungs, rubber boats, and other gear, we would pay them for their use and the replacement of any consumables we used up. With money being in short supply after Vietnam, this was something of a benefit to the active community.

The next thing we needed was an actual facility, a building. The base offered us what was called a Butler building. A Butler building was a temporary structure intended for rapid set-up in the field. It was little more than a bunch—maybe ten or twelve—of large shipping containers stacked on each other and interconnected.

So we had our building, if you could really call it a building. But a number of us in the reserve Team went into Coronado on our own time—and that covered a lot of weekends—and reconfigured our Butler building into what became the reserve SEAL Team facility. And it worked out pretty well.

The reserve Team conducted a lot of trips during our weekend drills. In the swampy, reed-filled area where the special boat unit trained with their small boats, we would field-train on weekends. Only instead of trucking or walking in, we would jump in for the exercise. Squaw Valley up near Lake Tahoe was another place we jumped in on.

So we quickly developed a very good training program. And the Navy Reserve hierarchy really took a liking to us. The head of the reserve contingent in Coronado became more directly involved with our training. They loved to go on rides in the helicopters and watch us jump out over the target area. The politicking worked out well, both for us and for the Navy.

The Navy Reserves are a completely different organization from the active Navy, a separate element really, and the active and reserve Teams were just as separate in an organizational sense. But we interacted with our brothers in the active Teams to a great extent and were treated as equals. Our capabilities remained sharp and up-to-date and we could augment the active Teams as needed.

A good UDT man or SEAL is a dedicated man, capable and skilled at his job, physically and mentally strong, and a levelheaded thinker. This man is willing and able to get along with other men who are like him and different at the same time. This is an individual who understands what it means to be on a team and what it takes to work together. And old saying is that a team is only as good as its slowest member. But in the UDTs and the SEALs, the rest of the team is willing to help that slowest member get a little faster.

The mission of the Teams grew in complexity over the years. From the hydrographic surveys of WWII to the bridge demolition attacks of Korea, the UDT developed more capabilities and skills as the scope of their missions grew wider. When counterguerrilla warfare became a more important aspect of combat, the SEAL Teams were commissioned from the UDTs. This was another natural progression of skills and capabilities.

Individuals made themselves part of the whole in the Teams. And people didn't seem to try for much in the way of personal recognition. There were a number of highly decorated individuals, but even they mostly just wanted to be considered as operators who just did their jobs.

There were individuals you learned about, historical figures in the story of the Teams. Admiral Draper Kauffman, who was the father of the UDTs during World War II. Frank Kaine was also one of the men who developed and guided the Teams through the postwar years and on through the 1960s. One man who I consider the father and architect of the SEAL Teams is Captain Wendy Webber, though his *contribution had more to do with instigating and moving forward the SEAL team concept and figuring out the administrative details, allocating resources, operational commitments, and things along those lines.*

When I think of the Teams, it's not individuals who come to mind. Instead it's the pride I feel in being one of these men, a member of that group of accomplished individuals. It's a fraternity, a group of people who had an equal beginning in adversity and who went on past that to become part of the whole.

Garry Bonelli, Captain, U.S. Navy Reserve

My thirty years in the Teams started almost from my first moments in the Navy back in 1968. After my enlistment, I was placed in the first-ever UDT-SEAL boot camp up at the Great Lakes Training Center north of Chicago. After I graduated boot camp, I went on to Coronado, where I started UDTR (Underwater Demolition Team Replacement, later called BUD/S) training with Class 50 on 3 January 1969. But that wasn't the class I graduated with. Right after Class 50 had completed a winter Hell Week, I broke my collarbone.

The instructors must have figured I was worth the trouble, as they rolled me back to complete my training with Class 51. That gave me the time I needed for my collarbone to knit. Training was tough, no matter what class I was with. I was one of those guys who barely held on through the hardest of the training. The only reason I made it was the instructors. At nineteen years of age, I was terrified of those men and there was no way I was going to walk up to one and tell him "I quit."

I just hung in there during training. The only thing I could do passably well was the swimming. Neither running nor the constant push-ups was something I was very good at. But I was a body, and they needed qualified people in the Teams.

At least I was motivated enough for the instructors. After I had been rolled back to Class 51 because of my injury, the instructors told me that I "probably" wouldn't have to go back through Hell Week again.

There was that little word "probably" in the conversation, though. When I asked what "probably" meant, the instructors told me to just take them at their word.

So I started training again on day one with Class 51. When that Sunday night before Hell Week rolled around, I mustered out with the rest of my class, standing there on the grinder facing those long, dark days. And I was all ready to be secured from Hell Week when the instructors pulled their little surprise. "No, you're going to go through Hell Week again," they told me.

So I was pretty well shocked, but there wasn't anything to say about it. There was no way I was psychologically prepared, but I faced another Hell Week. And I hung in there again. It wasn't until Tuesday that the instructors decided that I was motivated for the program and they dismissed me for the balance of Hell Week.

It's kind of hard for me to figure out just exactly what it was that got me through that first Hell Week, or both first phases, since I when through that part twice. Probably, it was my buddies, my boat crew, holding us all together, that got me through that first part of Hell Week the first time. By Wednesday or Thursday, I was just a zombie and whatever the instructors could do didn't matter. They couldn't hurt me, I was just numb.

When I was finishing Hell Week, the instructors had let the winning boat crew, that group who had done the best, be secured the night before the rest of us were. It was part of the Team's philosophy of "it pays to be a winner."

My own head was still straight enough, or at least I was cognizant enough that I would have loved to stop Hell Week right then as well. But the rest of us had to keep going. But at least we knew we were getting close to the end of our trial.

The next morning, when the instructors told the rest of us to secure from Hell Week, I kind of had mixed feelings. For one thing, I was really glad that I had personally made it through. Class 50 had started with maybe 136 guys. By the time we had gotten to Hell Week, the class was down to about 36. At the far end of Hell Week, there were 24 of us still standing on the grinder.

By that time we were only about a third of the way through training. The greatest single trial was behind us. But I was still worried about the training that was still in front of us. Could I keep going?

But I did keep going. Even though I was rolled back to another class, I still kept moving ahead. Class 51 graduated in June 1969. Only when I realized at graduation that I was holding a certificate that said I had passed UDTR did the reality of my situation begin to sink in.

Here I was, a seaman apprentice, and all of nineteen years old. And I could walk up to a Navy captain who I didn't know, and feel like God. I was in the Teams, there was no task too tough, nothing I didn't feel I could do. I wanted to take on the world.

We had started training with guys from all walks of life. There were farm boys from the country, some without a lot of formal education. And there were sophisticated guys with Ivy League backgrounds. But the best thing about the Teams centered on the name. One you were out there, in a platoon or a squad, all of those differences among the men—morals, values, knowledge, and backgrounds—were going to blend together. We were going to make a very flexible fighting force that could take on a wide variety of missions and be able to complete them like no one else could.

We graduated on a Friday, and had our class party that same night. Even though we were still half in the bag, the next morning we had to take a bus from Coronado to El Centro. Once at the Navy air facility there, we got on a plane bound for Army jump school at Fort Benning, Georgia.

My plan was that once I finished the three weeks of jump school, I was going to take some leave and go back to New York City. There, I would spend some time with my parents and walk around the Bronx a bit, seeing the place where I had grown up.

But things were happening pretty fast. We graduated jump school on a Friday and my platoon commander called me up and said we had to get back to Coronado by Sunday. So much for my leave back home. We got back to Coronado that Sunday, and by the following Wednesday, I was in Vietnam.

Now I was a member of Underwater Demolition Team 12. I had gone from UDTR to jump school, was assigned to a Team, and then went straight to Vietnam. Here I was, a kid all of nineteen years old, and suddenly I was stationed at Da Nang. In spite of the rush and confusion of everything, I remember my first impressions of Vietnam very well.

Stepping off the aircraft at Da Nang, I fully expected to be right in the middle of a shooting war. Instead I found myself in kind of a small, metropolitan airport. The guys who picked us up were driving jeeps with "UDT" printed all over them. It seemed pretty strange to me that we were advertising to everyone just who we were.

But that was the way they did things. We piled into the jeeps and drove around the bay, Da Nang Harbor, until we got to our base. It was just like a desert island or some kind of retreat, a number of Quonset huts near a nice chunk of beach.

In spite of appearances, the seriousness of our situation hit me that first evening. One of the more senior petty officers, a guy by the name of Chet Osborne, gave me my H-harness [web gear, weapon, ammunition, magazines, and hand grenades]. Then he told me to drape them over the foot of my bed. The idea was that if we had to go somewhere real fast, I could just grab my gear and move.

So I had my rack, gear, and weapon, and a memorable first night in Vietnam. One thing I wasn't used to was the sound of mortars exploding in the distance and the wavering light of flares dangling from parachutes. All of that made for a pretty tough first night's sleep. But I wasn't sleeping in the mud and was staying in a pretty secure area, seemingly far removed from the war.

The next morning, I was awakened by one of the guys from the unit. Immediately I grabbed for my H-harness, thinking we were going somewhere. Well, sure enough, we were going somewhere, but not exactly where I had thought.

"No, no, no," the Teammate who woke me up said. "Leave your harness here. We're going to an R&R center."

"An R&R center?" I asked. "Rest and relaxation? What are we going to do there?""

"We're going to go surfing."

So my first full day in Vietnam, I had a surfboard under my feet and was working the waves of the South China Sea. That wasn't really how I pictured that the war was going to be.

But it was only a few days later that another of the many faces

Seawolf 301 of HAL-3, Det 5, lifts off from the USS *Harnett County* (LST-821) in the Mekong Delta area of South Vietnam.

of this quick-moving conflict was shown to me. On that same beach where we had been surfing, a detachment of us were doing a beach recon and search. What we were looking for where the bodies of several U.S. Army guys who had gotten so drunk, they had fallen into the surf and drowned. That was my first real shock of the war.

My UDT detachment were fortunate in that we really were detached from the shooting war. To even get to the war, you had to leave the UDT base by jeep and go to either a boat or a helicopter to move out to the active combat zone. And most of the operations we were doing at the time didn't involve much direct combat.

The UDT was doing some river reconnaissances, checking the clearance for watercraft, looking for enemy bunkers, and blowing the ones we found. We did set up out in the jungle looking for the bad guys. But we weren't interdicting or ambushing them, just making note of their numbers and points of passage and reporting it back to command. Essentially, the SEALs were doing a lot more of the direct action against the Viet Cong while we in the UDT were still trying to get into the shooting portion of the war.

At least that was my perspective on things as a nineteen-year-old. So my first tour in-country was relatively easy. And I was pulled out of Vietnam fairly soon after I had arrived. I was sent back to Subic Bay in the Philippines, where UDT 12 had their headquarters. There, I attended hardhat divers' school.

So I wasn't in on the bigger UDT operations of the Vietnam War. Things like Operation DEEP CHANNEL, or what the old Frogs called the Big Blow Job. Lieutenant (j.g.) Harvey, a reservist like myself, was in charge of part of that operation, the blasting of a channel wide enough for a PBR to travel through part of the Plain of Reeds within sight of the Cambodian border. That operation was the largest combat demolition job in the history of the Navy. UDT 12 used 60 percent of the free world's supply of Mark 8 high-explosive hose to blast almost six miles of channel open.

Those were the stories that made the rounds of the UDTs. The SEALs were more the hard chargers, at least to me. The SEALs were the guys who went out and picked a fight with the enemy. The UDTs were more related to the beach and the water. We did recons and demolitions. And usually you had to do your time in the UDTs before you could go over to the SEAL Teams, something a lot of the guys in my Team aspired to do.

I spent the entire time of my first active-duty hitch in the Navy with UDT 12. I did another deployment to Southeast Asia, this time down to the Mekong Delta, and was based on SEAFLOAT, just as they turned it into SOLID ANCHOR. SEAFLOAT had been a cluster of barges that the Navy developed into a floating support base. SOLID ANCHOR was the replacement for SEAFLOAT and was a shore facility at Nam Can.

SOLID ANCHOR was a totally different war environment than the one I had experienced up at Da Nang. You didn't have to go far to find the enemy areas; they were in the free fire zone, which was everything outside of the barbed wire and sandbag walls of the base.

We went out and operated a lot differently in the Mekong area than we had up at Da Nang as well. We were far removed from what I would call civilization. At SOLID ANCHOR, we rested up during the day and operated at night. Using patrol boats, we traveled the rivers looking for the enemy.

With his M16A1 rifle near at hand, this UDT operator prepares demolition charges to destroy a series of VC bunkers. The light-colored cord is detcord that will be used to connect the various C4 explosive charges together. Once the detcord is fired, all of the charges will detonate at the same moment.

Essentially, we were trying to help the boats navigate the delta. Only instead of blasting channels, we were blasting bunkers and the enemy. The PBRs would run into a lot of trouble from rocket [B-40] attacks from the VC along the shore. So our job became one of finding the enemy and stopping the attacks.

We still used our diving skills quite a bit in the Mekong. The

A UDT operator gets ready to place a single block of C4 explosive on a VC bunker. His M16A1 rifle is kept within easy reach even though several of his Teammates are on watch.

U.S. Navy

boats and ships would run aground and bend driveshafts or props. And we would be diving in that terrible brown water to repair the boats since no dry-dock facilities were available.

One of the easy things we did was get a bent prop off a shaft. Normally, this operation required lifting the boat out of the water with a sling or dry dock. Instead, we went into that brown water, with a maximum visibility of about six inches in front of your mask, and removed bent props the UDT way. After we had loosened the nut holding the prop on the shaft, just a few turns of det-cord were enough to knock the prop loose. Then we removed the bent prop, sent it up on a line, and they sent down a clean prop for us to install.

The water was warm, but it was like swimming in coffee. Your face mask would fill with liquid and you would clear it. Only you didn't have a leak, that was the sweat coming off your face and filling up the mask.

The Mekong Delta is the "rice bowl" of Southeast Asia. It is some of the most fertile land on earth. And it gets that way from all of the organic runoff coming down the river from the jungles and mountains far upstream. On top of that, the rice paddies throughout the

After an operation in the Rung Sat, SEALs and Vietnamese hand up their weapons to the extraction boat.

U.S. Navy

area were fertilized with human waste. And this water also ran off into the delta.

We didn't take much in the way of casualties from enemy fire. But almost everyone I knew in that UDT detachment came down with some kind of infection from working in that water. Ears and noses were the victims from germs rather than arms and legs from bullets. We were young studs who didn't think about being vulnerable to such things as infections, and we were very lucky that none of us came down with any kind of lasting injuries or disabilities.

The Vietnam War was winding down, with Vietnamization, the

turning over of operations to the South Vietnamese, taking over more and more. But even though I didn't see a lot of heavy combat, I never felt I missed anything. There was more than enough to do just trying to take care of myself and keep myself and my Teammates alive.

It was our platoon officer who really spent his time making sure the rest of us stayed alive. I never knew it for a fact, but the word was that if we had a mission come down that he thought was a little too crazy, he would improvise and not do exactly what he had been told. Our flexibility in how we conducted our operations let him get away with that. And it may have helped a number of us come home again.

I have two very different memories about what it was like to come home to the States after my deployments to Vietnam. Coming home after that first tour, we flew in and landed at the Coronado Air Station. As a young man, I felt that I had just helped save the world from communism, but as I walked down the ramp from the plane, I wondered where everyone was to greet us. The tarmac was empty, no crowds of family and friends, Navy bands, or anything. Instead, a single petty officer came up and told us to get on the bus and it would take us to the base.

So that was it, no big greetings or anything like the Navy units had received coming back from WWII. Instead, there was just a bus ride back to the base. I wasn't a returning hero, just another member of the Teams who had done his job.

Time helped make me a little bit smarter before I returned from my second tour. I had been home on leave before I deployed to Vietnam again. Going back to New York and the Bronx and seeing friends I had grown up with and gone to high school with and talking to them was an education. My old friends who had gone on to college told me that things had changed a lot. They were telling me that the war was unjust, that men like me weren't doing the right thing in fighting there.

This was a shock for me. As far as I was concerned, I had just come back from helping to save that piece of the world from communism. But what really hit home were the mixed feelings about the war. This wasn't like my dad's combat in World War II. There, we had 100 percent support from all of America. For Vietnam, there wasn't a fraction of that, especially among the young.

That saddened me in a way. I even started questioning myself to some degree. What I was doing and how was I doing it? This was a big thought because I knew I was going back overseas again. And on the next deployment, I already knew that I would be going down to the Mekong Delta and SEAFLOAT/SOLID ANCHOR.

Were we doing the right thing?

Although I had those questions in my mind, what gave me the support I needed was just looking around at my Teammates. These were great guys I was working with. They were doing the right thing, supporting each other. And I was fortunate to be serving with them. I didn't have a lot of questions as to what the right thing was after that. It was to be in the Teams and with my Teammates.

But you couldn't stay in the Teams forever, though some have tried. By the early 1970s, Vietnam was winding down and the Teams were being reduced in size. Within a few years guys were being pulled from the Teams and told to report to the regular fleet Navy or other standard diver units. I could see which way things were going and I left the active Navy and the UDTs in 1972 when my enlistment was up.

The first-ever SEAL reserve unit was started up on the West Coast in 1974. A lot of the guys who had left the Teams because of the postwar cutbacks had been pretty pissed off. They had worked hard to qualify to join the Teams. You don't go through Hell Week and everything else just to sail on ships.

Without those big, gray, steel ships manned by sailors with pride in their work, there wouldn't be a Navy. There certainly wouldn't be the SEALs or UDTs. But the men who had been in the Teams didn't want to just be told to go back to manning a ship, no matter how important it was. There had to be another way of using their skills and giving those who wanted it a means to operate again.

But some bright men had gotten together and convinced the naval reserve force to start a SEAL reserve force. The big pool of qualified SEAL and UDT operators both in the Navy and in the regular reserves could be drawn on to man the new Team. And those skills that had been so hard-won during wartime wouldn't be lost as easily as they might have been.

Initially, we had about thirty-six guys in the reserve Team. In the beginning, it was much like a professional athletic club, where we could come in one weekend a month and keep up our qualifications. What that meant was that we had the chance to do one more jump out of an airplane, dive to the bottom of the ocean, and blow things up. And we got paid to do it. It was a good deal for both the Navy and for us, and we didn't even have to get our hair cut to do it.

Back in those days, I was going back to college and had let my hair grow out quite a bit. In fact, I had an Afro-style cut and looked like Linc from the old Mod Squad TV show. But as long as we could fit our hair under a wig, we were good to operate.

At that time in the midseventies, there was definitely the active-duty side and the reserve side to the Team community. On the weekends when we would come in, it was pretty obvious that we would use their equipment, instructors, and assets to have what appeared to be just a good time. And it was, too.

That did cause some friction between the reserves and the active-duty SEALs. A number of the active-duty SEALs and UDTs were wondering just what they were getting from having a reserve unit. But we had a lot of good operators, and they let us stick around.

And the reserves were a good place for me to be. I remain in the unit to this day. Receiving my direct commission in the reserves, I had stayed in the Teams and moved up to a position of command. In the summer of 1990, I received the big phone call when Special Warfare Group One contacted me about bringing the reserves up. After eighteen years of being off of active duty, suddenly I was being activated back into the regular Teams.

Frankly, I thought the situation was just a drill and someone was having a joke at my expense. But that wasn't the case. A number of senior officers were called in and command told us the situation.

What was needed was extra manpower to augment the SEALs. Command wanted men who were qualified snipers, who were good with outboard engines, who were hot on the fast attack vehicles (FAVs), the stripped-down, armed desert patrol vehicles. The Teams were going to Desert Storm.

For myself and most of the reserves who were called up, we

didn't forward-deploy to Saudi Arabia. Instead, we filled empty posts in Coronado. A very select few, maybe less than two dozen of the hundreds of reserve SEALs called up, actually forward-deployed to the Persian Gulf and Saudi.

What seemed to have come full circle in Desert Storm was the development of the UDTs into the SEALs. Many of the missions performed in the Persian Gulf were the same kind of hydrographic reconnaissance that would have been familiar to the Frogs of WWII. The cycle seemed to have become complete.

When I think of the Teams, a rush of different feelings come with the memories. There's patriotism and pride that come with having served my country. There's the satisfaction and well-being that goes along with having a team of fighters at your side. And there's just the pleasure of having a bunch of good guys with you that make up the family of Navy Special Warfare.

Index

Page numbers in *italic* indicate illustrations.

British Special Boat Service (SBS), 292
Broncos/Black Ponies Squadron (OV-10s), *61*,
    61–64, *63*, 66, 120, 152, *153*
Brown Water Navy, 152
"Brushfire" wars, 205
BSUs (boat support units), 117
Bucklew, Phil H. (Captain), 93–94
Bucklew Report (Vietnam Delta Infiltration
    Study Group), 93–94
BUD/S. *See* Basic Underwater Demolition/SEAL
    Team (BUD/S)
Bump, Charlie, 101
Butler building, 313

Camaraderie of Teammates
    aftermath of Vietnam, 305–307
    cost of war, 162–163, 174, 177
    deployment to Vietnam, 99–100, 112–113
    detachments (dets), 146–148
    history of Navy SEALs, 66–67
    Hospital corpsmen, 231, 234, 249, 251
    last detachment, 273–274, 276, 291–292, 295
    Navy reserves, 308–309, 315, 325, 327
    overview, 21–22, 25, 29
    POW rescues, 270–271
    Seawolves, 133–134
    Underwater Demolition Teams (UDTs), 81–83
Camouflage, *218*
CAR-15, 174
Casey, Dave, 184
Cast/recovery, 83, *84*, 182, *183*, 257
Casualties, 156–177. *See also* Williams, Curtis
    (Quartermaster, Third Class)
    Congressional Medal of Honor, 157
    deaths, 156–157
    Medal of Honor winners, 157–159
    physical limitations, overcoming, 156
    Tet 1968, 198–199
    wounded, 156–157
Chau Doc province, 179–180, 189–199
Chieu Hoi (Open Arms) Program, 15, 55–56,
    209–210
Christensen, Clyde (Commander, USN (Ret.)),
    121–134
    athwartships, 128–129
    camaraderie of Seawolves, 133–134
    Ca Mau mission, 130–131
    Dong Tam mission, 131–133
    extractions, 126, 128
    fear, view of, 132–133
    "Hatfields and McCoys," 129–130
    helicopter takeoffs, 128–129
    light attack teams, 127
    medals, view of, 130, 134
    SEALs and, 125–126, *126*, 131, 134
    Seawolves' mission, 123–125, 127
    "slick," going in, 128

Vietnamese Army support, 129–130
    weapons of Seawolves, 127, *127–128*
Class 29 (Roat), 182
Class gift tradition, *160*
Climate of Vietnam, 5
Cold War, 30–31, 34–37, 49
Combat tactics, 219–225. *See also* Navy SEALs
    operations
    experience and efficiency, 219
    Gene E. Peterson, 220–225
    leave-behind ambush, 220–223
    tactics development, 219–220
Command and Control History excerpts
    aftermath of Vietnam, 298
    combat tactics, 219–220
    Dominican Republic, 68–69
    history of Navy SEALs, 30–43
    last detachment, 272–273
    Provincial Reconnaissance Units (PRUs),
        210–214
    Tet 1968, 180
Concept of operations, 40, 42
Congressional Medal of Honor, 157–159, 290–291
Corpsmen. *See* Hospital corpsmen
Counterterrorism actions, 292–294
Cuban Missile Crisis. *See* Dominican Republic

Dac To, 178
Deaths of Navy SEALs, 156–157
DeFloria, Joe (Lieutenant), 260
Del Guidance, David (Lieutenant, USNR), 30,
    47, 228
Democratic Republic of Vietnam, 3
Demolition (demo) pits, 27
Deployment to Vietnam, 91–117. *See also*
    Gormly, Robert (Captain, USN (Ret.));
    Marcinko, Richard (Commander, USN
    (Ret.))
    Bucklew Report (Vietnam Delta Infiltration
        Study Group), 93–94
    funding problems, 104–107
    Harry D. Felt (Admiral), 92–93
    Ho Chi Minh Trail, 91, 178
    Lyndon Johnson (President), 93, 178
    Mekong Delta, 94
    "Nasty"-class fast patrol boat, *92*
    Operational Plan 34A, 92
    Operation GAME WARDEN, 94
    Operation MARKET TIME, 94
    Phil H. Bucklew (Captain), 93–94
    Southeast Asia (Tonkin Gulf) Resolution, 93
    Swatow gunboat attacks, 92–93
    unconventional warfare, 12, 94, 105, 116
Desert Storm, 204–205, 326–327
Detachment Echo, 272
Detachments (dets), 140–156. *See also* Sobisky,
    Frank (Electrician's Mate, Third Class)

Leadership importance, 21
Leave-behind ambush, 220–223
Lein Doi Nguoi Nhai (LDNNs), 58–61, 272–273, 279
LeMoyne, Irve C. "Chuck" (Lieutenant), 99, 184, 311
Leonard, Duke, 204
Light attack teams, 127
Light SEAL Support Craft (LSSC), *106*
Loc Ninh, 178
LSSC (Light SEAL Support Craft), *106*
Lyon, Scott R. (Lieutenant Commander, USN (Ret.)), 8–29
  Army of the Republic of Vietnam (ARVN), 15
  Basic Underwater Demolition/SEAL Team (BUD/S) instructor, 22–29
  camaraderie, 21–22, 25, 29
  Chieu Hoi (Open Arms) Program, 15
  demolition (demo) pits, 27
  harassment, 25, 27
  leadership importance, 21
  officers and enlisted men, 20–21
  Phoenix Program, 14–15
  POW camp raid, 16–20, 53
  Provincial Reconnaissance Units (PRUs), 13–15, 19
  rock portage, 26–27
  SEAL operations, 12–13, 16
  SEAL team rivalry, 15–16
  SEAL training, 12, *14*, 21–22
  snatch, secure, transport of prisoner (film), 22–24
  swim buddy, 21–22
  today's vs. historical SEALs, 29
  unconventional warfare, 12
  Underwater Demolition Team Replacement (UDTR) training, 8–10
  Underwater Demolition Teams (UDTs), 10–11
  Warrant Officer, 52–53

M4 carbine, *88*
M14/M16, 75–76, 176
M16A1/M203 combination rifle, *187*
M60 machine gun, 19, 176, 277
M72A2 LAW rockets, 284
M79 40mm grenade launcher, 175, *175*
Machen, Billy W. (Petty Officer), 32, 50
Manning levels of SEALs, 33, 51, 296–298, 307
Marcinko, Richard (Commander, USN (Ret.)), 107–117
  aggressive attitude, 115
  Asian cultures, 116
  camaraderie, 112–113
  drugs vs. human responses, 112
  evolution of war, 113–114
  extraction, importance of, 111
  fear, view of, 112

  Harry Humphries and, 187–189, 191–192, 206
  insertions, 111–112, *114*
  Mekong Delta, 110–111
  Michael Thornton and, 292–293
  "military Mafia," 113
  psychological warfare, 115–116
  SEAL Tactical Assault Boats (STABs), 110, *110–111*
  small war, purity of, 116–117
  training for Vietnam, 108–109
  unconventional warfare, 116
Marine Corps. and corpsmen, 236
Marshall, Aden, 86
Martin, Philip L. "Moki" (Lieutenant, USN (Ret.)), 256–271
  ammunition factory operation, 261
  camaraderie, 270–271
  intelligence gathering, 262–264
  introduction to operating area, 260
  limpeteer attack, prevented, 264
  McGuire rigs, 261–262
  Naval Special Warfare Western Pacific Detachment (WESTPAC), 264–265
  officers and enlisted men, 270–271
  Operation THUNDERHEAD, 262, 267–269
  swim buddy, 257
  swimmer delivery vehicles (SDVs), 265–266, *266*, 267–268
  Underwater Demolition Team Replacement (UDTR) training, 256–257, 261
  Underwater Demolition Teams (UDTs), 258
  USS *Grayback*, 262, *265–267*, 265–269
Mattingly, Harry A. (GMG1), 212
McCarty, Fred, 100, 102
McCombie, Ryan, 280, 287, 290
McGuire rigs, 261–262
McPartlin, Greg (Hospital Corpsman, Second Class), *54*, 234–254, *235*, *243*
  camaraderie, 249, 251
  first aid teaching to teammates, 239
  friendly fire accident, 169–172
  hammer-and-anvil ambush, 239–240
  image of SEALs, 252–253
  Marine Corps. and corpsmen, 236
  McP's Irish Pub and Grill, 251–252
  medals awarded to, 242–243
  partying, 249–251
  reporter interview of, 246–247
  SEALs and corpsmen, 238, 242–243
  special operations technician course, 236–237, 253
  Stoner light machine gun, *54*, 244–246, *245*
  teammate, being accepted as, 242, 244, 253–254
  today's vs. historical SEALs, 251–253
  Vietnamese, treating, 241–242
  wounds received, 243–244

counterterrorism actions, 292–294
drugs vs. human responses, 112, 164
enemy, learning from, 207
extractions, 111, 126, 128, 222–225
friendly fire accident, 169–172
hammer-and-anvil ambush, 152–154, 239–240
insertions, 86, *87*, 111–112, *114*, 269–270
intelligence gathering, 32, 35, 40, 42, 98, 254–255, 262–264, 279, 281, 284
introduction to operating area, 260
leave-behind ambush, 220–223
prisoners, value of, 56, *57*, 58
psychological warfare, 115–116
retrieving Teammate, 286
river patrols and recons, 83–85
Rung Sat Special Zone (RSSZ) operations, 31–32, 34, 52–55
Scott Lyon, 12–13, 16
Seawolves and, 125–126, *126*, 131
"sneak and peek" engagements, 216
sniping, 74, *75*, 76
unconventional warfare, 12, 94, 105, 116
Underwater Demolition Teams (UDTs) vs., 36, 88–89, 149–150, 319–322
vulnerable point of missions, 99
water as best escape, 154
Navy SEALs training. *See also* Underwater
    Demolition Team Replacement (UDTR)
    training
Basic Underwater Demolition/SEAL Team (BUD/S) instructors, 22–29, *51*, 291, 295
Exotic Dancer exercise, 39
Fleet Training exercises, 38–39
Flintlock exercise, 39
harassment, 25, 27
Hell Week, 27–28, 37, 45, 160
Jump School, *38*, 47, 146–148, *149*
overview, 37–39, 48–49
physical limitations and, 156
quitting, 161
rock portage, 26–27, 45
Scott Lyon, 12, *14*, 21–22
sea daddy, 183
selection process, 203–204, 207
Strong Express exercise, 39
swim buddy, 21–22, 148, 257
Vietnamese commando training, 49
Navy SEALs weapons, 165, *165*
9MM Model 39 Smith & Wesson, 175
40mm grenade launcher, *187*
AK-47, *177*
ammunition, 176
AN/PVS-1 (starlight) scope, 71, 76
AR-15 rifles, 68, 73–75
CAR-15, 174
Emerson breathing rig, 71, 75, 87

M4 carbine, *88*
M14/M16, 75–76, 176
M16A1/M203 combination rifle, *187*
M60 machine gun, 19, 176, 277
M72A2 LAW rockets, 284
M79 40mm grenade launcher, 175, *175*
pistols, 175
Stoner light machine gun, 19, *54, 103*, 175–176, *177*, 244–246, *245*
Neirgarth, Charles, 9
Nelson, Tom (Lieutenant (j.g.)), 260
Ngo Dinh Diem, 4, 91
Nguyen Ai Quoc (Ho Chi Minh), 1, 3–4, *4*, 178
Nguyen van Kiet, 158
Nguyen Van Thieu, 178
Nicholas, David (Lieutenant (j.g.)), 239–240
NILO (Naval Intelligence Liaison Officer), 55, 215
9MM Model 39 Smith & Wesson, 175
Nixon, Richard (President), 291
Norris, Thomas R. (Lieutenant)
    Medal of Honor, 158–159
    Michael Thornton and, 280–281, 283–291, 294, *294*
    Strategic Technical Directorate Assistance Team (SDAT), 273
North Vietnam (communist), 4–5, 91
North Vietnamese prison cell, *255*

Officers/enlisted men, 20–21, 270–271
Olivera, Vince, 176–177, 274–276, 291
Open Arms (Chieu Hoi) Program, 15, 55–56, 209–210
Open-circuit SCUBA gear, *144*
Operational control, 39–40, *40–41*
Operational Plan 34A, 92
Operation BOLD DRAGON I, 179–180
Operation BRIGHT LIGHT, 255
Operation CHARLESTON, 32–33
Operation CRIMSON TIDE, *59*
Operation DEEP CHANNEL, 320
Operation GAME WARDEN, 94
Operation JACKSTAY, 31
Operation MARKET TIME, 94
Operation THUNDERHEAD, 262, 267–269
Organization of SEALs, 31, 39–40, *40*
Osborne, Chet, 318

Panama, 204
Partying reputation, 249–251
Patrol Boat, River (PBRs), *17, 101*, 117, *124*, 171, *171, 179, 190*
Patrol boats (PTF-3/PTF-4), *93*
Pechacek, William (LTJG), 32
Penn, Petty Officer Third Class, 32
Perry, Frank "Superman," 306
Peterson, Gene E., 220–225

Walsh, Cliff, 87
Warrant Officer, 52–53
Water as best escape, 154
Watson, Patches, 109
Waugh, Leonard "Lenny" (Senior Electronics
  Chief, USN (Ret.))
  bounties on PRU advisers, 217–218
  Provincial Reconnaissance Units (PRUs),
  214–218
  "sneak and peek" engagements, 216
  tax collector (Viet Cong), 216
  Viet Cong fear of Navy SEALs, 218
Weapons of Navy SEALs. *See* Navy SEALs
  weapons
Weapons of Seawolves, 127, *127–128*, 222–223
Webber, Wendy (Captain), 314–315
"Welcome Marines" tradition, *26*, 79
Westmoreland, William (General), 178
WESTPAC (Naval Special Warfare Western
  Pacific Detachment), 264–265

Williams, Arthur "Lump-Lump," 199
Williams, Curtis (Quartermaster, Third Class),
  159–177
  ambush operations, 164–169
  camaraderie, 162–163, 174, 177
  drugs vs. human responses, 164
  fear, view of, 164
  fire discipline, 176
  friendly fire accident, 169–172
  injuries to, 172–173
  research and development (R&D) platoon,
  173
  SEAL training, 159–162, 177
  Seawolves and, 167–168, 168
  weapons, 174–176
Wolfe, Dick, 238
Woodruff, William "Woody," 280, 289
Wounded Navy SEALs, 156–157

Zumwalt, Elmo (Admiral), 51, 246–249